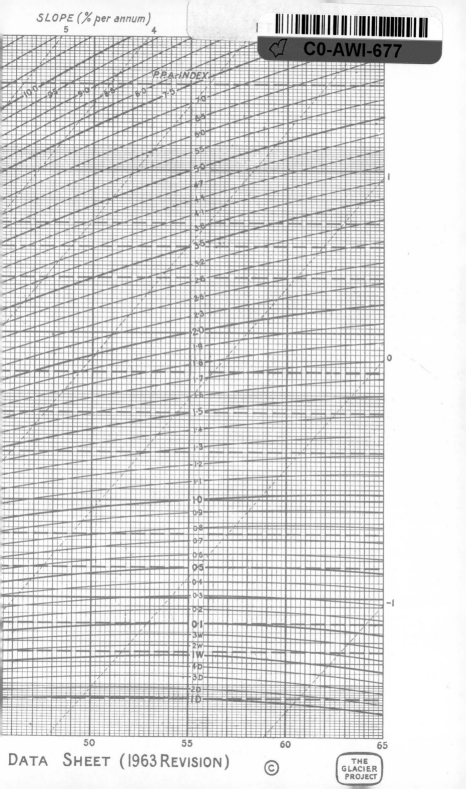

SLOPE (% per annum)

P.R.A. INDEX

DATA SHEET (1963 REVISION) Ⓒ THE GLACIER PROJECT

EQUITABLE PAYMENT

EQUITABLE PAYMENT

A general theory of work, differential payment, and individual progress

by

Elliott Jaques

M.A., M.D., Ph.D.

Southern Illinois University Press

Carbondale and Edwardsville

ISBN 0 8093 0374 4
© by Elliott Jaques 1961
First published 1961
Reprinted 1963
Second Edition 1970

First published in the United States by
Southern Illinois University Press

Printed in Great Britain by
Morrison & Gibb Ltd, London and Edinburgh

Contents

Acknowledgements

While working on this book I have had cause to look back over the events which led to my writing it. It has made me realize that more than fourteen years have now passed since I began my association with the Glacier Metal Company in a social-analytic consulting capacity. The interest of the Company has provided an unusual opportunity for continuous analysis of executive organization and industrial relations, an opportunity which must be unique not only because of the continuity of the work but also for the breadth and scope of the problems considered. The fact that the work has been carried on as an integral part of the Company's strategy for getting through a period of intense business competition and difficulties, has been gratifying.

It is directly upon the findings from one sector of this work in the Glacier Metal Company that the theories here presented have been built. My main acknowledgement, therefore, is to the Company and its members, nearly two thousand of whom I have worked with directly. Many of the managers and the representatives of members are mentioned in the acknowledgements in *Measurement of Responsibility*.

There are, however, a few individuals whose help I must mention specifically.

Mr Wilfred Brown (Chairman of the Glacier Metal Company) has read through early and late drafts of the manuscript, and his innumerable critical comments have proved immensely helpful in the rewriting of the text and in the developing formulation of concepts. His persistence in claiming the need for clear and explicit formulation has helped, for example, in a simplification of the statement of the time-span instrument and in the clarification and restatement of many other matters of equal importance to the text.

Mr J. M. M. Hill read through my first draft. In addition to his many criticisms he has also been of great assistance in formulating the basis of correction of earning data for the earning progression curves, and in handling many of the data on which my conclusions have been based.

Miss Rhoda Fowler has done all the secretarial work, and has maintained her usual careful scrutiny to ensure accuracy. Mrs Rosemary Perrins has drawn the diagrams.

Finally, I want to acknowledge my deep indebtedness to the late Melanie Klein, whose profound insight into the sources of human behaviour I have drawn upon personally, and whose discoveries and theories constitute the starting point for my analysis of group behaviour.

Preface to second edition

This book is a revised edition of *Equitable Payment**.

The most important change is the removal of part of chapter V and the whole of chapter VI from the first edition, and the substitution of chapters 3 to 8 from the *Time-Span Handbook*†. These new chapters have been combined into one to form chapter 5 of this book. The effect of this change is to introduce a simplified description of the technique of time-span measurement, that was developed after *Equitable Payment* was published. Readers who wish to have a fuller description of time-span measurement, with examples, are referred to the *Time-Span Handbook*.

Some changes have also been made in the formulation of the earnings progression curves. In particular, it will be found that Standard Earnings Progressions (SEPs) are now referred to by the more accurate designation of capacity growth curves. The 1963 revision of the data sheets which carry these capacity growth curves, has been used in this edition in place of the earlier data sheet. The reasons for this revision, and a more detailed description of the use of these data sheets, will be found in the *Progression Handbook*‡.

It may be of interest to note that time-span measurement, the equitable payment distribution, and the capacity growth curves, have now been tested independently in many countries. The results have been uniformly to support the UK findings. The evidence is strong that the findings derive from certain universal human characteristics.

*Heinemann Educational Books, 1961.
†Heinemann Educational Books, 1965.
‡Heinemann Educational Books, 1967.

Preface to first edition

I

My present object is to continue the theme of a previous book, *Measurement of Responsibility** – the theme of reasonable and fair employment in a society which aims to provide economic and social justice for its citizens. In that book I described the findings from some years of work at the Glacier Metal Company which had led to the identification of norms, intuitively known by individuals and shared in the working population, of what constituted fair payment for work. These norms of fair payment were identified by the use of a newly-developed yardstick for measuring the level of work in a job – a yardstick which I termed the *time-span of discretion*. This yardstick, employed within a social-analytic relationship with the firm†, made it possible to explore in some depth the feelings of members about their payment as related to level of work measured in time-span. Payment consistent with the norm was accompanied by a sense of relative fairness of treatment. Deviations from the norm produced characteristic symptoms of disequilibrium in the individual. If these deviations were widespread and affected socially connected groups of individuals, signs of social malaise and instability would ensue.

As I pointed out in the book itself, however, *Measurement of Responsibility* was not intended to be anything more than a preliminary or interim report. Since that time, just over three years ago, a number of developments have occurred which have made it possible to consider the whole matter of work, payment and individual capacity within a broader framework, and it is out of these considerations that the present general theory has emerged.

*Elliott Jaques, 1956.
† See *Measurement of Responsibility*, pp. xi–xii for a detailed description of the social-analytic relationship, and see also footnote on pp. 145–6 of this book.

First, some of the gaps in the work so far reported can now be filled. The instrument for measuring level of work – the time-span of discretion – has been more accurately defined, and has been used by others. This instrument will be described in sufficient detail to make it accessible to those who may wish to test for themselves the results to be described.

Second, it had not previously been found possible to use the time-span of discretion form of measurement with any consistency as a measure of level of work in manual jobs*. The initial problems have now been overcome. It will be shown that the level of work in both manual and non-manual jobs can be measured objectively by a common yardstick.

Third, with the building up of additional data, it has become possible to specify more closely the differential distribution of payment which corresponds to the individual sense of fairness of pay in connexion with the level of work carried in a job. This distribution has been separately established as an independent instrument which I have called the *equitable work-payment scale*. Some of the characteristics of this scale can now be stated, owing to the opportunity to study the way in which it has moved with shifts in the level of the wages index.

Fourth, a new instrument has been developed for following the growth in capacity of individuals to carry responsibility. This instrument comprises an array of curves which I have termed *capacity growth curves*. These curves conform broadly to the pattern of biological growth, and portray the course of progress in level of work which an individual of any given capacity will follow if his employment opportunities and his physical and mental health are such as to allow him to use to the full his capacity to carry responsibility.

II

Three separate instruments have thus become available – (1) the time-span of discretion, (2) the equitable work-payment scale, and (3) the capacity growth curves – which have made it possible to consider as independent variables the range of level of work in a person's job as measured in time-span; the payment he is

* *Measurement of Responsibility*, chapter 6.

actually receiving in relation to the equitable wage or salary bracket for the range of level of work in his job; and the capacity and growth in capacity of the individual.

By means of the use of these three instruments it has been possible to extend very considerably the scope of the original study, and to explore in some detail the effects of conformity, and of varying degrees of non-conformity, between an individual's capacity, the range of level of work in his job, and his payment and progress. Moreover, it has been possible to trace the effects through time of the interplay of changes occurring quite independently in work, payment and capacity: changes in an individual's capacity as a result of his own rate of growth; changes in the level of work in his job through changes in the work he gets to do; and changes in the differential level of his payment. To the data obtained through work in the Glacier Metal Company have been added data from five other firms, each in a very different line of business – banking, chemicals, food, woodworking, and heavy engineering. And, in addition to these data, it has become possible to trace the careers of a small number of individuals, but in some detail, during the period before they joined the Glacier Metal Company, for some years during their employment with that Company, and for up to three years after leaving its employ.

It was through this separate consideration of work, payment and capacity as independent variables affecting the individual in his relation to his work, that very marked consistencies in the behaviour of individuals and of economically connected groups of individuals were discerned. These consistencies were sufficiently regular for the prediction of individual and group behaviour about work and payment. They have made possible the development of new procedures for the administration of payment, and for the regularization of the way people are progressed in level of work and salary as their capacities progress.

From these observations of regularity in the behaviour of individuals and of groups, it has become possible gradually to put together the main elements necessary for the construction of the present theory of work, payment and progress. In broad outline this theory is about the conditions – psychological and economic – surrounding the allocation of work to individuals and the distribution of economic rewards for that work, which will provide dynamic equilibrium within the individual and within a society. The theory has to do with differentials: it recognizes that there are differences between individuals in their capacity to carry responsibility, differences between jobs in the level of responsibility they contain, and differences in the levels of payment regarded as fair and equitable for different levels of work. And the theory is dynamic: it not only takes into account the continually changing capacity of the individual, the changing level of work in jobs, and the changing position of individuals and groups relative to each other in payment, but it is concerned also with the effects that changes in the state of prosperity of the total economy have upon the norms of what constitute equitable differentials in payment.

I have summarized the theory in a separate section. Those who find it useful to have in mind a map of the total ground to be covered may wish to look at this summary before starting the book.

III

The findings I shall present (the observation of a normally expected rate of growth and development in the capacity of each individual, and of the existence of norms of equity in a differential pattern of payment) and the speculations built upon those findings have already, on occasion, aroused strong criticism. Notions about differential payment inevitably do. Without anticipating too much the material I shall be presenting, it may still be useful to refer now to one particular type of criticism which I would contend is the product of reasoning distorted by emotion, and which has already been levelled against preliminary reports of my findings. It is criticism to the effect that the findings show a particular political bias.

The striking feature of this criticism is that those critics professing to a left-wing or Socialist point of view say there is a 'right-wing bias' in the findings, and those critics professing to a right-wing or Conservative point of view find in them a 'left-wing bias'. The former believe, for example, that these findings smack of a kind of 'neo-feudalism', a reactionary return to an outmoded philosophy that each man is born into his own estate and ought to be content to rest there, and, moreover, that the workers will suffer because if the level of work in their jobs is reduced they (so it is said) will lose out in pay. The latter, on the other hand, are wont to accuse me of being unduly pro-working class, because my evidence is that many types of manual work, as well as of office work, appear to be inequitably paid; it is argued, therefore, that I favour a further narrowing of the gap between the working class and the middle class, and a relative depression of middle and upper class standards of living.

I believe that time will show these criticisms to be very wide of the mark. But I mention them because they raise an issue of such very great importance to social research – the responsibility to observe and record as accurately as possible the attitudes and reactions which characterize social behaviour, regardless of whether or not these observations fit any particular social or political theory of how people ought to feel and act. The reply that I would offer, therefore, to this kind of criticism is that my findings are factual and objective. They just do not fall into such categories as reactionary or progressive; or feudal, or capitalistic, or socialistic. They are observations about human attitudes and behaviour which have been made under special conditions which I have taken considerable pains to specify so that they may be repeated by others. In the same vein I have tried to state the theoretical conclusions which I have drawn from these findings in a form which will allow of empirical investigation of the theory, and its verification or disproof or modification. In a few places I have ventured to express views or opinions which do not derive immediately from my own social-analytic findings – this is the case, for example, in my background comments in Part One – but I hope I have made it patently clear whenever I have done so, and that I have sufficiently explained my reasons for these departures. In short, my goal is that of scientific observation and theory construction, and not that of political or quasi-political commentary.

My further comment upon such criticism is that the instruments I have developed for measuring work and the equitable value of that work, and for assessing progress and capacity, cannot, if correctly understood, be used to bolster up any particular political platform. Their use points towards full employment of the inherent capacity of individuals regardless of their social background. It leads in the direction of recognition of differential responsibility carried in work. I think many political programmes might subscribe to these ideas as objectives. The problems tackled in this study, however, have to do not so much with objectives as with the development of practical instruments: to establish norms of equity in payment differentials, to assess individual capacity, and to measure level of work. It is easy to subscribe to objectives in the absence of any means of achieving those objectives. The testing time comes when the means become available. It is my hope that the instruments and findings to be presented will prove sufficiently valid and reliable to change the framework within which wages negotiations and political arguments about distribution of wealth take place.

IV

It is not part of my endeavour to influence public opinion in the sense of saying what norms people ought to have. It certainly is my goal, on the other hand, to proceed as far as I possibly can with the scientific endeavour of discovering and displaying the objective properties of psychological and social phenomena. I am fully aware that to succeed in this endeavour – particularly in the field of psycho-economics – must inevitably have political repercussions. But clinical experience in psycho-analysis, uncovering the unconscious forces which motivate human behaviour, strengthens one's confidence in the value of conscious effort in resolving human difficulties, as long as the factors, conscious and unconscious, affecting a particular problem are sufficiently perceived and comprehended. When these problems occur in the sphere of social organization and social relations, the operation of the conscious will can take the form of constructing explicit social procedures, regulations, and laws, within which the otherwise socially unregulated effects of unidentified or unconscious motives and attitudes may be brought under control. If this outlook is accepted, then uncovering social and psychological reality must be to the eventual social and political good.

My experiences at the Glacier Metal Company during the past twelve years have strongly reinforced this outlook. My social-analytic work with members of the firm has been specifically designed to help discover the realistic organization and manning requirements for a wide range of problems which they experienced. I can list a few of the projects worked on, by way of illustration: responsibility and authority of managers; sanctioning of executive authority via representative and managerial legislation of entitlements of members; specialist organization; pricing and costing; status and payment arrangements; progression of individuals; top management relationships; statement of Company policy; management training; policy on direct management contact with employees during negotiations; relations between management and trade unions; and many others besides.

In every single instance where it has been possible to assist members of the Company to achieve an analysis of the real properties of the situation giving rise to the problem, then it has been possible for them to work out requisite policies and procedures to overcome the difficulties. By 'requisite' I mean policies and procedures which derive from the real social and psychological properties of the situation under scrutiny; to use the dictionary definition, an analysis which sorts out what is 'required by the nature of things'. Requisite social-analysis in the industrial situation starts with the realities of the work task of the enterprise, and of the employment contract by which members are associated with the enterprise and its work. The present theory of work and payment differentials is one example of the results which can be achieved. A great deal more material is to be found in a book* written by the Chairman (who was also formerly Managing Director), which outlines many of these developments as seen from the point of view of the firm itself.

One of the most striking things to me about these developments is the extent to which the results have been implemented

* Wilfred Brown: *Exploration in Management*, 1960.

17

in the Company. The following sequence has been repeated many times. A problem arises, and, for one of many reasons, is raised with me by the members of the Company concerned. It may be an individual, a committee, a whole department, a group of managers, a manager and his immediate subordinates – the pattern has many variations. Analysis of the problem is directed towards discovering wherein the situation as perceived and described differs from the actual situation and, when the actual situation has been perceived, towards uncovering such internal inconsistencies as there may be in the actually operating policies, procedures and organization.

This work of analysis often involves the members of the firm in an arduous process of exploration in which they may, for example, query my reformulation of the problem in terms of its actual rather than manifest content, or reject my observations on inconsistencies in which I think they are caught up. It has usually been possible, however, gradually to tease out the actual situation – over a period of weeks or months or, in some large-scale projects, years – so that the members are in a position to consider what requisitely they ought to do to sort the matter out. The requisite procedures, policies or organization seem to emerge pretty naturally at this stage. The experience and intuition of the members come into full play on a groundwork of reality, my own responsibility being to keep their own developing solutions under analysis and to point out any inconsistencies or apparent non-requisite features.

If the process of analysis has led towards a genuinely requisite solution of the problem, then difficulties over implementation do not arise to any great extent. Implementation just seems to occur. Anxieties about change have been worked through in the process of achieving the requisite analysis. The anxieties which remain are more about the possibility of remaining in the problem situation than about the adoption of a thoroughly worked-out organization, or policy, or procedure, which approximates to social reality.

I am not stating an aspiration. I am describing a factual sequence in the course of which some very large-scale changes indeed have occurred in organization and in policy. In the process, a variety of basic conceptions have emerged and have been made explicit, which I hope will contribute to a general theory of executive organization and industrial relations. In short, human intuition and human consciousness are powerful instruments for social good if they can be freed from the fruitless wrangling which results from being caught up in a tangle of unrealistic perceptions and concepts, and directed towards the discovery of social reality.

Summary of the theory

I

1. There are three main types of economic work: shareholding, directorial work, and employment work. (Entrepreneurial work combines the first two, and self-employment combines all three.) The theory of this book is concerned with employment work.

2. Employment work is defined as the exercise of discretion in discharging a contract to carry out tasks set by an employer, within prescribed limits and policies which he fixes.

3. It is the type of work for which salaries or wages are paid, and which constitutes the subject of individual payment differentials.

4. Level of employment work can be measured in terms of the time-span of discretion in a job; that is to say, by the maximum period of time during which the use of discretion is authorized and expected, without review of that discretion by a superior.

II

5. There exist shared social norms of what constitutes a fair or equitable payment for any given level of work, these norms being intuitively known by each individual.

6. The totality of these norms constitutes a pattern of equitable differential payment for differentials in level of work carried.

III

7. Each individual is endowed with a given potential capacity for work, this potential capacity showing a characteristic pattern of growth and decline with age, as represented in the standard earning progression array.

8. Each individual is unconsciously aware of his own current potential capacity for work, the level of work in the role in which he is employed, and the equitable payment level for his role.

9. Each individual is therefore unconsciously aware of the extent to which his role fulfils his potential current capacity, and the extent to which his actual payment conforms to equity or deviates from it.

10. The unconscious awareness of these judgements is experienced in feeling, but is difficult to verbalize in a manner precise enough to match the accuracy of the judgement. Moreover, this unconscious awareness exists regardless of the fact that a person may at the same time have grandiose or omnipotence phantasies about himself, or masochistically denigrate himself.

IV

11. There is an optimum level and rate of consumption for each person, in the sense that consumption at that level and rate is consistent with dynamic psychological equilibrium, and consumption above or below that level and rate leads to increasing psychological disequilibrium.

12. This optimum consumption is related to the individual's level of capacity for discriminating expenditure.

13. There is a direct correspondence between each person's level of capacity for discriminating expenditure and his level of capacity in work.

14. There is, therefore, an optimum level of payment for any given level of work: it is that level of payment which will provide a person whose capacity is just up to that work, with an income which matches his capacity for discriminating expenditure and his level of satisfaction consumption.

15. Although the total consumption requirements for a married man and his family will differ from those of a single man, this does not affect the theory of paying the equitable rate for a given level of work. Variations due to family requirements are matters of national policy to be handled in taxation, family benefits, and welfare and other procedures such as social insurance*.

*Indeed, I have little doubt that a social-analysis would reveal the existence of unconscious social norms about the value to a person of having a family, and how much national taxation and social benefits ought to influence the net incomes of single and married employed persons.

22

V

16. Individuals differ in level of capacity in work.

17. Individuals differ also in level of capacity for discriminating expenditure and in level of satisfaction consumption.

18. The work and income distribution which gives dynamic psycho-economic stability in a society is therefore a differential one, and corresponds with the character of the distribution of capacity to work and capacity for discriminating expenditure among the individual members who compose it.

19. It is this differential pattern which generates the norms of equity in payment distribution.

20. In an under-abundant economy the equitable distribution of income is less differentially steep; the more impoverished the economy the flatter the equitable distribution.

21. Under mere subsistence conditions, equity is served by equality (except for the special needs of the ill, the infirm, and the helpless); that is to say, equilibrium is obtained by a non-differential distribution, everyone alike receiving that amount necessary to remain alive.

VI

22. The actual distribution of payment in any society at any given time will be mainly determined by the interaction of two sets of forces: first, impulses of equity in the members of that society, which cause them to seek to establish a differential distribution which corresponds to the equitable distribution: second, the destructive impulses in the members of that society which cause them to seek personal gain at the expense of others, by means of power bargaining and regardless of equity.

23. In the absence of equitable regulation of payment, imperfection in the labour market for whatever reasons, makes it possible for the destructive impulses to be expressed in the form of exploitation by the favoured groups to bring about deviations between the actual distribution of payment and the equitable payment distribution.

24. Imperfections in the labour market can be exploited – whether by employers or employees – only to a certain point.

At about twenty per cent departure from equity an explosive situation develops, the outcome of which would be difficult to predict.

VII

25. Abundant employment (in contrast to full employment) is that condition which provides not only a job for every individual who seeks to work, but a job at a level of work consistent with his capacity.

26. Psycho-economic equilibrium is best achieved in the individual by a level of work corresponding to his capacity, and equitable payment for that work.

27. At a level of work greater than his capacity, a person will fail; at a level less than his capacity, disequilibrium will show either in dissatisfaction or in psycho-pathology characterized by acceptance of non-utilization of personal capacity in work.

28. At an over-abundant level of income, disequilibrium will show in squandering and waste, or in defensive behaviour against squandering; at an under-abundant level of income, disequilibrium will show in feelings of impoverishment and economic want.

29. The reaction to disequilibrium will be critically influenced by the extent to which the notion of equity is accepted by a society and obtains in it.

30. The greater the acceptance in society of equity in income distribution and employment opportunity, the more will psycho-economic disequilibrium in the individual express itself in the desire for social cooperation to establish and maintain equity and abundance.

31. The greater the rejection in society of these conditions, and the greater the reliance upon bargaining for the price of labour, the more will psycho-economic disequilibrium in the individual express itself either in resentment against those who are differentially in a preferred position, or in unenlightened self-interest by those who are in that preferred position.

24

VIII

32. Each individual has a normal pace of work and intensity of application, which he will apply to his work as long as his conditions of work do not inhibit him.

33. Equity in payment and abundant employment are necessary conditions in the long run to avoid inhibiting normal pace and application to work; inequitable payment and fear of unemployment in the long run inhibit pace and application.

IX

34. Under conditions of inequitable distribution of payment and uneven opportunity for employment, any given individual may not be able to do much to affect his own personal position, and may have to accept it; but individuals receiving common treatment (i.e., favoured or unfavoured payment or employment) will tend to cooperate in collective action to protect a favoured position, or to improve an unfavourable one.

35. In the short term, inequitable distribution of income may be maintained and supported by established social and political *mores* and traditions which decree the rightness of relative economic hardship suffered by certain sections of the population; these states of inequity are, however, fundamentally disruptive of social cohesion since they are based upon economic exploitation of one sector of society by another, lead to social disequilibrium, and may eventually lead to forceful suppression or forceful overthrow.

36. In the long term, social cohesion will best be gained by societies which can maintain abundant employment and accept and conform to their own real norms of equity in income distribution. Even in an under-abundant economy under these conditions, social cooperation to enrich the total economy may be stimulated.

PART ONE

Introduction

CHAPTER 1

Current system of wage bargaining

I

WORKING for a living is one of the basic activities in a man's life. By forcing him to come to grips with his environment, with his livelihood at stake, it confronts him with the actuality of his personal capacity – to exercise judgement, to carry responsibility, to achieve concrete and specific results. It gives him a continuous account of the correspondence between outside reality and his inner perception of that reality, as well as an account of the accuracy of his appraisal and evaluation of himself (even though he may not always desire to observe the account). And more, in the quality of enthusiasm or apathy which he brings to his work, he is faced with the state of the balance between the forces of life and the forces of death within him. In short, a man's work does not satisfy his material needs alone. In a very deep sense, it gives him a measure of his sanity.

In confining attention to work that is for a living, I wish to delineate that particular type of work which is embedded in the most primitive and powerful urges having to do with survival – with food, shelter, warmth and comfort: not merely personal survival, but the survival of dependants as well. The economic foundation and framework of family life are encountered – parental responsibility expressed through the medium of providing the material comforts and other things that money can buy, and childhood experiences of being looked after and cared for in these terms.

The actual place occupied by the individual and the family in any social and political system can be judged by the provision made for work. To call itself well-ordered, a society must of a certainty be able to provide work for every citizen who wants to work. But it must do more. It must provide work which enriches the individual by allowing him to exercise his full wit and capacity in his work – and indeed by calling upon him to do so – giving him room to progress in responsibility as he progresses in capacity. It must provide an economy so regulated as to ensure a fair and balanced distribution of wealth in connexion with work: fair in the sense that each man is assured of his due measure of reward for the level of work he is employed to carry out; and balanced in the sense of giving each one that standard of living which he can enjoy without on the one hand experiencing the bitterness of want, or on the other being prey to idleness or tempted into compulsive and wanton expenditure. Plato has pointedly remarked: 'Wealth and poverty are the two causes of the deterioration of the arts. Wealth is the parent of luxury and indolence, poverty of meanness and viciousness, and both of discontent.' Somewhere between, the balance must be struck so that the reinforcement of primordial envy, rivalry, greed, aggression and fear, by outside economic circumstances, can be reduced or eliminated, and the individual faced with both the opportunity and the responsibility for fulfilling his own personal destiny. A human society, to be deserving of that name, must provide such a balance: to the extent that it does not, it cannot expect to be able to rely upon the cooperative identification of its citizens with the common social good.

II

The problem which confronts us is that of regulating the connexions between a man's work, his capacity, and the payment he receives for his work: it is a part of the more general problem of regulating the distribution of wealth. These connexions are presently handled within a framework set by a complex of bargaining and arbitration procedures built up by custom and practice, and carried out within established labour law. The arbitration procedures are intended to bring some order into the working of the labour market on those occasions when, if left to itself, the market mechanism leads to chaos. But they are primitive procedures: the bargaining rests upon the relative power of the contending sides; and arbitration, when used, is based upon the wisdom and personal good sense of the particular individual who has been chosen to arbitrate. What is required is to supplant custom and practice by genuine principle – principle which can be objectively defined – or at least

others, additional national awards having occurred meanwhile. They may be full-scale adjustments on a percentage basis; they may be only partial adjustments. Sometimes adjustments are said to occur unconnected with national awards on the score of payment for scarcity value. We shall have grounds later for examining this last notion.

Regardless of the reasons for any particular demand for a wage or salary increase, regardless of the industry, and regardless of the political outlook of those concerned (and with the possible exception of those few industries which have some type of sliding scale agreement in force), it is tacitly accepted by all sides – employees and employers, government officials, economists, the press, leaders of opinion, and the community at large – that little if anything should happen with regard to wage or salary increases or adjustments unless and until the organized workers, through their official representatives, take the initiative and make demands. Even the proposals to increase earnings by some established increment such as, say, two per cent per annum in years when productivity has increased, still leaves initiative with employees to decide whether they consider the increase to be satisfactory, and to take action if they do not. The main initiative which is commonly expected of the political stereotype of the employer is to find ways of decreasing his labour costs regardless of the welfare of his employees. Any exception to this practice – workers' organizations voluntarily taking a decrease in pay, or employers' organizations voluntarily offering an increase – occurs only in very special circumstances, as for example, in the introduction of fringe benefits.

The situation is then that, after an appropriate interval has elapsed since an increase, the organized workers or staff in one industry put in a claim for a new wage or salary increase, regardless of their current level of earnings. The size of the demand will be determined by a number of forces; the strength of the organization of the workers or staff; the intensity of the feeling of grievance as influenced by such factors as increases in cost of living, or dividends paid in the industry; the political policy of the Union; the sense of rightness or fairness of wages or salaries in that industry as compared (in no very precisely formulated manner) with wages or salaries in other industries or occupations. A bargaining increment is added to give a margin for compromise in the negotiation situation, it being taken for granted that the demand will automatically be rejected by the employers' organization.

The employers do reject the claim. They may argue the case for no increase, or put in a counter-offer sufficiently lower than the claim to allow them to move upwards to some extent once the bargaining gets under way.

The claim may be settled by the process of bargaining. It may not be. If it is not, there may be a show-down – a strike – in which the two sides test their relative strength, the one to go without work and payment, the other to go without production, and each to maintain group solidarity in the face of this trial. Or the issue may be sent to arbitration, the Government acting as intermediary helping the two sides to choose an acceptable arbitrator who will hear both sides of the case and give his decision (or help the two sides to arrive at agreement if his recommendation has not been established as binding).

IV

The bargaining process described (there are steps which have not been mentioned but which do not alter the broad picture) is carried on as though all concerned in it took it for granted that the arguments and counter-arguments are based on certain principles, on an objective and demonstrable rationale, so that if only one's points are sufficiently telling, the force of logic and reason must sway the other side – or at second hand, and perhaps more important, sway public opinion (for the public is listening intently to the proceedings) so that the solidarity of one's members may be increased as a result of public favour for the justice of their case. If the matter is considered more deeply, however, the impression forms that the character of these bargaining arguments is designed rather to sway the passions and stir feelings of justification, to appeal to the logic of the emotions, than to constitute a logically watertight complex of reasons why an increase of some particular amount is either justified or not justified at that particular time.

Consideration of these bargaining processes leaves the distinct impression that all concerned – employers, employees and arbitrators – are trapped by well-established but largely unrealistic conceptions and, premises. No matter how hard they may try to avoid the position, and to be realistic, the results of their deliberations are inevitably dominated by the inadequate frame of reference they are forced to adopt. Attempts to achieve a deeper line of logical reasoning and principle are persistently frustrated by the outmoded framework. This impression that objective and consistent arguments for or against an increase simply do not get stated, is much hardened once we consider some of the main explicitly formulated points of debate. These explicit arguments seem to be attempts to express some deeper-lying line of reasoning which remains buried in feeling, and is itself extremely difficult to identify, formulate and express.

Take, for example, arguments about what is fair and just with regard to the differentials of value applied at any given time to different types of work and to the skills and experience required in order to do these jobs. These attitudes, as expressed in negotiations, and in arguments about differentials, are typified by a quality of evanescence – a will-o'-the-wisp quality. They are difficult to pin down, in the sense that the reasons for the view that one job is inherently worth more than another are simply not stated – the differences in value being presented as manifestly self-evident. Or, if reasons are advanced, these reasons, as I have had occasion previously to demonstrate*, tend to be used in an exceedingly inconsistent manner. The same arguments, whether about skill, experience, responsibility, versatility, or training required in doing the job, or about the complexity, difficulty, size or other quality of the job itself, are used in whatever manner will best support the case it is desired to make. If a job appears relatively complex and requires specialized training and qualification, these features will be cited by those seeking to emphasize the value of the job, and the fact that no finger dexterity or quickness of movement, or

*Measurement of Responsibility, chapter 1.

lifting of heavy weights is required will be omitted. If, however, the latter characteristics are outstanding, then they and not the factors of complexity, or training or qualification will be put into the foreground for the purposes of negotiation. Contrariwise, those seeking to argue the case against any increased valuation of either job, will emphasize the importance of those qualities or characteristics which are more noteworthy in other jobs, and will make light of those which are noteworthy in the job in question.

The essential difficulty in resolving such arguments about the relative value of different jobs is that the criteria used do not apply equally to different jobs, nor are they quantifiable. If the skill, or the training, or the experience, or the complexity of the work, or the physical character of the work, or whatever other criteria or sets of criteria were used, applied in similar fashion to all jobs, comparisons could be made. But they do not, and attempts to force comparisons frequently end up *in absurdum* – as in the case, for instance, of arguments about the relative skills, arduousness, and worrisomeness of, say, the work of a surgeon, an engineer, and a schoolteacher. And attempts to generalize the argument by neat but false quantification of various factors by job rating schemes so as to make some sort of comparison possible, end up in a masking of the real difficulties in the problem* (a technique, moreover, which works only so long as it is possible for those engaged in the dispute to agree on the quantitative values to be assigned to various qualities of the job and of the type of person required to do the job).

Or, again, consider arguments concerned with the cost of living. If the cost of living goes up, there are three possible courses of action: (1) give the same percentage increase to everyone to balance, or partially balance, the rise; (2) give no-one an increase; or (3) give an increase to some groups partly or wholly to balance the rise, and not to other groups. The first two courses of action leave the relative position unchanged, and do not constitute a basis for industrial dispute except in so

---

*I have dealt at greater length in *Measurement of Responsibility* (pp. 6–12) with the non-objective character of job rating schemes.

far as there are groups which are already dissatisfied with their relative position. It is the third course which gives rise to differential change and which most commonly sparks off disputes. These disputes are of two types:

(a) regardless of what is happening to other groups, should not the standard of living of this particular labour group be maintained in the face of rising living costs; or, contrariwise –

(b) is not the standard of living of this particular labour group falling with rising costs to a greater extent than has happened to others, and ought it not therefore to be corrected?

In short, although disputes are frequently argued in terms of cost of living, the point of dispute is in fact solely concerned with the question of how various groups should fare relative to each other in balancing changes in cost of living.

V

Nor, to take another common basis for negotiation, can differential wage and salary levels be linked in principle to levels of productivity. Increase in productivity, either within an enterprise or in the national output, is mainly a matter of invention and discovery or of investment. It arises from a complex of technological advances and of improvements in the organization and deployment of resources. It is rarely, if ever, connected with increased effort on the part of any particular group – except perhaps for spurts carried on for short periods of time for special reasons or in response to special and limited appeals. Realistic rewards for increased productivity would fall, therefore, into two categories: payment in the form of *ex gratia* awards for inventions and discoveries, or for occasions when special efforts have been applied: and participation in an increased standard of living for everyone, whether by a national round of increases in every wage and salary, or by reduction in the cost of living, or by both. To increase the relative wages and salaries of any particular sector because of a high investment rate in that industry, or because the opportunity for rapid technical advance makes it possible for the productivity of the members of that sector to be increased without their assuming a higher level of work consonant with the relative gain in

37

earning level, will provoke economic unrest among those in sectors where like opportunities for investment or technical advance do not exist.

I am suggesting, therefore, that wage disputes settled in whole or in part in terms of increased productivity, or promise of increased productivity, in the industry, are not based upon a realistic premise. (Nor can governmental policies of higher pay for higher productivity be shown to have any realistic meaning.) They assume that an increase in output can be so analysed as to enable it to be attributed explicitly, in part or as a whole, to the increased effort of some particular group. Moreover, they imply that the members of that particular industry have begun to work harder than those in other industries who have not received an equivalent increase – a fact which is not only highly unlikely but which it would be extremely difficult (if not utterly impossible) to prove.

In thus criticizing as unrealistic settlements of wage claims on the basis of productivity, I am aware that by the same token I am rejecting the notion of settling wage claims on the basis of the capacity or incapacity of an industry to pay. The work which employees are given to do does not necessarily vary with the success of an enterprise. But it is the work they do for which employees presumably are paid. If an industry pleads lack of success, or lack of capacity to pay, as ground for not granting an increase – or asking for sanction for a cut – then it is asking its employees to invest a portion of their wages or salaries in the industry – that portion represented by the amount they would supposedly have received had the industry been more prosperous. Or, conversely, if an enterprise or industry has been highly profitable beyond its investment needs, that may be a reason for an all-round bonus, perhaps in recognition of special effort or perhaps just because of the high profits. But it is not a sound reason for arguing a change in the wage and salary levels of that industry relative to other industries.

In similar vein, profit-sharing schemes beg the question of what constitutes a reasonable wage or salary for work. For profit-sharing simply has no bearing upon the question of the differential pattern of wages and salaries within the organization or the industry, nor upon that of the relation of its actual wage and salary structure to the wage and salary structure in other industries.

I am not here trying to argue for or against the notion of employees investing in the organization or industry for which they work, or sharing in its success or lack of success. Nor am I considering the pros and cons of private profit-making as against nationalized industry. I am merely pointing out that investing in an organization and working for it are two different things, requiring in principle entirely different types of return; investment, that of sharing in its profits or losses; work, that of being paid for the responsibilities one discharges on its behalf. Mixing the two together by bringing about unidentifiable investment through reduced wages and salaries, or sharing in profit by an increase in wages or salaries rather than by special bonus, blurs and obscures both processes: the individual employee has no record of his investment, and does not reap direct personal gain or loss in relation to the amount of his investment; and the real issue in wage and salary questions, namely the differential pattern, is left untouched. And it works both ways: neither high nor low productivity can be arguments in principle in favour of either high or low wage and salary levels in a particular industry or organization.

Responsibility for the profitability and productivity of an enterprise lies upon its directors and their immediate agent, the head of the enterprise. If an employee discharges his contractual obligation by doing in a satisfactory manner the work he is given to do, then in equity that employee is as much entitled to the wage or salary appropriate to that work as an employee engaged on the same work in a more profitable enterprise. If he is not doing his job satisfactorily, then he ought not to be retained in it. If he is performing satisfactorily, then apart from special spurts from time to time, there is nothing further that he can do to affect the profitability of the concern. The price paid by the employee for working in an unproductive and unprofitable concern is insecurity of employment and diminished opportunity for advancement. To add to this price that of a less than appropriate wage or salary is to spread indiscriminately over everyone employed by the enterprise a responsibility requisitely residing at the top.

The point can be clearly illustrated by reference to nationalized industry. For to plead lack of profitability in such a case is to ask the employees of that industry, in the interest of maintaining their own jobs, themselves to support an industry whose lack of profitability ought in fact to be a charge on the nation at large. If in the national interest it is considered necessary to keep a particular industry or service in being, even though it is unlikely to be profitable, then it is not for the employees in that industry to be expected to pay for that policy. If on the other hand it is considered that the industry ought to be capable of being run profitably, then it ought to be put in the hands of a board and a chief executive who can succeed in doing so. The same pattern applies in principle in precisely the same way in the private sector of industry.

The argument most often put forward to justify differentially lower rates of pay in unprofitable industries and differentially higher rates in profitable ones, is that unprofitable industries ought to contract while the profitable ones are encouraged to expand. The differential payment structure is to encourage the appropriate movement of labour. I think this principle confuses a number of issues: that of the wage and salary structure, that of special payments, and that of reducing establishment.

In the first place, if it is decided that a given industry must of economic necessity contract, then it ought to be contracted in an open and executively decisive manner – namely, by reducing its establishment in a planned way connected with the realistic requirements of the economic situation. If the opportunities for advancement and security of employment in expanding or otherwise favoured industries are not sufficient to attract the necessary labour, then, for example, special one-time payments should be offered, either as one lump sum or in parts spread over a finite period. Such special payments, separated from wages and salaries, leave the wage and salary structure intact.

To manipulate the wage and salary structure to stimulate movement of labour is a crude course of action, which, even though it may achieve its immediate goal, leaves a trail of disturbance in its wake. It allows managements to avoid their executive responsibilities for controlling establishment, by allowing them to underpay all their employees, so that even those whom they wish and need to retain are financially penalized. It sanctions a technique of wage and salary inflation for carrying on the competition between enterprises for personnel. And it contributes to further instability of the wage and salary structure, since further adjustments have to be made in due course when the desired transfer of labour has taken place and the contracting industry has reached its planned or economic size.

How these problems may be differently tackled is the subject of the whole of this book. How the relationship between profitability and wage and salary levels may be dealt with, I shall comment on in my final chapter.

VI

One special feature of all the usual arguments put forward to prove the validity of any given claim for a wage or salary adjustment must be noted. They all contain the implicit but usually unrecognized assumption that there is a wage or salary which would be fair and reasonable for the job or jobs in question as compared with other jobs. To argue that one job is worth more than another is to assume that there is some principle which can be used to compare the jobs. If it can thus be used to compare jobs, then this must imply that all jobs can be ranked in order of worth one compared with the other. There is implied, in short, a fair differential payment pattern.

The same assumption is made unwittingly by those who put forward the argument that payment ought to be adjusted in relation to profitability or productivity. The implicit standard is inherent in the idea of there being some appropriate level of payment in relation to profits – a level somewhere near that being demanded. Otherwise why a demand for that particular amount? Or why had there not been demands before the profits increased? To reply that the labour supply and demand situation did not allow such demands is to deal only partially with the question, for demands for adjustments to payment are very far indeed from conforming simply either to the supply of labour or to the organized strength of the contending parties. And rarely are there any downward adjustments with falls in profits and productivity.

These unrecognized assumptions about fair and reasonable rates are manifested more explicitly in the form of the rather vague and unspecific notion of the rate for the job; that is to say, if we are doing the same sort of job, we ought to get the same rate. A more precise statement of what I think is usually intended by this standard is that jobs carrying equal responsibility ought to carry equal pay. In practice, however, most people seem to shy away from the idea that this principle could be applied in any very practical way, despite the fact that intuitively they are applying it all the time.

VII

The lack of realism in the modes of settling payment disputes, which I have described, emphasizes to what extent outmoded or non-requisite concepts and perceptions can dominate the conduct of human affairs in such a way as to bring about the defeat of constructive human aspirations and intellect. Unworkable assumptions lead to confusion and despair, which in turn not only unloose hostility and suspicion, but provoke actual behaviour patterns which substantiate for each group the validity of its hostility and of its suspicion of others. Effective and constructive social intercourse needs more than goodwill. It requires that the growth and change in society be accompanied by the discovery and establishment of both the understanding and the techniques which are needed to regulate the new modes of expression of social forces.

The current lack of requisite concepts and procedures has a most debilitating effect upon industrial relations, and is connected with a number of socially disruptive phenomena which it may be useful to summarize. I say connected with rather than caused by, for it would be difficult to say which is cause and which is effect, or whether both are symptoms of some deeper-lying cause. These phenomena are familiar enough, but appear to be so taken for granted or accepted as inevitable that their existence causes no comment whatever.

(*I*) Wage increases normally have to be claimed or demanded. The main initiative in making demands comes from organized staff and manual workers, although of recent years professional groupings too have instituted procedures for negotiating salary scales. A group which demands nothing can ordinarily expect to get nothing other than consequential increases arising out of successful demands made by other groups.

Consequently, society allows itself to break into two major organized groups, and a large unorganized group in between. This breaking up into opposing groups is strongly decried in most quarters as a situation which reinforces historically-determined class splits and class warfare. Nevertheless, the procedure which heightens the split – that of requiring organized staff and manual workers to demand and force increases from their employers – is accepted without demur.

(2) Leadership in industry is turned upside down in its most important single aspect. For work is done for a living. The notion that workers will not get any increase unless they demand it means nothing less than the fact that in times of inflation they will not be able to maintain or better their standard of living unless they demand it. It is accepted – no less by the employers themselves – that employers cannot be counted upon to behave reasonably or fairly with regard to a man's living unless that man organizes to make his demands. The stereotype of the employer who, left unchecked, would be selfish and exploiting, is more than a caricature – it is a factual statement of the role into which employers as a group – whatever may be their outlook as individuals – allow themselves to be cast in our wage bargaining procedures.

As a result, initiative having been passed to organized staff and manual workers in getting a living wage, leadership also passes into the hands of the leaders of the organized staff and manual workers on this most important score. Employers in industry, conversely, have lost their leadership role in this respect. It is a most important respect. All the stress upon the importance of managerial leadership in industry, all the exhortations to managers to lead their men, cannot overcome the simple fact that when it comes to earning a living out of their work, the men lead themselves. Thus to emphasize the negative aspect is not to deny that any leadership is possible. Good leadership does occur in spite of these circumstances. But for it to occur, a manager must be able to overcome by his personal qualities the social matrix in which he works. Good managerial leadership is hindered all the way. It must drag the full weight of economic conventions which eat at the foundations of leadership. This situation is concretely reflected in the conflict between managers and shop stewards in industry as to precisely who has the main leadership function *vis-à-vis* manual workers. In view of the fact that whenever a man's living is at stake it is to his shop steward and not his manager that he looks for initiative, leadership and concern, the importance so widely attributed to good managerial leadership and the emphasis on leadership training for managers take on something of a hollow sound.

This leadership from below in industry has become quite formally accepted. Trade union leaders, for instance, are exhorted to adopt responsible attitudes to the welfare of the nation in putting forth their wage claims. They are asked to act with restraint, and to accept their full responsibility for preventing inflationary pressure on the economy which would be caused by too high demands. Such exhortations betoken acceptance of the fact that the initiative lies with the men and their representatives. It is in no way seen as odd or unusual that employers do not lead in this basic aspect of the contractual relationship in work. The weakening and rending of the fabric of managerial leadership seems not to be recognized or even suspected.

In similar vein, the situation is taken for granted on the shop floor. It has become a widespread custom, if not indeed a universal one, that managers, in discussing the arrangement of particular wage structures within establishments, should not take the initiative and go direct to their employees to make their views known to them*. Such matters are to be discussed only with duly accredited representatives of the men, it being

* For a detailed analysis and discussion of this most important point, see the chapter on the subject of managerial contraction in Wilfred Brown: *Exploration in Management*.

the responsibility of these representatives to act as go-betweens, keeping to themselves all direct contact with the men. For most employers this arrangement seems to offer a welcome relief from a difficult and onerous responsibility. But the price is a disruptive split between managers and workers inside the establishment. This split extends into the minutiae of daily working life, when eventually it becomes the responsibility of the shop steward, and not of the manager, to be concerned about the welfare of the men in every respect, taking up their grievances about every aspect of working conditions*. The assumption is that if the shop stewards are not complaining, the men are satisfied. And yet whenever shop stewards do take up grievances, managements frequently feel themselves persecuted and played up. They are unsure whether the shop stewards are acting maliciously and without valid cause, and resent that very loss of direct contact with their men which they themselves have sanctioned.

In short, if in industry an employer of men cannot take the initiative and give the lead in paying his men for work in such a manner as to be seen to be behaving in a fair and equitable way, then he cannot expect to be perceived as giving that full and rounded leadership which is entitled to full and rounded respect. To be able to do so requires that he have some objective and demonstrable standards about the relative values of the jobs he has established.

(3) In the absence of any objective and lawful basis for adjusting payment differentials, the sole available method of giving a real relative increase to one group is to increase its level of payment. All real adjustments, therefore, contribute to inflation. There are no means whereby real – that is, differential – payment adjustments can be made between various jobs at all levels from shop floor to managing director, dropping some and increasing others in accord with agreed principle, while yet maintaining non-inflating wage and salary levels so that general increases in standard of living may come about through greater

---

*I have discussed this point at some length in my analysis of the split at the bottom of the executive system, in *The Changing Culture of a Factory*, 1951.

productivity, lower prices, and, if circumstances warrant, a general upward movement in wages and salaries.

A system which necessitates the making of demands for wages to be adjusted is a system which is using wages inflation as its wage correcting technique. It is inconsistent therefore to decry the fact that the inevitable result is wages inflation. And it is inconsistent to ask workers to forego use of the mechanism because of the threat of the inflation which must ensue.

A most striking fact is the extent to which the differential feature in wage negotiations tends to be denied and pushed to one side. If group A feels unfairly paid relative to other groups, the fact that its demand for a relative increase may be inflationary is really quite beside the point. Society provides no other means of redress for such an economic injustice. The one possibility that is usually not faced up to is that other groups – and genuine equity would not necessarily limit such groups to shareholders – might explicitly allow an increase to one group without claiming one themselves, thus suffering a relative reduction of real wages in order to right an economic inequity and at the same time avoid adding to inflation.

(4) The public acceptance of inconsistent and non-objective arguments as though they were objective and consistent, stimulates the need for leaders representing both employers and organized workers who are skilled at concealing power bargaining behind a façade of apparent rational argument. An advantage in the competition for leadership roles is handed to the aggrieved and the demagogue. The more stable and constructive leader must conform to some extent to this mould – and the inherent socially destructive nature of the negotiation system makes it easy to do so. A disrespect for rational thought is engendered.

(5) Work is de-humanized by making it a fit subject for primitive bargaining. The creativeness in work and its value as a human activity are debased by the crudeness of the arrangement for paying for the employment of that creativeness. Sermonizing on the virtue of work does not overcome this fact. When men enjoy their work, as they do, it is in spite of the system of industrial relations.

(6) Finally, when genuine changes occur – as does happen from time to time – in the responsibilities carried by any given occupational group such that its members move higher or lower in the hierachy of industrial responsibility, there is no objective mechanism either for noticing the change or for giving financial recognition to the fact of its occurrence. So-called anomalies are built up which in due course become very difficult to put right.

VIII

If the system of wage negotiation is as powerfully negative in its effects as I have described, then why, it might be asked, does not the whole system cease functioning, break down, disintegrate? Because the negative effects are balanced by sufficient common good sense and social cohesion. This balance ought not to be taken for granted, however. Industrial disputes are a chronic canker upon our social life, causing unnecessary wastage of constructive effort, and severe and deep-rooted disaffection against the pattern of regulation of our economic life. This disaffection readily spreads into confused misapprehension about the modes of regulation of our social and political life in general. Should this picture of social pathology seem excessively pessimistic, consider for a moment the intensity of bitterness unleashed against the social system in periods of economic insecurity, and the impulse potentially available for release to destroy that system in all its aspects, both good and bad.

It might be argued that it is the law of supply and demand which holds the balance and prevents chaos from developing over the establishment of a differential pattern of payment in industry. If only the law of supply and demand were allowed to operate unfettered, then the greater would be the stability and equilibrium. But the law of supply and demand does not operate unfettered; perfect competition does not exist. On the contrary, there are many important restrictions preventing it from doing so, set by governmental regulations, trade union organization, employer organizations and public opinion.

Whether or not these restrictions ought to be, or could be,

diminished and the law of supply and demand allowed to operate more freely is a question which I do not believe it would be very profitable to consider. Not only is it not a practical question. Worse, it presupposes a continuation of power bargaining as an integral part of settling the pattern of distribution of income. There is another and different route which I propose to follow, which I believe leads more readily to a possible solution to the problem of payment differentials. It depends upon the finding which I have already reported* that there exist norms of what constitutes fair payment for any given level of work, regardless of the type of work, productivity, scarcity of labour, or of other conditions connected with that work.

What would the result be if we did take seriously the fact that we do have a sense of a fair rate for the job? My previous work has led me to conclude that a more systematic and objective regulation of the pattern of wages and salaries might be achieved by conforming with these norms. Such a view assumes that there are powerful limiting forces preventing the differential payment structure from deviating too far from the norm, and setting decided limits within which the law of supply and demand operates and negotiations are carried on. Further, it assumes forces inside each one of us such that we are in a state of equilibrium when in receipt of the norm of fair pay for our work, and in a state of disequilibrium or tension when we are not. The arguments in favour of this assumption of internal equilibrium in each of us have been put forward by J. M. M. Hill†, and need not be pursued further here.

If the case can be established for this view, then it will be possible to move towards a systematic regulation of payment differentials based upon demonstrable social norms. The implementation of equity in payment could replace the socially accepted and stereotyped working assumption that employers, whenever they are in a position to do so, are attempting to force down wages and salaries as far as possible, while employees, whenever they are in a position to do so, are agitating

*Measurement of Responsibility.
†J. M. M. Hill: 'A note on time-span and economic theory', 1958.

for more pay, or changing jobs, or downing tools. It might also eliminate the false dichotomy between the notions of paying in accord with a social principle as against paying in accord with the economic conditions of the industry. It may be possible that payment in accord with equity ought to prove economically sound as well as socially just, because it diminishes wrangling and encourages efficiency. Genuinely sound efficiency, and justice for the individual, are opposite sides of the same coin.

I shall begin my consideration of the case for equity by turning to the problem of defining and measuring work.

CHAPTER 2

The nature of economic work

I

THE problems of payment and of individual progress which we have set out to examine are connected with work: payment for work; individual progress in work. The question remains: what is work? A practical and realistic definition of what is meant by work is of fundamental importance to our inquiry. It is the absence of explicit definition that precludes the possibility of any explicit statement in principle of the connexion between employment work and financial reward for that work.

I shall first consider the definition of work in general. Then I shall turn to the question of economic work – that is, work directed towards an economic objective. It will be necessary to sort out the main types of economic work – in particular, to distinguish between entrepreneurial work and employment work. In so doing, we shall be able to establish the framework within which employment work occurs, and to set out some of its basic characteristics. That will allow us to return to the question of definition, and to establish a conceptually rigorous definition of employment work which will lay the basis for systematic measurement.

In physics, the concept of work has a special and precise definition – the operation of a force in producing movement of mass through space. Such a definition does not of course apply to work in the psychological sense. Although the physicist may not consider Atlas to be doing physical work in supporting the world, nevertheless in the psychological sense he would most certainly be considered to be working. It is the essence of this psychological definition of work – the work which goes on inside the individual – which we must seek. All my references to work, therefore, unless otherwise specified, are to psychological work.

The dictionary definitions, reflecting common usage, are not precise enough for our purpose. They refer to something that is done – an act, or a deed, or occupation, or business, and more especially action involving effort or exertion directed to a definite end, a means of gaining one's livelihood. The short-coming of such definitions is not only that they give a variety of different meanings, but that none of them indicates how the psychological content of the work it defines might be measured – why one act is greater than another, why the exertion or effort in this occupation may be considered greater than the exertion or effort required in that one. Sometimes, for example, the term is used to refer to physical exertion – it is more work to lift a heavy load than a light one. At other times it means mental activity – so-called brainwork. But whether brainwork is more difficult, or more fatiguing, or more valuable, than physical work is a question which I must leave open for the moment. The difficulty in finding a definition for work illus-trates the absence of any common social frame of reference within which the whole issue of the value of work may be con-sidered.

The economic view of work is not much more helpful. Work is approached via the value of labour, or its productivity. It will be noted, however, that neither value nor productivity takes us nearer to the heart of the problem of what is meant by labour in the sense of psychological work. Labour, as a commodity, as a resource to be acquired or dispensed with, may be considered in terms of its marginal utility. But this is to describe certain aspects of the functioning of the labour market. It provides no basis for the analysis of psychological work. Nor will we find conceptions of work in terms of productivity to be of much more help. Productivity describes the result of work. It is an end product of a complex of activities carried out by directors, managers, technicians and workers. Hence it is of no use for our purposes unless we can find a means of ascribing to a particular individual his particular and specific contribution to that productivity: in order successfully to be able to do that, we have to be able to define and measure what we mean by that individual's work, and we are back where we started from.

In seeking for a definition of work which will best suit our purposes, two sets of criteria must be met. First, the normal conditions of any scientific definition must be served: the definition must be objective, in the sense that what is defined can be observed by anyone who follows the definition; it must be both comprehensive and exclusive, in the sense of identifying what it is intended to refer to and excluding the rest of the field; and it must serve as a basis for quantification, for if a definition is objective, then the amount of whatever is so defined ought to be open to measurement. Second, the definition must encompass the notion of responsibility. For no sooner do we consider the question of the relative value of different types of work in terms of payment differentials than we find ourselves in the field of argument about the relative degrees of responsibility in the various types of work under consideration. Payment in the sense of value of labour or work is intimately associated with felt weight of responsibility carried.

In *Measurement of Responsibility*, work was defined as the exercise of discretion within prescribed limits in order to reach a goal or objective. This definition I thought met the foregoing requirements. It is entirely consistent with common usage, in that it includes the notion of activity or effort directed towards a goal or objective. But it is a refined definition in that it distinguishes between two major components of the activity: (a) the discretionary content, comprising the discretion, choice or judgement which the person doing the work is expected to exercise; and (b) the prescribed limits, comprising the rules, regulations, procedures and policies, the custom and practice, and the physical limits of plant, equipment or tooling, which set external limits within which the discretion has to be exercised.

This definition of work in terms of discretion, prescribed limits, and a goal or objective to be achieved, lends itself to quantification in terms of the maximum length of the span of time during which discretion has to be continuously exercised before the quality of the discretion becomes assessable – the longer the span of time, the greater the size or level of the work. Subsequent experience with this conception of work has brought about modifications in detail which have sharpened the method of measurement and increased its objectivity.

II

This definition of work, however, is quite general in scope, covering every type of psychological work. Before turning to the detailed consideration and its measurement, therefore, a further delimitation is required of the field of work with which we are here concerned. The different broad areas of work are distinguished by the goal or objective; for example, economic work, artistic work, or charitable work. The different types of work are distinguished by the character of the discretion which has to be exercised and the prescribed knowledge required; for example, manual work, mathematical work, personnel work, teaching, or secretarial work.

But for our present purposes two broad categories of goal, and hence of work, may be separated – economic and non-economic. By economic work is meant all work whose designated goal is part of the social network connected with the creation and distribution of goods and services. Under the rubric of non-economic work are included all other types of work in connexion with which labour services are not offered for sale – as, for example, family, recreational, and some charitable work. By way of illustration, and not detailed description, the work of the housewife comprises such matters as judgement in the upbringing of children, choices in the running arrangements for the house and for meals. She operates within the limits of the family financial means, cultural custom and practice, and a variety of other geographical, social and psychological constraints.

Our main endeavour being the exploration of the nature of economic work, however, we need be diverted no further into considering other forms of non-economic activities. Economic work aimed towards the production and distribution of goods and services comprises the manifold activities broadly encompassed within the field of economics – primary production of food and raw materials, manufacturing and processing, transportation, distribution including wholesaling and retailing, and the planning and organization and administration of economic work, including governmental planning and administration, accounting, supply, technical, personnel, and other specialized functions essential to the running of the economic process.

An obvious feature of work in the economic sphere is that those so employed are participating in the production and supply of the material requirements of living. In more primitive economies – where exchange is at a minimum and is carried on by barter – the material fruits of a person's labour are reaped and handled by himself, and hence are directly and tangibly apparent to him. Differences in standard of living among different members of the community are more immediately relatable to individual differences in capacity to produce – to farm, to fish, to build, to hunt. By comparison with the relative directness of perception of rewards in primitive production, there is an absolute quality to the intangibility of the appropriateness of individual economic reward in our own society. In an industrial economy based on large-scale organization of production and distribution in which individuals are deployed on more or less detailed aspects of the total process of production and distribution, and with money excluding for all practical purposes the trading of goods as a means of exchange, the relationship between the material outcome of one's own work and the material value of one's reward is totally obscured from conscious assessment.

III

There are two main forms of economic work, each generating its own form of economic return – entrepreneurial work (including shareholding and directing work), and contractual employment work. It is contractual employment work with which the present study is mainly concerned. In order to define the problems of employment work, however, it is necessary to define entrepreneurial work as well. It is within the total setting of entrepreneurial work that the full character of contractual employment work may be made manifest. I shall briefly set out the main features of each type of work with particular emphasis upon the type of discretion which must be exercised.

Entrepreneurial work is that of deciding which kinds of economic enterprise are likely to prove profitable by virtue of the demand for the particular goods and services which they provide, investing appropriate amounts of capital in the establishment or purchase of such an enterprise, employing an organization to carry out the work, and directing how it shall be operated by its employees in order to fulfil its objectives. The amount and character of the shareholding of the entrepreneur – be he an individual or a financial combine – if he attracts capital other than his own, must be such that he retains effective financial control of the enterprise.

In short, the entrepreneur owns enterprises outright, or financially controls them, and directs their operation. His judgement and discretion are concerned with setting objectives or goals in work, in deciding what goods and services are to be produced, providing the resources necessary for their production, and setting general standards for the development, production and sale of those goods or services in relation to the resources provided. The prescribed content is contained in company law, Stock Exchange regulations, and other regulations governing the running of companies. The risk is a personal risk – that of loss of the personal resources invested in the enterprise. The rewards are the personal return on investment to be gained from the operation of the enterprise. Most important from our point of view is the fact that, while the risk is personal, at the same time the control of the enterprise is personal. The entrepreneur takes his chances with his own capacity to foresee sound areas for investment and business activity, and his capacity to direct his enterprise towards the objectives he sets.

Employment work, by contrast with entrepreneurial work, is that of carrying out designated tasks within the executive organization of an enterprise with which the person has a contract to work, the contract ordinarily not having a specified time limit for which it holds good. Employment work does not carry responsibility for setting goals or objectives. Although it may not always be obvious, what an employee is to do and the results to be achieved by his work are *always* set for him. This fact need not be obscured by the fact that there are employees in managerial positions who set the results to be achieved by their subordinates.

Every manager has had his own objectives set for him, and is authorized to allocate to his subordinates only that work which will enable him to discharge his own responsibilities. That is to say, he is limited to allocating work consistent with the objectives and goals of the enterprise.

Employment work is that type of work, then, carried out by every single member of an executive organization established by a company to do its work. It includes the work of the chief executive employed by the company, and of all the managers, technicians, specialists, and workers employed by him or by his subordinates. In this regard it is useful to keep firmly in mind the true distinction between a company – the legal entity whose members are the shareholders – and executive organizations established by a company to do its work, whose members are *employees* of the company and not *members* of it.

The discretionary content of employment work has to do with deciding what steps to take to achieve the results prescribed – how best to do the jobs allocated – within the resources provided, company policies and regulations, set methods, administrative procedures and routines, and other prescribed limits. In return for discharging the responsibilities which he was employed for and which he has contracted to carry out, each employee is paid a wage or salary which is ordinarily the greater the more the responsibility carried in a job.

IV

Full scale entrepreneurial work in the hands of one person or of a small combine or partnership has become far less common in present-day industry than a splitting of entrepreneurial work into two main components with the establishment of a public company; namely, the investors or shareholders who are legally the members of the company, and the directors who act as elected agents of the shareholders. This division of entrepreneurial work throws up two separate types of work, entrepreneurial shareholding work and directorial work.

Entrepreneurial shareholding work is that of judging in which kinds of enterprise – and, more specifically, in which particular enterprises – it is worth buying shares. The individual investor relinquishes liquidity in favour of a prospective yield either through appreciation in the value of his capital through the success of the enterprise, or through a steady return on his capital at or above the ruling rate of interest, or both appreciation and steady return. His risk is personal. He uses his own discretion (even where he takes friendly or professional advice, responsibility for the final decision is his), and the financial gain or loss is his own. If he chooses to gamble on enterprises where there is uncertainty about producing goods or services which it is known would have a definite value if they were produced, or where there is uncertainty about the likely value of the goods or services themselves, then the risk is his, and so are the rewards, if any.

The investor's relationship with the enterprise is a financial one. Having decided to invest, there is no obligation upon him to do any further kind of work for the enterprise. His work is that of selecting the enterprise and buying his shares in it; and his work continues in the form of periodic review of his investment and his decision to continue it or to sell out at the best price he can get, depending on his assessment of the current situation. He may take part further in setting the course of the enterprise, by his influence, along with other investors, on the directors. But such participation is his right in protecting his investment, and is not an obligation.

Individual shareholding work must be sharply distinguished from *corporative investment* – whether governmental or non-governmental – in which the nature of the risk is obviously and significantly different. Whether the government of the day decides to invest in the nationalization of a particular type of industry, or a particular economic development such as atomic energy, or whether the directors of a large insurance company decide to invest in a particular enterprise, the financial risk involved in the investment is not personal to those whose discretion decides what investment shall be made. The investment decisions are made by investor-agents and not directly by the shareholders who take the financial risk. They do not give up the liquidity of their personal assets. Their risk is the risk of loss of the office or position they hold. Whereas the individual shareholder gets his return in the form of a yield on his invest-ment,the investor-agent's reward is not related to the investments he arranges. He gets the salary or the fee for the position he occupies.

The existence of a business enterprise, whether public or private, requires that the general objects of the business have been defined. These objects indicate the economic activities which the enterprise may pursue. Which of these activities the business will pursue and how in reality the objects will be achieved, is for the directors to decide on behalf of the share-holders (although in some instances the directors and share-holders may be the same persons). In short, *directorial work* is that of exercising discretion in determining broadly how the resources of an enterprise shall be deployed among various possible economic activities which could be pursued in further-ing the objects of the enterprise. Directors, as the title implies, set the direction of activity, decide what work shall be done, what goods and services shall be provided for the market.

Directors are appointed or elected for a specified period of time. They are subject to the will of the shareholders in very general terms: that is to say, in the sense that the shareholders, if they are dissatisfied, may replace their directors by others who would propose to pursue some alternative general course. They carry financial risk only so far as they are financially committed as shareholders. The personal risk is that of loss of appointment as director. The method of payment of directors is by fee. This method of payment – in effect a fee for services rendered to the shareholders in seeing that their money is wisely employed – derives from the nature of the role. The fee is a fixed payment, usually common to all the members of the Board, for sharing the responsibility for corporate decisions*.

* In passing, it may be noted that the work of the *self-employed person* – physicians, solicitors, architects, accountants and others providing profes-sional services; private dealers, traders and agents; professional artists and entertainers – combines elements of individual investor, director, and employee. He is personally liable for his investment and for the expenses incurred; he must personally direct the course of his activities; and he personally carries out these activities (sometimes with the assistance of additional employees).

The composite nature of the payment arising out of the composite nature

It will be apparent that there is a considerable difference between the role of full-scale entrepreneur and that of director alone, because of the difference in the financial risk involved. The division of the entrepreneurial role into shareholding and directorial work has thrown up a form of industrial organization in which the directors are subjected to strong pressures from shareholders, employees, and customers, and hold the balance between them*. It is a characteristic of such organization that the directors' concern is the maintenance of a sound and developing enterprise, giving a due return to investors and due payment to employees, without that necessary predilection for the shareholder which inevitably occurs when shareholder and director are the self-same entrepreneur. Indeed, it is a very common feature of such organization that some if not all the directors are employed in full-time executive roles in the enterprise as well as carrying their directorial role, a fact which brings into the Board Room an increased intuitive sense of questions of wage and salary differentials.

V

It is by separating the question of shareholding and directing work from that of employment work, that it may be shown that the analysis of employment work to be presented is general in scope in the sense of being independent of type of ownership. A public company, a nationalized enterprise, and a cooperative society, for example, differ in the structure of shareholding, in the mode of distribution of profits, and in the mode of appointing directors and setting policy. But they do not differ in the

---

of the responsibility in self-employed work can be illustrated most clearly in those instances where an individual is established as a company, and can thereby receive income from his work as follows: dividends as shareholder in his company; director's fee as a director of it; and a salary as an employee of it. Even where no formally established company exists, it is possible to distinguish between the profit (or loss) made as a result of the year's income and business expenditure, and the money which is periodically drawn (as a salary) for the personal and family expenditure of the self-employed person.

*See Wilfred Brown: *Exploration in Management*, for a more detailed analysis of this point.

way they get their executive work done. They all employ executive organizations of precisely the same kind. They organize their work in the same general manner, and they compete for labour in the same market.

The differential conditions of work and payment which govern executive organizations apply to all levels of the organization. Top management, as much as manual workers, are employee members of the enterprise, and work in its executive organization. Our mode of analysis of employment work must, therefore, be capable of exploring the work content of all the levels in the executive organization from managing director to shop floor. It must be able to compare these levels of work by reference to a common yardstick, and to establish a differential payment structure which includes every single position in the executive hierarchy.

In short, it must be recognized that all contractual employment positions are part of one common area of social organization, different from the shareholder area and from the director area. It is not sufficient to deal separately with the structure of wage and salary differentials applying to manual workers and the bottom level of clerical workers, and to treat the salary differentials of managers as though they were something different. Managers and workers are part of precisely the same executive organization, employed to do the work of a business enterprise. To sort out the problem of work and payment differentials, we shall have to learn to see these executive organizations as total systems of interlocking positions, including the various levels of manager, the technologists and technicians, the administrators, and the office and manual workers*.

*I should emphasize that my views about payment and sound industrial relations have developed against a background of the results of other projects in which I have been involved at the Glacier Metal Company. I cannot review these results here. I must mention, however, that I assume a particular and rigorous definition of the concept of manager; a certain conception of requisite executive organization; the existence of full-scale employee participation in the legislation of all social policies and individual entitlements; and an effective individual appeals procedure. (See *The Changing Culture of a Factory* and *Exploration in Management*.)

CHAPTER 3

Employment work

I

EMPLOYMENT work begins when the directors of an enterprise purchase labour services in order to get work done in pursuit of its objectives. They can appoint one or more persons. Theoretically, with growth in the work which has to be done the board could go on appointing an increasing number of people to do it. In practice, a board cannot control large numbers directly and appoints usually a single person as chief executive who, on the board's behalf, establishes subordinate to him a hierarchy of positions for which he and his subordinates choose candidates. The number of these chief executives may be increased to make possible the establishment of a number of separate executively conducted businesses under the same board.

In these very simple and very familiar procedures lies the establishment of an executive hierarchy. Executive organization of this type is as old as civilized man. It is used not only to get industrial economic work done, but in the organization of the Church, the Army, the administrative organ of the state, and every other kind of work where those responsible for the accomplishment of the work need to employ more than one person to do it. It is the basic form of organized human effort. It makes possible the mobilization of human effort in large-scale endeavours which would otherwise be impossible.

Why hierarchical forms of organization inevitably occur whenever an enterprise establishes an executive organization to do its work is a question of great importance. Why do not other types of organization occur*? What are the human

---

*It may be thought that I am overlooking cooperative communities like the Kibbutzim in Israel, or the many Utopian communities which have been established throughout the world. I am not. These communities organizationally have the form of large partnerships. They are not executive organs in the sense in which I am describing them – that is, executive organs

61

characteristics which dictate that the employment of a multitude of persons shall precipitate a hierarchical structure? If we were able to direct our attention to these questions, might we not be able to discover other means of organizing human effort in doing work? These questions are not necessarily wide of my main theme; the answer to them would undoubtedly deepen our understanding of that theme. But my data do not take me far enough at present to tackle them*. We may note, however, that this form of hierarchy accords with the employment of a hierarchy of individual capacity. It is to be suspected, therefore, that the existence of executive hierarchies is a social response to the distribution in society of individual capacities, making possible the employment of available capacity.

II

Hierarchical executive organization, then, enables an enterprise (through the board of directors on its behalf) to employ individuals to work for it. The directors are able to confine their activities to deciding what they wish to get done, to employing a chief executive who will arrange for the necessary work to be done to achieve the objective, and to periodic review of the results of the chief executive's work to ensure the work's getting done in a satisfactory manner. The chief executive

---

employed by an enterprise to do its work. And they are subject to the limitation of large partnerships, in that there are definite upper limits to the number of persons who can cooperate in this manner – a limit imposed probably by the fact that the members must be known to each other, a factor essential to genuine partnerships. Large-scale endeavour such as occurs in industry, the Church, the Army, appears to be impossible to achieve under such forms of organization. I include industrial co-partnerships in my comment, for these are not real partnerships. They are large employment organizations whose employees enjoy a bonus scheme related to some extent to the profits.

*I do propose, however, to undertake this analysis of hierarchic organization in due course, in connexion with the analysis of certain general characteristics of production organization which have emerged from the social analysis of factory organization at Glacier. See, for example, the description of unit and section organization in Wilfred Brown: *Exploration in Management* for a report of these developments written from the company's point of view.

may be a member of the board itself – a managing director – or he may be employed by the board to carry out their policy without taking part in board-room decisions – a general manager.

In either case – managing director or general manager – the board specifies the results to be achieved and controls the general direction in which the activities of the enterprise are to move. The manner in which a board specifies results and controls direction may vary from the setting of very precise and explicit terms of reference, to the setting of very loose ones. Targets may be set in the form of profits and turnover to be achieved and cost limits to be bettered; or the goal set may be to do the best possible under the economic conditions to be encountered, whether or not the best possible has been done being a matter for retrospective assessment by the board in the light of the results achieved. Whatever the form in which they are set, however, terms of reference will be discovered always to exist, even though many of their aspects may frequently remain unrecognized until such a time as the chief executive attempts to exceed them.

It is the responsibility of an appointed chief executive to see that the work he has been set gets done – by his own efforts and through his management of the efforts of his subordinates. How he does so is, within the prescribed limits, a matter for his own discretion. From his point of view the position is much as follows. Whereas the members of the board (including himself if he too is a director) are corporately accountable, he in his position as chief executive is individually accountable. How well or badly he manages the organization and its business is his responsibility alone. To him personally goes the credit or the blame. His continued employment as chief executive depends upon his performance. He gets from the board the necessary assets in the form of sanctioned capital expenditure, and allocation of existing material resources in the form of property, buildings, equipment and plant. The quantity and character of the assets put under his control constitute the first limit on the scope of his activities.

The chief executive also gets from the board his terms of

reference, stated in more or less general terms (and deriving in the first place from the articles of association governing the enterprise as a whole), or not formally stated at all but rather just there and understood without its being necessary to state them. These terms of reference set the limits on the products or services which he may seek to develop, produce, and sell, on the methods by which he may provide them, and on the markets within which he may seek to trade. These limits are ordinarily set and modified in practice each time the board considers proposals from him with regard to opening up new markets, developing new lines of business, or scrapping current processes or procedures in favour of new ones. What constitutes a *new* market, or line of business, or method, is usually a matter of custom and practice, involving intuitive rather than explicitly formulated judgement. Certain matters seem quite naturally to climb to board level (sometimes, but by no means always, because they require sanction for capital expenditure which has not previously been authorized). Other matters, also to do with markets, business and methods, seem to be straightforward, or covered by some previous capital allocation, or are a natural part of what are often called day-to-day operations, and the chief executive proceeds to deal with them, usually without a second thought about whether or not board sanction is required. What it is in each particular instance that distinguishes which issues require board sanction and which do not, is a question which may be answerable once we consider the question of work within a time-scale.

Within the policy – however manifest or however implicit – established by the board, the chief executive must exercise his own discretion on a host of issues, predictable and unpredictable, which he encounters in his working life. He must to a certain extent decide on company objectives, since many of the decisions he is forced to take have to do with matters on which company policy is shadowy and only vaguely defined. His discretion must be exercised also, for example, with regard to pricing, sales activities, establishment, production methods, maintenance of plant, wages and salaries, manpower planning, budgeting, quality of product, research and development, advertising, purchasing, stock levels, trade union relations. These and countless other questions he must deal with, some in terms of long-term plans to be adopted, others in terms of immediate actions to be taken. In all, he has freedom to exercise his own judgement within the policy set for him by the board, deciding which from among the variety of possible courses of action will in the particular circumstances stand the best chance of fulfilling the work he has been set to do.

Thus it is the fact of the existence of both prescribed and discretionary responsibilities which enables a Board on behalf of the enterprise both to control its chief executive and to allow him freedom. The prescribed limits delineate the area within which he has freedom to act. The paradox in this situation is that the prescribed limits are as necessary for genuine freedom of action as are the discretionary responsibilities. It is from having been set realistic and sufficiently clear prescribed limits that freedom to use discretion ensues. There is perhaps nothing more likely to inhibit the application of effective discretion than for the bounds of that discretion to be so utterly vague, indefinable and diffused as to give no frame for executive decision and action.

Just as the chief executive is bound within the prescribed limits of his activity, so are the positions in each subsequent layer in the hierarchy bound within narrower and narrower limits, each within the whole. Part of what is discretionary at one executive level becomes prescribed at the next lower level. The chief executive delegates to his subordinates work over which he has discretionary control. He sets terms of reference, parts of which may be explicit and parts implicit, within which he expects them to exercise their judgement in carrying out his instructions, just as the board limited his own field of action in doing his work. The subordinates, in their turn, may delegate work to their subordinates, setting terms of reference which define the limits within which discretion may be used.

In this manner the total system is gripped within a controlling framework extending from the top to the bottom, ensuring that the whole is working towards a common end. The prescribed framework makes it possible to ensure that the discretion exercised by each person will be linked and dovetailed with the discretion exercised by every other, so that if every one of the firm's employees exercises adequate discretion, the managing director can be assured that the work he wants done will be done. What happens to the resources of the enterprise as a result of the work done by the executive organ it employs, is a responsibility which rests with the board. Whether or not the enterprise is commercially successful will depend upon the wisdom of the board in many respects: its choice of chief executive; the soundness of the objectives it has set; its standards of efficiency; the facilities and budgets it has made available; the congruence between its objectives and the work upon which it engaged its executive organ; and its sense of what constitutes a necessary executive organization to carry out that work. It will depend also upon external circumstances beyond the control of the board.

III

This brief description of hierarchic executive organization is in its essence self-evident. I hope I have not unduly laboured the matter. The next point also is self-evident – indeed axiomatic. It may prove to be so obvious as to leave our argument open to the criticism of being overly careful. It has been my experience, however, that if a common understanding is not arrived at on these simple starting points, then they arise to bedevil every subsequent point in the discussion. It is by far the safer course, even though slightly the longer one, to make no assumptions as to which points can be taken as commonly agreed and accepted.

The point I have in mind is that of what constitutes responsibility. What do we mean when we say an employee is responsible for something? It is a term which lies at the very heart of the meaning of work and calls for the greatest caution and respect. But it tends on the contrary to be carelessly treated and loosely used. Confusion arises as a result. The main abuse is that of applying it in far too general a sense. Thus, for example, for reasons which I shall state in a moment, it is not correct to describe a research department manager as responsible for his firm's new products, a sales manager for the sales figures, a secretary for the letters she sends, a goods-inwards inspector for the quality of the goods taken into stores, a railway engine driver for the safety of his passengers, a safety officer for the prevention of accidents, an employment officer for the quality of personnel intake, a progress officer for delivery. The list could be multiplied over and over again. In each case there is some reality in the statement. But the statements are only partially true. Each of the employees contributes by his work to the outcome mentioned. But he cannot by himself be said to be responsible for that outcome.

What do we mean then by contributing to the outcome? How does each one contribute? Clearly he contributes by doing something, by carrying out certain activities. Is that, then, all that he is responsible for? But surely, yes. Work refers to activities. We shall not go far wrong if we stick very closely to the elaboration and description of specific and detailed activities when we talk of responsibility, and resolutely avoid being led astray by more high-sounding but misleading broad and general statements which give no idea of the actual work activities to be carried out.

By responsibilities I wish to refer, therefore, simply to the particular activities to be carried out in the job, with the results to be achieved stated in concrete terms of the specific things to be done. It is entirely inaccurate, for example, to describe a night watchman's job as carrying responsibility for the security of a factory. We must ask ourselves 'What is he supposed to do?' He goes on certain specified rounds at specified times. He tests doors and locks. He checks certain supplies. He writes reports on certain specified topics, and if he notices anything that in his judgement is untoward, he reports it or takes appropriate action within a previously laid-down policy. If he carries out his job, he contributes to the security of the factory; but he cannot be said to be responsible for it.

Nor can his manager be said to be responsible for the security of the factory, even if he is in charge of all the security force or works police. He is responsible for working out the times and plan of the rounds. He checks over the reports. He devises special security measures, buys or specifies locks, inspects storage methods, trains and keeps his police up to scratch, and inspects their work from time to time. He may have many other such duties which contribute to the security of the factory, but he cannot be said to be responsible for it.

This particular example could be elaborated further. At each succeeding managerial level new and more general types of responsibility for security are found, the discretionary responsibilities at each level setting the prescribed framework for the activities carried out at the level below. Thus, activities at the next higher level might include determining the number of police to be employed and sanctioning the types of work on which they are employed, along with responsibilities for activities in other spheres, such as, for example, managing a purchasing department and a department concerned with protecting materials and equipment from damage and deterioration. Finally, the level of the chief executive himself is reached. Even he, however, cannot usefully be described as responsible for security. It is much more accurate, again, to outline the steps which he must make decisions about and take action upon – such as prescribing company policies on searching of personnel, budgeting for expenditure on security arrangements, or deciding whether his managers are sufficiently security-minded.

Indeed, it is only when the level of the board is reached that it can really be said that responsibility in general terms for security is at last found. It is the board which can accurately be described as responsible for security, and for every other generic responsibility as well. For it is the board, and the board alone, which can be said to be responsible for the enterprise, on behalf of the shareholders or the state.

The fallacy in the loose use of the notion of 'being responsible for' which is characteristic of so much job description, can be further illustrated by substituting in the above example of 'responsible for security', the following: inspectors responsible for the quality of goods; operators responsible for the rate of production; engineers responsible for the level of efficiency; salesmen responsible for the level of sales; research workers responsible for inventions and new products; buyers responsible for what is purchased; production control responsible for delivery on time; etc., etc.

The responsibilities of employee members of the enterprise have to do with the carrying out of activities in the enterprise, and as I shall show in Part Two, it is a description of these activities which constitutes the only accurate description of their responsibilities. In short, if you wish to answer the question, 'What are the responsibilities of an employee?', ask what are the specific activities which that employee is supposed to be engaged upon – precisely what decisions is he authorized to make, and what is he supposed to be doing.

IV

One further axiomatic point emerges from the foregoing, one which Hill* has accurately emphasized. It is the fact that employment work is definable not in terms of what an employed person may be doing in his job, but in terms of the work which a manager is authorized to allocate and required to control on behalf of the employing organization. The orientation of our analysis towards the discovery of the work sanctioned and allocated by a manager on behalf of the employing organization is absolutely fundamental. It leads to a method of measuring employment work in terms of what the manager in charge of the work is authorized and expected to do, rather than by observing and measuring the activity of the employed person at work – although such direct observation may often be helpful in discovering the content of the work being allocated.

The reality of this way of looking at employment work can be shown by the fact that an employment job comes into existence at that point in time when a manager has been authorized to get specified work done through a subordinate. This job can be analysed and, as I shall show, measured regardless of whether an actual subordinate has been hired and is doing the job. Indeed, it is always assessed by some means at this stage, since in order to advertise the job and to select and appoint an incumbent for it, it is necessary to establish its level so that a

* J. M. M. Hill: 'The time-span of discretion in job analysis' (1957).

69

salary can be fixed which will attract candidates with the necessary capacity to do it.

The definition of employment work, then, must begin with the set of responsibilities which a manager has been authorized to allocate. But, it may be argued, this definition cannot be realistic, since in many instances an employed person creates his own job, or in any case changes it by his personal efforts once he gets into it. It may happen that a firm does not have too clearly in mind the job it wishes to fill; it may wish, for example, to introduce chemical, or metallurgical, or statistical control processes, and have no one already in the firm with experience of such work. It appoints a person with likely qualifications to do the work, counting upon him to demonstrate the possibilities of the new methods. Does not the job in question, then, require to be analysed in terms of the activities carried out by the new appointee?

The answer to this last question is that to define the job in terms of the work the new appointee begins to do on his own initiative, is to lose sight of the most fundamental characteristic of employment work. The new appointee will be allowed to do his work only to the extent that he conforms to the policies of the firm, stays within the prescribed limits of cost and facilities provided, and, most important of all, directs his efforts towards achieving the results he has been employed to achieve, using his knowledge and discretion – the content of which his employers may understand little or nothing about – to accomplish his assigned tasks. Employees are always taken on for the purpose of carrying out certain activities, explicit or implicit, however great the difficulty of expressing exactly what those activities are. That this statement is true can be demonstrated by the fact that if an employee at any time begins to depart in his work from the activities which he has been employed to conduct, he soon learns about it. In other words, it may often be easier to point to an employee's responsibilities in terms of what he is not to do than in terms of what he is to do – but that does not gainsay the existence of definable responsibilities which may be discovered by analysis.

Similarly, an employee who appears by his own act and

efforts to change the responsibilities attaching to his position is not in fact making the decisions to establish such a change. Even if no one higher up says anything, or indeed even if no one becomes knowingly aware of the change, the establishment of that change is nevertheless requisitely the decision of his manager and the responsibility of his manager. Again, this fact of executive organization can be demonstrated negatively. It is most often the case that it is undesirable – indeed a nuisance – from the point of view of the employing firm for a subordinate to begin to change the content of his job by adding to his responsibilities, or contracting them, or simply switching some of his responsibilities for others. If an employee does so, he is acting outside his terms of reference, and his manager is being irresponsible if he remains unaware of what is happening. Equally that manager is in reality accountable in those special instances where the subordinate's action happens to coincide with the needs or desires of the firm*, or perhaps even opens up new lines of endeavour which are subsequently endorsed.

In short, an employing organization employs its personnel to discharge the responsibilities set by the concern, and not those arrogated by the employees. I would not wish, however, to be interpreted as saying that employing organizations never in practice allow their employees to determine to some degree the responsibilities they carry, or at least enable them to do so by default. Indeed it does happen. But to the extent that such a practice exists, no systematic wage and salary structure is possible. A kind of executive anarchy has been substituted for executive authority. This anarchic situation would itself have to be straightened out, and realistic executive responsibility established, before systematic analysis could begin.

These issues have great practical importance for the type of work analysis and measurement which I shall describe. The first step required for the analysis is for the manager in charge of a position to discover just what responsibilities he is in fact

---

* See Wilfred Brown: *Exploration in Management*, for a description of how unallocated work which needs requisitely to be done tends to get done, thus changing the responsibilities in roles in a manner often unrecognized by either the occupant or his manager.

allocating to that position. I have yet to come across a manager who found this an easy task on his first attempt. Once they did become more explicitly aware of just how they were dividing up and allocating responsibilities, managers have not infrequently found themselves confronted by inconsistencies and inefficiencies in their mode of organization, and faced with the task of refashioning their organizations more in line with the demands of the work they were responsible for getting done. The explicit definition of employment work, and systematic analysis of that work, require that a manager should know on behalf of the employing organization just what work he is allocating.

PART TWO

Measurement of level of work

CHAPTER 4

Prescribed limits and discretion

I

WE may now turn to the measurement of level of work in terms of the time-span of discretion. Before we do so, I must make two brief comments about the concept of measurement.

By measurement of level of work, I do not mean job evaluation*. Evaluation and measurement are not at all the same thing. To evaluate the height of a hill, or how far away it is, is to judge it, to make as good a guess as the circumstances allow. To measure its height or distance is quite a different matter. It requires operationally definable measuring instruments used in an operationally defined way. In similar vein, job evaluation is based on judgement and opinion – and in the hands of a good and experienced judge may give a good measure of a job. It is not possible to know, however, how accurate any particular evaluation is. And when the opinions of two judges differ, there is no yardstick against which to resolve the difference. Level-of-work measurement, in contradistinction to evaluation, requires the explication of an objectively definable instrument which can be used in an objectively definable manner, without guesswork and opinion.

The second point is that measuring something does not automatically tell you all about the thing you are measuring. Nor do you have to take all the properties of something into account in order to measure one of its aspects. These observations may seem obvious. And yet, the criticism has frequently been levelled against the time-span method of measurement that it fails to take aspects of a job other than time into account. Surely, it is argued, such factors as the type of responsibility, or the variety or number of kinds of responsibility, or the importance of the responsibility, or the consequences of bad discretion, or the

* A brief critique of the principles and practice of job evaluation will be found in chapter 1 of *Measurement of Responsibility*.

difficulty of the discretion exercised, ought to be considered. Are they not equally important as the time-span of the discretion? Maybe so. But it is not my endeavour to make these comparisons. The length of a column of mercury in a graduated capillary tube constructed under certain conditions cannot in itself tell very much about the structure or functioning of the human body. But it is useful in measuring its temperature.

Thus, for example, if you want to know the area of a surface with an irregular periphery – say a leaf – it may not immediately seem relevant to take a length of wire bent at right-angles at each end, hold it loosely at one end, and trace around the periphery of the leaf with it. In fact, if you do so, and mark the position of the free end of the wire at the beginning and end of the operation, you have the essential data for a calculation of the area of the leaf*. This procedure describes the hatchet planimeter for measuring surface areas. Why such a procedure should give surface area is an intriguing question. But the fact remains that it does. The instrument may not tell us anything about the properties of the surface measured, but it does measure its area.

In similar vein, in describing the time-span instrument as a means of measuring level of work, I do not wish to imply that either the time-span of a role or its level of work is the most important thing about that role. To the extent that it is useful to be able objectively to measure the level of work in a role – and there can be no doubt about the practical value of doing so – then I think time-span measurement is useful in that it gives a measure of precisely that characteristic of work. It may not tell us all the whys and wherefores about level of work. Measuring instruments do not do this. But I will present the evidence which leads me to conclude that it does give an objective and real measure. In a more general vein, I believe that time-span measurement is one illustration of the fact that genuinely objective measurement is possible in the social sciences.

---

*The distance between the two positions is measured in a particular way, and the value multiplied by a set factor, to give the area of the surface.

II

In the light of the previous chapter, we may attempt to construct a more precise definition of employment work. It is *the application of knowledge and the exercise of discretion within the limits prescribed by the immediate manager and by higher policies, in order to carry out the activities allocated by the immediate manager, the whole carried out within an employment contract for a wage or salary.* Two concepts appear in this definition, both of which we have used already, but without their having been adequately established or defined. They are the concepts of the prescribed limits and the discretionary content of responsibility. They constitute two of the foundation stones of our definition and measurement of work.

There are always to be found two different aspects to the responsibilities which a manager sets out to be discharged. He sets them out partly in prescribed limits; that is to say, in such a manner that his subordinate will be in no doubt whatever when he has completed his task, and completed it as instructed. And he sets them out partly in discretionary terms; that is to say, in such a manner that his subordinate will have to use his own discretion in deciding when he has pursued the particular activities to the point where the result is likely to satisfy the requirements of his manager. In the case of the prescribed limits of the responsibility, the subordinate knows when he has done his job because the result to be achieved or the regulations to be adhered to have been established in objective terms such that anyone would know when the work had been done as required. In the case of the discretionary content of the responsibility, no one can know definitely if the work has been done as set out by the manager, until that manager himself – or someone else officially on his behalf – has reviewed the results of the work and accepted it as satisfactory or rejected it as sub-standard.

The prescribed limits of responsibility are laid down. They exist in external reality. They can be observed independently by any number of observers. They refer to the genuine rules and regulations; but they do not include so-called rules which are not really meant to be rigorously adhered to; such, for example, as those rules in the rule books of many enterprises which, if strictly worked to, would lead to the shutting down of the enterprise. In order for an aspect of work to be prescribed, there must be an externally defined and observable control such that a departure from regulations is immediately apparent without the exercise of judgement. These prescriptions may be given by means of physical controls, such as jigs, or railway tracks; mechanical controls such as automatic temperature regulators, or signals such as a light or a bell which do not require to be interpreted; administrative controls such as explicitly laid-down procedures to be followed, perhaps on or by specified dates; technical controls which require a particular technique to be employed in doing a job; or policy controls such as the delimitation of particular markets or customers or categories of customer with whom business is to be done.

The following are examples of aspects of limits stated in prescribed terms: follow this routine; get such-and-such records out each Friday; use British standards in drawing; keep double-entry books; use the Matrix intelligence test; travel via trunk road A3; keep below the speeds, as shown on a speedometer, specified for each curve on a railway; confine yourself to air ejector systems in designing these machine tools; advertise only in the national daily newspapers; see that a random ten per cent of all goods is inspected before dispatch; visit all customers with more than a given turnover at least once a month. The language of the prescribed limits is always concrete and specific in the sense of having an external reference which can be pointed to.

If the external control eliminating choice for any particular aspect of an instruction cannot be objectively identified, then that aspect is not prescribed but is discretionary. Thus, for example: make sure you buy enough stamps; use the best method in the circumstances; design advertisements with public appeal; keep a satisfactory standard of finish; select the most capable of the applicants. All such instructions are prescribed in the sense only that they tell a subordinate to do *something* about stamps, best methods, appealing advertisements, satisfactory finish, or capable applicants. In the absence of any further and objective definition of what the manager intends by these terms, the meaning of the instruction and the sense of what would constitute its being carried out properly are left for the time being to the discretion of the subordinate. He must judge his manager's requirement on the basis of his previous experience of the work combined with his know-how or sense of what is required in that particular job.

It is impossible for any manager to issue an instruction that has no prescribed limits. There are always prescribing policies, limits, results to be achieved. On the way to achieving these results, however, some discretion must be used, since it is only the end result which is prescribed. Therefore, there is no such thing as an executive instruction which does not incorporate both prescribed and discretionary elements.

At minimum, the person doing the work must use his discretion on how it is to be organized and on the pace to be maintained in order to get the work done on time. Thus, for example, a manager may instruct his subordinate to carry out a series of chemical analyses on a certain material so as to determine its composition. He may, having decided in his own mind on the likely composition, specify precisely which tests he wants done and in which order. He leaves the pace of work and possibly certain judgements of observation to the discretion of his subordinate. Or he may simply instruct his subordinate to analyse the material, laying down no particular test, but perhaps setting certain limiting conditions such as ascertaining all the components present in amounts of 0.5 per cent or more, but leaving smaller traces unanalysed. With such an instruction, it is left to the judgement of the subordinate to determine the range of tests he will use, as well as the organization and sequence of the tests.

At times it may seem that so much of the content of responsibility may be prescribed that little or no discretion appears to be left in a job. For instance, in operating an adding machine there is discretion with regard to personal modes of operating the machine. Such discretion may seem too insignificant and too unimportant to be worth mentioning. Any such conclusion can be shown not only to be completely unwarranted, but to lose sight of some of the most important characteristics of what it is to do work.

When an adding machine operator – the same analysis would apply to copy-typing and, indeed, to the operation of all machines – is at work, much of what is going on is under his own control; it is not prescribed or regulated. He himself controls the way he sits, the movement of his arms, hands and fingers, how hard he strikes the keys, the number of times and the way he refers to the columns of figures he is transcribing, his sizing up of how much work there is to be done, his adjustment of his pace of work in order to complete so much by, say, lunch-time or by the end of the day, or before the regular midweek rush comes in the following afternoon. This control may not be wholly conscious; it is being exercised all the same.

The significance of recognizing the control being exercised by the operator is simply this. The way he exercises control determines the efficiency of his work. We are dealing here with the differences between – on the one hand – the clerk who gets on with his work quickly and easily, requires no supervision, is usually on top of the load of work, forestalls crises, and does not get into flaps, and – on the other hand – the awkward clerk who tends to be slower, is irregular in pace of work and needs intermittent supervision if occasional piling-up of work is to be avoided. The importance attaching to these apparently insignificant features of control of work by employees, is that they are usually precisely the aspects of work that are the target for work study specialists. The aim of standardization or routinization of work such as that described, is to reduce the amount of discretion by such means as regulation of the flow of work, and the introduction of appliances designed to lessen the frequency of insertion and removal of cards, to hold materials and data in pre-arranged ways, and to give mechanically controlled intensity of print by electrical key operation.

The nearest to a completely routinized job that I have known in which operators were used was that of watching filaments in electric light bulbs passing an inspection point. The bulbs passed by on a conveyor moving at a controlled speed – the operator having to watch the bulbs as they passed, rejecting those with broken filaments. Judgement was not required in determining which filaments were satisfactory and which were not, those in which there was an obvious break being the only ones to be rejected. During the years in which the job was organized in this manner it was a constant trouble spot from the point of view of labour. Women were employed, but simply would not stick to it. Pay for the work was increased to a level commonly agreed to be artificially high for the responsibility carried. But nevertheless, the job was regarded as highly undesirable, operators remaining at it for only short periods of time despite the relatively high pay. It was hated work – regarded as soul-destroying. The light bulbs moved by – the broken ones calling for an automatic response by the operator. There was nothing to do but watch – dominated by the pace at which the conveyor presented each bulb for scrutiny as it went by. The difficulty remained unresolved until the management brought itself to face the inevitable expenditure and installed a simple automatic inspection rig to reject the bulbs with broken filaments.

The essence of human work lies in the use of discretion within a framework of regulated procedures. Reduction of the discretionary content of a job to near zero is to de-humanize it. It can be better done by a machine.

III

Adherence to the prescribed limits of responsibility demands knowledge. The person doing the job must have been taught, or must otherwise have learned, the particular routines, or the signals, or the tests, or the policies, or the techniques, which he has been instructed to use in carrying out his assigned activities.

In contrast to the prescribed limits, the performance of the discretionary content of responsibility demands know-how, wisdom, gumption, *nous*. The person doing the job must exercise his own control and judgement from within himself. He himself must decide, choose, judge, feel, sense, consider, conclude just what would be the best thing to do in the circumstances, the best way of going about what he is doing. He may take his knowledge and previous experience into account, but knowledge and experience are not in themselves sufficient. They are insufficient in the sense that they cannot be automatically applied. They can be used only as guides when new features in a situation call for slight or radical variation on past activities, or sometimes for entirely new solutions based on hunch and guesswork, solutions for which there may be little precedent, or no precedent whatever.

The essential difference between the prescribed limits and the discretionary content may thus be noted. In the case of the prescribed limits, a person's assessment and control of his working activity can be achieved by reference to objective standards external to himself; in the case of the discretionary content, assessment and control of his working activities must be achieved by reference to intuitively sensed standards within himself. The prescribed limits, since they exist in external reality, can be described in concrete terms; the discretionary responsibilities, since they refer to standards which a manager has in his mind, can be described only in subjective terms. If, therefore, a person were carrying out a prescribed series of tests and he were to be asked why he was doing them, he would reply that he had been told to. Sitting quite still, he would be able accurately to enumerate which tests, and in what order, so that anyone else who had knowledge of that field of work would himself know precisely what tests to do if he were given that job.

In the case of the discretionary content, however, a very different pattern of behaviour can be observed. If the same question were asked of a person who had been given the job of analysing certain materials – which tests he did and in which order being left to his discretion – the answer would be something to the effect that he was doing a series of tests which he thought would be the best method of analysing the material he had. If asked why, he might say that the colour of the material, or its surface characteristics, or its feel, led him to suspect certain elements. He might have started with certain other tests, but on balance he thought that the particular sequence of tests he was using was most likely to give him the most accurate results most quickly. If pressed to explain why the colour or

82

surface characteristics or feel gave him the impression he had received, he might get some way towards putting his impression into words, but there would come a point at which words would fail him and he would be reduced to vague references to experience, or hunch, or simply to the fact that it just felt right. Meanwhile, he would be seen to be unwittingly moving his arms and hands in that kind of eloquent pawing into space which is substituted for words which are simply not there to express the touch and feel of intuitive judgement in doing a job. It is like the imitative gesture which inevitably accompanies a skilled worker's attempt to describe what he means by putting 'just the right amount of force' into tapping delicately with a hammer, or applying a tool.

The use of this gesture for the purpose of filling in gaps in speech is uniformly characteristic of descriptions of the use of discretion. Whenever, in interview, a person begins to use his hands rather than words to explain how and why he does particular aspects of his work, then it can be taken for certain that he is talking about a discretionary aspect. The essence of the use of discretion is that it is intuitive, touch and feel, the sense of the job. It is non-verbalized knowledge – the kind that is carried in one's bones.

One further distinction arises from this analysis of discretion. It is the distinction between discretion and decision. The use of discretion is a process internal to the person. It cannot be seen from outside. It has to do with thought, judgement, sense, feel, discrimination, comparing, wondering, foreseeing, and other contents of mental work – both conscious and unconscious. Decision, by contrast, is concerned with action. I shall use the term decision only in the full executive sense of action taken. I shall not use it in the loose sense of someone 'deciding' to do something. An executive decision exists only when a manager or his subordinate has committed himself – issued an instruction, or otherwise actually carried out some observable work. Intentions do not constitute a decision. They are part of the process of discretion leading up to the taking of decisions. No decision in the executive sense occurs until the member has acted on his own discretion. Good discretion is thus definable as discretion which leads to good decisions; sub-standard discretion leads to sub-standard decision*.

IV

If there has been failure to stay within the prescribed limits in work, then the person doing the job was either lacking in the requisite factual knowledge and ought, therefore, never to have been appointed, or, if he had the requisite factual knowledge, he must either have made a clear-cut mistake, or else he must have been guilty of negligence or insubordination or down-right dishonesty. For if he knew his job, he must have known objectively and without any reasonable doubt that he had failed to carry out his orders. He must have known that he had failed to give the required signal, or to conform to a specified policy, or to employ a standard method.

If, however, there has been a failure in the discretionary content of a job, then all that can be said is that the person doing the job has failed to exercise the necessary judgement and discretion, leading to inadequacy in the results achieved. The results may have fallen short of those set by the manager. Or they may have taken too long to be achieved, or have been achieved by methods requiring greater expenditure of resources than would otherwise have been necessary. But questions of negligence or insubordination or dishonesty simply do not arise as they do in the case of failure to conform to prescribed regulations. All that can be said is that sub-standard work has been done. The subordinate has not been up to the task in hand. He has not done as well as he was expected or called upon to do. Such occurrences are everyday matters. Niceness of judgement is always a relative matter – a matter of more or less góod, rather than of clear-cut right or wrong. There is no such thing as perfect discretion exercised by a subordinate; the issue is always one of his being good enough – in contrast to the pre-scribed limits of his work in which strict and clearcut con-

---

*This distinction between discretion and decision is upheld by etymology. Discretion, from *dis-cernere*, has the sense of separating out, analysing, the elements of a problem. Decision, from *de-caedere*, has the sense of cutting apart, that is, of taking an irretrievable step.

formity, correctness or incorrectness, is very much the issue.

Failure to conform to the prescribed limits constitutes a mistake or negligence because the essence of a genuinely prescribed instruction is that it provides a continuous feed-back to the person doing the job – a feed-back from outside himself which allows him to know unequivocally whether or not he has done what he was supposed to do at the time he was supposed to do it. He does not have to wait for his work to be inspected, or otherwise to be told if he has succeeded or failed. He knows then and there, on the spot, at the time, by reference to the externally given datum line upon which the instruction has been based.

The discretionary content is different. There is no external feed-back at the time the work is being done, no external datum line. The person doing the job can never be sure how well he has done until his work has been reviewed by his manager. While he is doing the work, therefore, he can never quite be sure whether he has done it well enough; whether, for example, he ought to spend just a bit more time on it, do just a bit more, get it just a bit more exact, get out just a few more data, put a slightly better finish upon it, carry on the interview a bit longer, modify the tools slightly before putting them into use, give his subordinate one more chance, press for a slightly higher price from a customer, etc.; or whether, on the contrary, he has already spent too much time and effort, has done well enough for all practical purposes, and ought to call a halt.

The exercise of discretion always poses the problem of when a job has been done *just* well enough. Who says what just good enough is? We come here to one of the primary facts about economic work. The standard of quality which an enterprise offers to its customers is a decision of the highest order. It is made in general terms by the managing director, within a very broad, and usually unstated, policy of the board establishing the quality inherent in the company's trade mark. These quality standards figure prominently in the expense of manufacture, and in the price at which products are offered to the market. The important point to be noted is that the trade mark standard of quality is a guarantee that a particular quality will be achieved

– it is definitely never a guarantee that the very best possible quality is given. The best product can always be improved in quality by doing still further work upon it.

The art and the necessity of economic production, therefore, is to ensure that the executive organization produces goods or services just at the company's policy on quality standards – but neither above nor below those standards. In order to achieve this end each member employed in the executive organization must work within standards which have both an upper and a lower limit – his work must be just good enough to contribute to an efficient organization, and to a product that is fair and reasonably consistent with the standards offered to customers at the quoted price – good enough, certainly, but never the very best possible, never the maximum. Exercising discretion is therefore like walking an invisible tight-rope. If one is too careful, the job will take too long and be too expensive, and one's work will pile up. If one is not careful enough, however, the work will not be good enough. And there is nothing outside to tell you whether you are doing well enough until you have committed yourself, carried out the activities assigned, and your work has been made available for your manager to assess (by what methods of review, we shall consider in a moment).

It is because of these circumstances that it is so important to achieve internal consistency between the prescribed limits and discretionary content of work. If a manager is not satisfied with the discretionary content of a subordinate's work, he can express himself as dissatisfied, criticize the work as being substandard and even, in the final analysis, conclude that his subordinate is not up to the job, does not have the necessary capacity or *nous* to do it. But he would not be correct to criticize him on the score of negligence or insubordination. If he wants to achieve an automatic control he must construct and implement prescribed controls. The discovery of prescribed controls which give the necessary rigidity of support to the work of subordinates while yet leaving them the necessary discretion to cope with unpredictable variations in the circumstances of work, is an essential aspect of efficient and imaginative management.

It may also be worth noting that there is no magic in setting the standards governing the exercise of discretion. The particular standards of quality and efficiency of any given enterprise, are nothing more than the standards laid down by the managing director and implemented in detail throughout the various parts of the enterprise. The standards themselves require the exercise of discretion. There is nothing absolute which can tell a managing director, or a board, that any particular standards are economically advisable in the sense of guaranteeing a volume of business and at a selling price that will realize a satisfactory profit. Setting standards is a central part of the art of running a business. If the members employed by the executive organization are not held to these standards within appropriate limits, the continued existence of the enterprise is threatened.

V

If we now ask what it is that an enterprise seeks when it employs a person to work in its executive organization – what is it that it pays a wage or salary *for* – we get a two-fold answer. First, it employs that person's capacity to understand the prescribed limits and to conform to them: he must know enough to do so. Second, it employs his ability to exercise sufficient discretion on his own account to cope with uncertainties, the vicissitudes, the unknowns, in the job: he must have enough capacity and experience – the know-how or the *nous* – to do so. It has seemed to me that one of the most intriguing and telling findings revealed by our social-analytic studies* was that it is the second of these responsibilities – the exercise of discretion – which is mainly connected with the sensation of the amount of responsibility in a job. We appear to derive our sensation of level of work or responsibility from the discretion we are called upon to exercise, and not from the regulated or prescribed actions which have been set and which we have learned and can carry out automatically.

Why should it be that we react to the regulated aspects of our work as though there were no great effort required in adhering to them, whereas carrying out the discretionary aspect imparts the sensation of personal responsibility? Conforming to

* See *Measurement of Responsibility.*

regulation feels like doing work which someone else has already decided about, and if it goes wrong it is 'his' doing and not your own. When required to use your own discretion, however, it feels like doing your own work, it is you yourself who carry the responsibility, and it is to yourself that you turn if things go wrong, for it feels as if you yourself are to blame.

As he carries out the discretionary part of a job, an employee must rely upon his own skill and *nous*. The skill and *nous* employed determine how well or how poorly his work is done. I am using skill and *nous* in a manner which I wish precisely to define. Skill is the capacity of a person to exercise sensory and perceptual judgement in carrying out the discretionary aspects of his work. *Nous* is his capacity to exercise mental judgement for the same purpose. Skill is made up of the capacity to respond intuitively to the sense of touch, sight, hearing, taste, smell, or balance, and physically to guide and manipulate one's work according to the sense or feel of the job in the course of doing it. *Nous* is made up of the capacity to weigh up available information, to sense what other information, if any, ought to be obtained, and mentally to proceed on the basis of what feels like the best course of action where many factors in the situation are only unconsciously assessed, and some of the factors – perhaps even the most important ones – are simply unknown.

It is precisely this element of uncertainty, of having to rely on our own judgement, to guide our own actions, without knowing the result until the work has been completed and reviewed, that makes the feeling of weight of responsibility come from the discretionary content of the work. By contrast, the prescribed content leaves no room for uncertainty and makes no such demands.

I have presented elsewhere* findings based upon my clinical psycho-analytic work which lead to the conclusion that, in the unconscious mind, many of the deeper-lying anxieties are mobilized precisely by this uncertainty in the discretionary aspect of work. To be able to work requires sufficient willingness

*See my paper 'Disturbances in the capacity to work', 1960. This paper elaborates and deepens the analysis of the effects of uncertainty which I first presented in *Measurement of Responsibility*.

and ability to accept both consciously and unconsciously the anxieties arising out of the uncertainty in work, and to exercise and continue to exercise judgement and discretion in spite of them. Although these anxieties are usually mainly unconscious, everyone from time to time has the experience of their breaking surface. There are occasions when, for shorter or longer periods of time, either because of an increase in personal anxiety, or encountering a particularly difficult job, or a combination of both, a person becomes quite uncertain which way to proceed with his work, but has to push on nevertheless and find his way through the difficulties as best he can. It is on such occasions that the anxieties of which I am speaking may become conscious, leaving him unsure and on edge until such time as the results of the work he has done are subject to review and he discovers whether his worries have been warranted or not.

The intensity of the uncertainty and anxiety comes from the fact that the discretion of which we are speaking is discretion in action. It leads to decisions, to committal of actual resources – either the use of time, or the use of time plus the using up of physical resources as well. If the discretion has been inadequate, so will the decisions be, and resources will have been wasted. Extra expense will have been created, costs will have increased, and all without any chance of going back and starting again as though the waste had not occurred.

Thus, to the question raised earlier when we first considered the nature of work in the psycho-economic sense – 'What constitutes the effort in work?' – we may now reply that the essence of the effort in work is to be found in the anxiety engendered by the uncertainties which are part and parcel of the exercise of discretion. A man lifting heavy weights is not necessarily doing more in the psychological sense than a man dealing with very light and delicate articles. He may be doing more work in the physical sense. Which of the two, however, is exerting the most effort, doing the hardest work in the psychological sense, will depend upon which is subjected by the discretionary content of his job to the most extensive uncertainty and anxiety.

The foregoing analysis applies at all levels of executive work.

More than that, the same relationship between the prescribed limits and the discretionary content of responsibilities applies in all roles at all levels. It is not true to say that higher-level roles become relatively less prescribed and relatively more discretionary. Certainly the discretion to be exercised becomes increasingly extensive. But so do the prescribed limits become increasingly extensive. The larger the scope for the exercise of discretion, the larger is the prescribed frame required to contain it in the sense of allowing for bigger commitments of resources.

The question remains, however, of how the extensiveness of the uncertainty in work is to be determined. An answer to this question was suggested by the most important of the findings presented in *Measurement of Responsibility*. It was simply that the longer the period of time that discretion had to be exercised in a role without the results of that discretion possibly coming to the attention of the immediate manager, then the greater was the psychological effort required for the work. In short, the longer you have to tolerate and stand up to uncertainty and yet keep on with your work, the greater is the responsibility. Looked at the other way round, the longer the employing organization leaves a member to carry on exercising his own discretion in his work, making decisions based on that discretion and committing resources of the firm in so doing, then the greater is the reliance of the firm upon him and the greater is the responsibility allocated to him. As I have previously reported, there is evidence to confirm the view that the length of this span of time corresponds with the financial value of the losses which would be caused by sub-standard discretion.

VI

But how does a manager review the results of the discretionary content of his subordinate's work? And, conversely, how does the subordinate know that he has carried out the discretionary content in a manner that will be satisfactory to his manager? Surely, by the manager seeing the result, looking at it, examining and scrutinizing it, deciding whether it is what he wanted and expected, and telling his subordinate whether or not he is satisfied. In principle such an answer seems inevitable. In practice, the matter is far from being so simple. The occasions when a manager himself *directly* reviews the results of the work of his subordinates are much rarer than the occasions when he does not. What happens most commonly is that the manager does not himself review the work when it is finished. He allows the work to continue on the assumption that, if it is not quite up to scratch, he will hear of it. So long as he is not receiving any complaints from elsewhere about the quality of his subordinate's work, he assumes – without necessarily being aware that he is doing so – that the work is satisfactory. In other words, an indirect review has occurred, a review of omission rather than of commission*.

One of the reasons why managers rarely themselves directly review the results of the work of their subordinates is that the work rarely passes back to the manager. Most commonly the job of the manager is to see that work gets done and passed on, rather than to have it done in order to use the results himself. The cases where the tasks he allocates get passed back to him, occur mainly in connexion with secretarial and development work; for example, a secretary typing letters for her manager; research assistants subordinate to a research investigator carrying out special tests, or trials, or projects, for him; or draughtsmen subordinate to a designer doing component drawings for him. Apart from these special instances, the manager himself does not get the chance to see directly the results of the discretion exercised by his subordinates. For example: one operator's work passes on to the next operator or operators, then to an inspector, to stores or despatch, and out to a customer; the discretionary content of a salesman's behaviour in negotiating with customers is rarely seen by his manager; a time-study engineer does his work out on the shop floor away from the scrutiny of his manager; a personnel interviewer works in conditions of privacy, the applicant interviewed not necessarily being seen by the personnel manager; a cost accountant works out a budget with a departmental manager, and the works accountant is rarely in a position directly to assess

* This distinction between direct and indirect review is described by J. M. M. Hill in his paper 'Time-span of discretion in job analysis'.

whether he would have exercised the same judgements under the existing conditions; electricians and millwrights are working on their own, out in the factory, away from their managers, completing the repair of one breakdown and moving on to the next.

A manager is thus rarely in a position to keep under direct review by his own first-hand scrutiny the quality of the discretion being exercised by his subordinates. Moreover, even in the above special cases where the work of a subordinate is passed back to the manager, direct scrutiny of the discretion in the work does not necessarily take place, and indeed rarely does so. Usually only a cursory scrutiny occurs, and it is only blatantly sub-standard discretion which can be detected by such means. The detection of more marginally sub-standard discretion in any one task requires extended examination. This point may require illustration.

The situations are legion where there is all the appearance of managers' learning about the quality of their subordinates' discretion, but where the appearance is totally misleading. Perhaps one of the most important – albeit a special case – is that of the annual general meeting which apparently scrutinizes the discretion exercised during the previous year by the board of directors and its appointed chief executive. In the vast majority of such meetings, nothing could be further from the truth. What any given annual report reflects is not the work of the previous year, but a conglomeration of the results of discretion exercised over the previous several years (in the case of large corporations, as many as five to ten years and more), the shareholders being in a position to review little other than the degree to which there has been conformance to the general policy of the enterprise (a policy which is usually neither very explicit not consciously recognized). As far as discretion is concerned, information can be built up only by watching the trend of activities and results over a period of years, and investigating the circumstances in detail and by special means, should there be any dissatisfaction.

Or we may take another illustration: a designer who gives his draughtsman the job of getting out some drawings of a particular component part of a larger design. He prescribes what the component is to do, its size, the frame into which it must fit, perhaps the material from which it must be made, the lubrication which must be used, the stresses to which it will be subjected, etc., etc. In getting out his drawing, the draughtsman will still have to exercise much discretion; for example, discretion with respect to.the exact placing of fitting screws, types of moving rig, exact size and strength of various parts, type of finish on its surfaces, etc., all of which will affect the efficiency of operation of the component, and its accessibility and ease of maintenance; and discretion with respect to the laying out and labelling of the drawings themselves, which will affect the ease with which they can eventually be read and interpreted by those who will have to use them when the component is being made.

When the designer receives the drawing from his subordinate, he is faced with two possible courses of action: either to carry out a detailed review, or to rely on his subordinate's discretion. He may, for example, consider the drawing and, if on the whole it seems what he required, accept it without considering whether a better job might have been done in the time taken; with such a cursory scrutiny, the manager is really continuing to rely upon the quality of his subordinate's discretion – reliance which is the rule rather than the exception if work is to be got done. He is in effect saying, 'The job looks good enough – I'll let it go and we'll see later if there are any snags I haven't noticed.' It may turn out later that the layout had not in fact been quite convenient enough. If the manager wanted to forestall any such possibility – that is, if he were not content to rely on his subordinate's discretion – he would himself have to spend perhaps some hours mentally going through in summary fashion the process which his subordinate went through in designing the component. He would have, further, to question his subordinate on why he had decided on this or that point of detail. By going through such a process, he could himself decide whether the design was to his own personal satisfaction, and could be said to have conducted a direct review.

In the one instance, it will be noted, the manager – even though he has seen the immediate result of the work – cannot be said to have reviewed the discretion. Direct managerial review requires a specific act of scrutiny of the discretion involved. The manager must be in a position to judge whether, under the given conditions of work, the subordinate has exercised the necessary judgement to overcome the difficulties encountered within the confines of the job, and has done so in a reasonable time. He must have examined the particular difficulties encountered. These difficulties are infinite in their variety in different types of work – the unusual variations in materials, new circumstances, special pressures of work, machine breakdowns, subordinates absent, minor variations in customer demand, complications in the available mix of work, let-downs by suppliers, new and unfamiliar features in the job – the details of work are always fluctuating, usually imperceptibly in minor respects, but sometimes rapidly and extensively, and a manager must rely upon his subordinate to take these minor variations in his stride and to call the larger ones to his own attention.

My experience has led me to conclude that the occasions are probably infrequent when a manager himself *directly* reviews the discretion in the work of a subordinate. Even when a subordinate brings a supply requisition, or a report, or a proposal direct to his manager, and the manager countersigns or accepts it, a review does not necessarily take place. In many cases the manager's counter-signature or acceptance may imply only that he has no immediate reason to doubt the efficacy of his subordinate's discretion; it indicates that he backs his subordinate's judgement. The only common situation which I have encountered in which a manager does carry out a direct review is where he has a subordinate who is in training or still on probation, and whose work he cannot as yet rely upon. Apart from such special instances, managers generally keep only a loose direct grip on the on-going work of their subordinates – ensuring that no grossly unsatisfactory work is being done.

VII

Under ordinary circumstances managerial review takes place by indirect means. The subordinate carries out his allocated activities. The manager gets on with his own work. If the subordinate's work fills the bill and causes no trouble elsewhere, then nothing need be done. This method of review is not so careless or passive as it might seem. For, if a subordinate is doing sub-standard work, his manager can in fact be sure that it will come to his notice. This fact of automatic and assured feed-back of information on sub-standard work arises from the interwoven character of work in executive systems.

The nature of the feed-back of information about sub-standard work may be illustrated in the following examples. If the draughtsman we mentioned earlier uses sub-standard discretion, the sub-standard work, or reports upon its ill effects, will be sent to his manager, the designer, by those who had to make and test or use the component; if an operator does not quite sufficiently fettle his work after completing his operation, so that it is slightly too rough to the touch, the unsatisfactory work will soon come back from the supervisor in charge of a succeeding operation who finds that his own operator has to touch up too many of the pieces coming through in order to get a proper set; if a salesman uses marginally too high pressure in his dealings with customers, this fact will come to his manager's notice by customer complaint or via colleagues of the manager who deal with those customers either themselves or through their subordinates; if a time-study engineer is slightly too lax in his rate fixing, supervisors and operators will begin to want him on the job instead of others; if a final inspector is slightly too tight in judging quality of finish, there will be complaints from the shops about their work being rejected, and if he is too loose, customer complaints will increase; if the manager in charge of a millwrighting and maintenance department does not adequately organize the services he provides, his manager will be criticized about the quality of the service given. It is possible to give similar illustrations for any and every type of work. In the case of the discretionary content of any job, information about sub-standard discretion always filters back eventually to the manager in charge of the job. In the absence of such information, therefore, the manager may take it that his subordinates are working satisfactorily.

If, on the other hand, a subordinate decided to avoid any possibility of his work being sub-standard in quality by working very carefully, this excess of care would come to light, for his pace of work would be slowed down. Those who were waiting for the work to be done would begin to be hampered. Demands for work would begin to reach the manager by the same routes. And he himself would at the same time be in a position to note that he was not able to allocate to his subordinate as much work as he thought reasonable for the job.

The uncertainty in connexion with the discretionary content of work has an important effect. If you are hearing nothing wrong about your work, you can assume that it is all right. You are much less likely, and at best infrequently, to hear directly that your judgement and discretion were satisfactory. Indeed, I believe that it is mainly because review of discretion tends to be indirect rather than direct, that bad work is criticized systematically whereas good work is so very rarely mentioned. We may note, therefore, that our measure of how long a job requires its incumbent to exercise discretion without managerial review, will have to be in negative rather than positive terms. We shall have to define it in terms of how long it would be possible to exercise inadequate discretion before that fact would come to the attention of the immediate manager.

VIII

Sub-standard discretion may range all the way from patently bad discretion – a 'howler' – to discretion which is nearly but just not quite good enough. It will readily be manifest that the more seriously bad the discretion the more quickly its effects are likely to show, and the more readily observable are its effects. In considering review mechanisms, then, what degree of sub-standard discretion are we to assume? And how are we to measure the degree to which the discretion is sub-standard?

There is a characteristic of employment work which makes it possible to resolve these problems. This characteristic is that quantitative limits of quality and time can always be discovered within which a manager lays it down that his subordinate shall work. (We shall enlarge on this later.) For purposes of measurement, therefore, we may fix on discretion which is just marginally sub-standard, and take this as our datum line. Marginally sub-standard discretion is discretion which produces results which are just outside the limits of the standard set. It is a boundary concept. One is not here considering grossly bad judgement which is quickly spotted by many people. Marginally sub-standard discretion is not usually immediately observable. Its effects are cumulative. It can be ascertained in the following manner.

Sub-standard discretion may occur in either of two directions: it may be due to the exercise of too much care in work, so that the results may be better than the standard set, but a significantly longer time is taken to do the job than would otherwise have been required; or it may be due to the exercise of just not enough care, so that work gets done quickly but by means of short cuts and other too quick decisions which produce results that are below the limits of the standards set.

It may at first sight have seemed imprudent to classify work that is consistently much better in quality than the standard set, together with work that is not quite good enough, and to regard them both as sub-standard. This classification, however, is entirely consistent with the character of employment work. Every job that is allocated always has implicit in it the instruction not only to do the job within certain limits of quality or effectiveness, but also to do it within certain limits of time. More frequently than not, these limits of quality and time are neither explicitly stated nor consciously known. They exist, nevertheless, and can be discovered, as I hope to show (see chapter 5). Every job, therefore, requires the person doing it to be constantly weighing his pace of work against its quality. The art of good work is to do a job that is just good enough – avoiding any tendency towards perfectionism on the one hand, and insufficient care on the other – while at the same time getting on with the job so as to keep the work flowing at the required pace. During flaps and crises, a very fine judgement may often be required so as to speed up the pace of work to that point where quality is just good enough to get by, and the pile-up of work is diminished. The essence of employment work is not just to be able to do a given job, but to be able to do it within the time limits allowed.

CHAPTER 5

Time-span measurement

I

Summary outline of time-span measurement

TIME-SPAN measurement gives the level of work in a role rC, by measuring the work which the manager B is assigning into role rC*, as authorized by his own manager A. The tasks may be directly assigned, or indirectly assigned through general responsibilities.

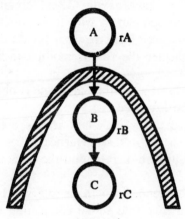

FIGURE 1

The definition of time-span of discretion is:

The longest period which can elapse in a role before the manager can be sure that his subordinate has not been exercising marginally sub-standard discretion continuously in balancing the pace and the quality of his work.

This definition leads to two formulae for measurement – one for multiple-task roles, the other for single-task roles, as follows:

* I shall use the convention of a capital letter, say B, to refer to the occupant of a role, and the capital letter preceded by a small r – rB – to refer to the role itself.

(a) *Level of work in* ____ *Time-span of target completion time of*
    multiple-task role ‾‾ *longest task*

(b) *Level of work in* ____ *Time-span of target completion time of*
    single-task role ‾ *longest task (direct review), or longest*
    task sequence (indirect review)

The main steps in measurement are as follows (detailed description of them is given in the sections of this chapter indicated in brackets):

1. To measure the level of work in rC, see the manager B in charge of the role, and ascertain the information in steps 3, 4 and 5 (section II).

2. If possible, see subordinate C and obtain the same information so as to compare it with (and possibly supplement) the information received from manager B (section II).

3. Ascertain whether the role is multiple-task or single-task (section III):

(a) the time-span of a multiple-task role is obtained from the time of the longest extended task;

(b) the time-span of a single-task role is obtained from the time of the longest task or task sequence.

4. If it is a multiple-task role, find the longest extended task (section IV):

(a) discover the extended task in the role, which has the longest target completion time (the actual completion time may differ from that originally set, because of manifold unforeseen circumstances);

(b) in doing so, explore –

(i) any routinely recurring tasks,

(ii) any development projects, and

(iii) the time allowed to C for the induction and training of his newly appointed untrained subordinates.

5. If it is a single-task role, find the longest task or task sequence (section V):

(a) ascertain what happens to the work if the subordinate C works quickly enough buf is just marginally sub-standard in the quality of the discretionary aspects of his work;

(b) ascertain the review point – whether the review is direct or indirect – for marginally sub-standard work;

(c) draw a chart showing the time-span of a succession of tasks and their review points;

(d) find the time-span of the longest task or sequence of tasks.

6. Confirm with manager-once-removed A that level of work as assigned by B is within his policy, and thus that he authorizes the time-span measurement, and the payment level.

II

Time-span measurement – general

This section sets out how time-span measurement is initiated, and the objectives in doing so. It takes the process of measurement through to the stage of establishing whether the role whose level of work is being measured is a single-task role or a multiple-task role. The final steps in measurement are pursued separately for each type of role in sections IV and V.

WHO YOU SEE

The main person to see is the immediate manager B of the role rC whose level of work is to be measured. The manager B is accountable for knowing, or for being able to discover, the kinds of task he is assigning, as authorized by his own manager A, into his subordinate role rC. He is accountable also for knowing, or for being able to discover, the means by which any sub-standard discretion exercised by the occupant of role rC would come to his own attention.

If the role rC is occupied, the information obtained from manager B may be supplemented by your seeing subordinate C. C may sometimes have a more detailed picture of what he is doing than B has. Thus, for example, it may occur that certain activities which B would approve if he knew of them have accrued to rC without B's having intimate knowledge of them. If there is disagreement between B and C about C's actual activities, the disagreement can be resolved by reference to the reality of the case. Has C, or has he not, been carrying out certain tasks? Once the facts have been established, it is for B

101

to decide whether or not he shall authorize C to carry the duties in question, and to specify them in terms of prescription and discretion accordingly.

It should be noted, however, that discussion with C is not an essential part of the technique of time-span measurement – even though the results of measurement will eventually be communicated to C. The measurement can be carried out in discussion solely with B (and eventually authorized by A), since the data that are being measured have to do solely with the work that B is allocating, or wishes to allocate, into role rC. A discussion with the manager-once-removed A is held after a time-span measurement has been carried out with the manager B, in order to check with A that he in fact authorizes the work allocation which B has described and B's methods of reviewing his subordinate C's performance.

WHAT YOU SET OUT TO DO

The objective of the discussion with the manager B is to help him to organize his experience of allocating tasks and general responsibilities to a subordinate and controlling his subordinate's performance, in terms of the completion times that he is setting and the standards of quality he expects. Managers do not need, in their everyday work, to be consciously aware of all the tasks in detail that they have allocated to their subordinates. Time-span measurement provides an occasion when a manager can systematically consider these tasks and grasp them explicitly in his mind.

Managers are not necessarily familiar with the detail of many of the tasks that they allocate, or with the targets of quality and completion time that they set. This work is allocated in the round of day-to-day activities. Much of what is important in the work is intuitively understood by both the manager and his subordinate and does not need stating. That this intuitive understanding is a fact can be seen if the situation of the manager with an experienced subordinate is compared with that of a manager with a new and inexperienced subordinate. In the latter case, the manager has to explicate the tasks in detail, including the time in which he wants them completed; this is often a time-consuming and painful task, not because the manager does not know what he wants to get done, but because it is not easy for him always to put it into words.

A MANAGER'S DECISION IS AN OBJECTIVE FACT

As the target completion times, or the standards of quality, are made more explicit and formulated, the manager B is in a position to come to a decision. He must decide whether the time or quality standards exposed are satisfactory, or whether he wishes to modify them in the light of the analysis. Either way, *it is the objective of your analysis to require B to come to a firm decision* about the target completion times in the case of a multiple-task role, or quality standards in the case of single-task role, beyond which he would not be prepared to let his sub‑ordinate go without criticizing him for sub-standard work (see Sections IV and V for further elaboration).

These managerial decisions are the basis of time-span measurement. It is they which constitute the raw data on which the time-span measurements are taken. It is they also which make time-span a method of objective measurement. For managerial decisions of this kind are objective facts. They have manifest and observable effects on subordinate behaviour.

One point needs sharp emphasis. If manager B is unable to make a firm decision about target completion times and quality standard limits, then you cannot carry out a time-span measurement. The necessary data do not exist. It is as though you were trying to measure the length of an irregular wad of cotton wool. But you should also note that by the same token the minimum conditions do not exist for B to be called a manager. He is not in a position to set standards for C which will allow him to hold C accountable for his work. By effective time-span measurement, you can assist a manager to examine and decide his time and quality standards more explicitly, and by this means help him to review his position of executive leadership *vis-à-vis* his sub‑ordinates.

A WARNING

You will often be asked to do a time-span measurement of level of work in a role in discussion with X who is not the manager but who 'knows the job very well', or at least is pretty sure he does. Reject the invitation. It is simply not enough to 'know about a job'. You have to interview the manager, for it is he alone who can give you the fundamental data you require, namely, *his decisions* about the work he assigns and the time targets and quality standards he considers he is authorized to set.

In the absence of these managerial decisions, you are in the position of someone who is asked, 'Measure this piece of string, A, I am sure it is the same length as the piece, B, whose length we want to know' – but neither of you has ever seen piece B. How much reliance would you wish to place on the measurement of A giving the length of B? You are in exactly the same position in trying to measure time-spans without having access to real managerial decisions about work.

SUCCESSIVE APPROXIMATION

One means of helping a manager to structure his intuitive experience about the work he allocates and to make his standards of quality and pace explicit in quantitative terms, is to approach the analysis by successive approximation. Thus, for example, if you ask a manager when he expects a subordinate to have completed the development of a design, he may reply that he could not give any exact date; he expects the subordinate to get on with it as quickly as he can and to get it done along with a number of other tasks that he has been allocated. If you then ask whether it would be all right if the subordinate completed it within the next ten years, the manager will probably laugh and say, 'Oh, no! He doesn't have that much time.' Does he expect it to be completed within the next few hours? No, it would be quite impossible for him to do so; he would need at least some months to do it along with the rest of the work that he has to do. You might then ask him if he would allow the subordinate, say, a year to complete it, to which he might reply 'No, not that long – possibly something more like six months.' You can then refine the questions and help the manager to converge upon the maximum number of months that would constitute the longest target completion time that he would allow the subordinate when he allocated the task.

What seems to happen when the method of successive approximation is used, is that the moment the manager has realized that he would not allow, say, ten years for his subordinate to complete the task, he realizes also that he must have some target completion time in mind. There begins to form more consciously the longest target completion time that he intuitively assumed when he allocated the task under consideration to his subordinate.

LIMITS OF ACCURACY OF TIME-SPAN MEASUREMENT

The accuracy of time-span measurement depends upon two main factors. It depends first, as with all measuring instruments, upon your skill in using the instrument; in this case, upon your skill in eliciting the necessary information about the assigned tasks. It depends secondly upon the precision with which manager B can make and state his decisions about time and quality standards.

This question of limits of accuracy in measurement is not to be confused with the question of the realism of manager B's decision, nor with the question of whether or not C is capable of carrying out the assigned tasks within the time and within the standards of quality set. Just because a manager sets unrealistic tasks for a subordinate, or because the subordinate is not up to a task, it does not alter the time-span measurement. It simply means that the task as assigned may not be accomplished. I shall return to this matter in section VI.

In practice you will find that unless there is something grossly disturbed in the executive organization, managers are gripped in a more general plan of work, and must complete their own work as scheduled. Thus in turn they must have completion times and quality standards in mind when assigning tasks to their own subordinates. Successive approximation can help to reveal these times and standards.

The successive approximation technique may seem to provide little chance of revealing completion times and quality standards with any accuracy. The opposite proves to be the case. In dealing with time-spans of a few days, for example, you will find that tasks are assigned for completion within a specified number of hours or parts of a day – say, by the end of the succeeding day, or by midday of the day after that. In cases of time-spans extending over some months, you will find that there is some particular period which the manager has in mind, such as completion before the summer break, or before Christmas, or in three months' time. In the case of time-spans extending over some years, you will find that completion time targets are set in terms of, for example, completing a particular project or development in eighteen months' time, or getting some large-scale order ready for delivery in twenty-four months' time, and so on.

Accuracy to the week in high-level roles, or to the day, the hour or the minute in others, is not required. You will find that tasks of time-spans of 5 years and over are commonly assigned to be taken to the nearest year; time-spans of 2 years to 5 years, to the nearest half-year; time-spans of 6 months to a year, to the nearest month; 1 to 6 months, to the nearest week; 1 to 4 weeks, to the nearest day; under a week, to the nearest hour, or half-day; and under 1 hour, to the nearest 5 to 10 minutes.

TIME-SPAN MEASUREMENT OF OCCUPIED ROLES

When the role rC whose level of work is being measured is occupied, it is important to be clear about the tasks the manager B has in mind. Is he speaking, for example, of the longest extended tasks he is allocating to the present, say, average good incumbent? Or the longest extended tasks that would be just acceptable from any incumbent? Or of the longest extended tasks that he would have available for allocation to the very best possible incumbent? Or of the longest extended tasks he is allocating to the present incumbent, who, say, might be below the standard really required so that the time-span would be dysfunctionally low?

Different time-spans would be obtained for each of the above cases, just as different measurements would be obtained if you were to measure an extending telescope shut, half-extended, and fully extended. From these time-span data, what you can get is the range of levels of work within which the manager B is currently authorized to fill the role rC. They also give an indication of the likely range of level of work available to subordinate C if he has the potential for growth in capacity to progress to, and possibly above, the level of work available in the role as currently structured.

TIME-SPAN MEASUREMENT OF NEW ROLES AND UNOCCUPIED ROLES

Time-span measurement can be carried out with respect to unoccupied roles as well as occupied roles. It demands only that manager B should decide what tasks he requires to allocate into the unoccupied role rC. Thus, for example, in a discussion in preparation for recruitment and selection for a vacant role, he might indicate what are the very longest extended tasks he would require, and what are the extended tasks he could just get by with if they were the most that a new subordinate could manage. In this way, it is possible to measure the highest level of work the manager would require in a new subordinate, as well as the lowest tolerable level at which he could fill the role.

If the vacant role is a new role, the problem of measurement is no more difficult, but it may be more difficult for the managers A and B to make up their minds as to what they are expecting. The first problem, therefore, is for them to decide what kinds of task they are setting up the new role for. They have to do that anyhow, and the more clearly they can do it, the more precise will be their recruitment and selection. When they have decided, time-span measurement is nothing more than the measurement of those decisions. The decisions, of course, may be very tentative. In that case the level-of-work measurement would be subject to change as the specification for the role changed.

III

Discovering the tasks

You may encounter a number of difficulties in sorting out with the manager just what constitutes a task. I shall describe some of the more important of these difficulties. You will notice that they are of a kind characteristic of all measurement. They are not connected with the act of applying the measuring instrument; that is relatively easy. They are connected with the problem of sorting out the data ånd getting them into measurable form in the first place. Thus, for example, it is easy enough to measure the voltage of an electric current in the sense of reading from a voltmeter; the problem is to understand enough about the phenomenon of electricity, and about the particular electrical circuit, to get an electric current into the voltmeter under conditions which allow a reading to be taken.

It is the same with time-span measurement. The difficulty is not in taking readings of times. You will encounter your trouble in forcing out into an explicit and measurable form just what tasks are being allocated. It is not that the tasks do not exist, nor is it that they do not have discoverable objectives and target completion times. It is simply that you cannot expect a manager always to be able readily to state the objective of the task he has assigned, or the tasks implicit in general responsibilities, or to be able to tell you his time targets. They are often set as a matter of intuitive understanding between the manager and his subordinate. You may have to help him discover the objectives and time targets he has been implicitly setting, by using successive approximation. In order to do so, you will have to learn about the task content of roles. The prime experience required in measuring time-span is a wide experience of the task content of all the kinds of roles with which you will be concerned.

I have tried to help overcome some of these difficulties by the examples given in sections III and IV. In more general terms, however, it may be found that the trouble will arise in distinguishing between tasks on the one hand, and general responsibilities, sub-tasks, part-tasks, series of tasks, or programmes of tasks, on the other. I propose in this section to consider each of these difficulties in turn.

ASSIGNED TASKS AND DIFFICULTIES IN ASCERTAINING OBJECTIVES

If it is a manager's first experience of time-span measurement, you may have to explain the meaning of a task. In doing so you may find it useful to emphasize the fact that the objective of the task is always set by him in terms of quality standards and maximum allowable time for completion. Sometimes he will not be explicitly aware of setting such precise quality and time standards, and the fact may come as a surprise to him. In such a case, the successive approximation technique can assist you to let the manager see that in fact he is implicitly setting such standards.

I have found it useful to carry the point further, and to show managers that unless these quality and time standards were either implicitly or explicitly set, then no task had been allocated to the subordinate. For a task without ascertainable time and quality standards cannot in fact exist. It is a phantasy. It can have no definition in the mind of the subordinate, unless he himself picks standards which he thinks will satisfy the manager.

I have found that many managers deny this view of assigning work. They like to believe that they are leaving initiative and opportunities for creativity to subordinates by giving them open-ended instructions, as, for example in managers of research work. If you ask a research manager when he expects a subordinate to complete a given task, his reaction often is that he does not know because it is hard to tell when research will come to fruition. Such an answer is the result of the common misconception that research in industry is an unstructured search for knowledge. In fact, research workers in industry are assigned explorations to carry out which may or may not lead to positive results in the sense of discoveries being made. The manager has been authorized to employ the subordinate to carry out these explorations, it being the manager's responsibility to decide which exploratory work he requires to get done, and whether or not it is worth pursuing it any further.

The initiative of the subordinate is not reduced by this type of instruction. His creativeness will show in the discretion he exercises in carrying out his tasks, and in the initiative he takes in recommending to his manager new projects and profitable lines of investigation. If the manager fails to accept good recommendations, perhaps because he is not as good as his subordinate, that situation is not overcome by giving open-ended tasks. It requires that the subordinate be promoted out from under the manager. Whenever you come across apparently timeless tasks, look either for some kind of organizational problem, or for a failure to recognize that what is being described is in fact a general responsibility and not an assigned task (see under next heading, 'Tasks and general responsibilities').

Another example of a situation in which there is seeming obscurity with respect to the objective and end-point of an assigned task, is that of the salesman who is given the project of securing a new customer, or of launching a new product, or of opening up a new market. You will find that it is sometimes difficult for his manager to say just what target of time he has in mind. For example, he might say that it may take anywhere from two to ten years to establish business with a certain large potential customer who has always steadfastly done all his business with another supplier; how can he possibly put a target completion time upon it?

In such a case you will have to pursue the question of exactly what the manager thinks he has instructed his subordinate to do. Was it simply a wide-open instruction to go on for as long as the subordinate found necessary to establish contact, even if it took ten years? You will find that a salesman does not have such open-ended terms of reference. The manager may sometimes think he does give such terms of reference: in such a case, refer the matter to A, the manager-once-removed. He will be in a much better position to realize that he cannot allow open-ended terms of reference to be assigned to a subordinate.

If you are to help sort out such a problem you will first have to be absolutely clear in your own mind that it is requisite for a manager always to set limits (whether explicitly or implicitly) on both the objective and the target completion time for tasks which he assigns*. He cannot otherwise hold his subordinate accountable for accomplishing the assigned task. In short, if there is neither an explicit nor an implicit target completion time, then no task can be said to exist!

Pursue the questioning of manager B so as to discover precisely what work he is allocating to C, and with what object. For example, he cannot expect C, in any absolute sense, to obtain the trade of a new customer, since there can be no guarantee

* If this point causes difficulty, refer to chapter 4, and to *Exploration in Management*, chapters 3 and 4.

110

about a potential customer's decision. But he can expect C to carry, among his other tasks, that of pursuing this potential customer so that, during the next six months (or twelve months, or eighteen months), he will have explored the needs of the customer, the organization of his purchasing department, his buying policies, etc., and will have taken steps to meet the chief buyer, or chief designer, or other significant persons, with a view to getting them to put some of his company's products on test, and will at least be able to state the likelihood or unlikelihood of being able to get business. Such an instruction gives the necessary framework to enable C to plan the intensity of his programme of work in relation to the potential customer. It also allows the time-span measurements to be made.

TASKS AND GENERAL RESPONSIBILITIES

Tasks are discrete and finite units of work which a subordinate must carry out. They have the characteristic of having 'to do this', to achieve a concrete and specifiable objective. Confusion may occur, however, because there are two major sources from which a subordinate's tasks may arise. The first source is directly from his manager in the form of an assigned task; that is to say, an instruction from his manager to do such and such. The second source of tasks is from carrying general responsibilities. It will be necessary to consider this latter source of tasks for a moment, since time-span measurement can be bedevilled by failure to recognize the important distinction between tasks and general responsibilities.

A general responsibility given by a manager to a subordinate applies indefinitely unless amended. It is an instruction to take appropriate decisions or actions whenever specified conditions occur. Let me give a few examples of such instructions: 'Whenever authorized persons come and ask you, give them the stationery (or other) supplies they request'; 'Give authorized maintenance, or decorating, or toolmaking, or accounting, or personnel selection, etc., services, on request under the specified conditions'; 'Whenever you discover potential new customers, decide whether or not to take steps to contact them'; 'When you think I may be missing possibilities in licensing or patenting new products or methods, take steps to recommend to me what you think I ought to do'; 'If you see a possible new development in your field, decide whether to do some initial exploratory work on your own, or whether to recommend some course of action'; 'Keep your establishment under review and take such opportunities as may arise to train and upgrade members of your extended command'; etc., etc.

The general responsibilities exemplified each leads to action at appropriate times. The storekeeper hands out supplies when asked; the maintenance engineer carries out maintenance or decorating projects; the tool room manager makes tools; the accountant carries out special accounting analyses; the personnel officer recruits and selects new personnel; the sales representative contacts potential new customers; the legal adviser makes recommendations on licences and patents; the research worker carries out exploratory research; departmental managers assess and train subordinates; etc.

These decisions and actions do not, however, result from specific task instructions given by the manager. The subordinate must initiate his own decision or action within the general responsibility he carries, the particular decision or action he takes depending upon his assessment of the circumstances with which he is confronted.

The tasks generated by general responsibilities will be found to have implicit maximum completion times. These times are set by the general prescribed limits on expense, time and quality standards which are implicitly set as part of the general responsibility. You will find that the manager and subordinate are intuitively aware of these prescribed limits, and can soon be made explicitly aware of them by means of successive approximation.

Neither the storekeeper, nor the maintenance engineer, nor the tool room manager, nor the accountant, nor the personnel manager, nor the sales representative, nor the legal adviser, nor the research worker, nor the departmental manager, will be discovered to be authorized to initiate long-term projects lasting many years and costing large sums of money. (Nor are those who might be requesting services likely to be in a position to request such activities unless they themselves have a very high level of work.) There are definite and discoverable limits to the tasks they may initiate within their general responsibilities. It is these limits which you must find if the tasks concerned turn out to be relevant for the purpose of time-span measurement in any given role.

TASKS WHOSE STARTING POINT IS DIFFICULT TO ASCERTAIN

Tasks arising out of general responsibilities may sometimes be found to have an obscure starting point. Thus, for example, a feature writer on a newspaper had a general responsibility for deciding what issues in his field of work were likely to become prominent or important in the future, and to begin to prepare himself to write about those issues if and when they became live topics of news.

First appearances seemed to suggest that this kind of role would have tasks of at most one week, since the writer had the assigned tasks of writing a new feature article each week. You have to ask, however, when the process of writing the article begins. Is there any preparatory work, for example? You may discover that the writer spends most of his week not in writing that week's article, but in seeing people, reading, doing research, taking trips, as preparatory work for future articles – the work arising out of his general responsibility. In all of these activities he is spending the firm's money, in terms of his own salary and in travelling and other expenses.

To measure the time-span of such a task, use the technique of successive approximation. Ask the manager if he would authorize his subordinate to carry out such expenditure of resources for an article he planned to write in ten years' time; here the manager would undoubtedly say 'No'. You can then help the manager by successive approximation to recognize whether in fact he is instructing his subordinate to begin preparatory work now for articles that are likely to come to fruition in, say, a month's time, or six months' time, or a year's time, or two years' time, or whatever it may be. In this actual example it has been my experience that the more responsible the feature writer's work is thought to be, the longer time forward he is expected to begin his preparatory work, and thus the longer the time forward he is authorized to expend resources.

This difficulty of ascertaining the starting point of a task may also be encountered with assigned tasks. The manager may say, for example, that his subordinate must start the task no later than a given date, but could start at an earlier date if he wanted to. In such a case, press the issue so as to require the manager to decide whether he is in fact instructing his subordinate to consider starting the task at the earlier date; that is to say, discover whether or not he would hold the subordinate accountable for taking that task into his active work programme. If so, the starting point is the earlier date. If not, the starting point is the later date, since the subordinate is not accountable for doing anything on that task before that date.

TASKS AND SUB-TASKS – THE TIME-SPAN OF PROJECTS

There is a generally encountered problem in measuring the time-spans of tasks in the form of projects. It has to do with distinguishing the completion point of a project from sub-tasks constituting elements in the project – the starting and finishing times being under the discretionary control of the subordinate.

Sometimes projects appear to be allocated in phases. Thus, for example, a machine tool is to be built in twelve months. This machine tool must incorporate a certain base which is usually completed within the first three months, and its completion can readily be observed by manager B. The project has what appear to be additional three-month phases of this kind. Is this a twelve-month or a three-month project?

From this much information it is impossible to say. But here are some questions that must be asked. Are, for example, the first three months to be exclusively devoted to the manufacture of the foundation, so that a progress report would take the form, 'I have now completed all you required me to do; shall I start the next phase?'; or are assemblies for other parts of the mechanism also begun during the three-months period, so that any report at the end of three months might have the character,

'I have finished the foundation and have the work for a number of other parts well under way, so that the whole project is progressing in a manner which will ensure that we will finish in the twelve months' allowed time'?

If the first type of report applies to all the phases, it is a series of three-month projects. If the second type, it is a twelve-month project. In other words, if the phases of a project are such that the instruction to the subordinate is to complete all aspects of one phase before beginning the next, then that phase is not a sub-task but the end-point of a task. For the manager has set the starting and end-points of the phases. If, however, the phases are interlocking, and their interaction is under the control of the subordinate, in the sense that it is at his own discretion to plan and decide the start and completion of these phases, then each phase constitutes a sub-task.

The problem of distinguishing between tasks and sub-tasks would not be so difficult if managers were less prone to try to allocate a task, and then to set tasks within the task rather than leaving it to the subordinate to find his own way. If the manager B, for example, in the above illustration, were to instruct his subordinate to complete the machine tool in twelve months, and were also to specify that he must complete the base in the first three months, he has in fact allocated two tasks: one is the task of completing the base in three months; the second is the task of planning all the other activities necessary to complete the machine tool in twelve months, and among other things, using the base that is completed in three. If he really wishes his subordinate to do the twelve-month task, then to set the three-month task is redundant. It is most likely an instance of managerial interference. He may be hindering rather than helping his subordinate to complete the machine tool in twelve months. For if he simply leaves it at the twelve-month task, it gives his subordinate freedom to judge how and when under the particular circumstances it is best to plan the completion of the base, and all the other sub-tasks.

In other words, you may find that in carrying out time-span measurement you will have to assist managers to improve the way in which they allocate tasks to their subordinates.

For the questions about the tasks they allocate inevitably lead into the realm not only of what they give their subordinates to do, but of how they leave their subordinates to get on with it.

TASKS AND PART-TASKS

Tasks frequently are made up of a number of parts; for example, the task of making one hundred of a certain type of article, or of packing fifty boxes of sweets per day, or of copy typing four letters and three memoranda. So long as all the parts are given at the same time, as one instruction, and are all to be completed as one order and handed over at the same time, they constitute separate parts of one task, and are to be treated as such for purposes of time-span measurement.

Managers may sometimes be uncertain about what they might erroneously call a part-task. Thus, for example, a manager has a six-month task to assign to his subordinate. But he does not have confidence in his subordinate's capacity to carry it through to completion. He therefore divides the task into three parts each requiring two months to complete, and assigns him each part in turn.

The manager may then think that he is allocating his subordinate a six-month task, for as he may put it, 'the task is six months – the two-month bits are only parts of the task.' Yes, from the manager's own point of view! But from the subordinate's point of view, three separate tasks of two months each are being assigned, and not a three-part task of six months.

TASKS AND SERIES OF TASKS

Sometimes a manager may, for reasons of convenience or through force of circumstances, assign to a subordinate a series of tasks. The instruction is of the type, 'I want you to carry out the following tasks, one by one in the order given, starting each task only when you have completed the preceding one. You will complete each of the tasks within the quality and time standards set for it.'

This form of instruction leaves a series of discrete tasks. The manager could stop the series at any point without there having been any work wasted on the succeeding tasks, for he has explicitly excluded his subordinate's doing any work on any task in advance of its prescribed point in the series.

From the point of view of time-span, each of the tasks in the series must be considered in its own right, with its own starting and completion time.

TASKS AND PROGRAMMES OF TASKS

Tasks and programmes of tasks ought not ordinarily to be confused, since a programme of tasks is the total complex of tasks being carried by a person in a multiple-task role. But they can be confused in the following way.

The series of tasks in the preceding example might have been erroneously thought of as a 'programme of tasks' if they had been assigned in the following manner: 'Here is a programme of, say, ten tasks (each of which could be completed in, say, three months). You are to get one of these tasks under way every month, so that you can complete them in the next year by appropriate switching of your subordinates from one task to the next.' In fact such an instruction can be seen to give a series of overlapping three-month tasks, and not a programme.

For a programme of tasks implies that the manager wishes his subordinate to plan the effort he expends on completing each task by borrowing from other intermittent tasks. The manager would thus have to set completion dates for each of the ten tasks, such that each one could be carried out as an intermittent task, in some such form as: 'Here are ten independent projects, each of which would normally take three months to complete. Start them when you wish, but project A is to be completed in four months' time, project B in seven months, project C in eight months, etc., and project J in two years' time.' Such an allocation is in fact a programme, which contains a longest extended task of two years, namely project J.

The fact that the subordinate might decide not to start project J until the second year of the programme does not shorten the time-span. For this is at his discretion, determined by the manner in which he has decided to plan and progress the total programme.

SINGLE-TASK ROLES AND MULTIPLE-TASK ROLES

When you begin your time-span measurement you will have first of all to discover whether the role whose level of work is to be measured is a single-task or multiple-task role.

In the single-task role the subordinate never has more than one task to work on at a time, and he works on that task until he has completed it – unless his manager interrupts him before he has finished and gives him another task to work upon, in which case he drops what he was doing and his single task becomes the newly assigned one.

Single tasks may be assigned one at a time, a new one being given out as each one is finished. Or a series of single tasks may be assigned, the implication of the instruction being to finish these tasks one by one in the order given. Or, the equivalent of a series of tasks may be given in terms of a general responsibility; thus, for example, a copy typist may be given the general responsibility of answering the telephone when the secretary is out of the office, and taking messages; in effect, the instruction is to work on her assigned typing task, but to interrupt it when the phone rings and continue it again when she has taken the message: a single-task role with possible interruptions, but with priorities always determined by the manager and not left to the discretion of the typist.

In the case of the multiple-task role, the subordinate will get a mixture of tasks. Some of them will be continuous; that is to say, once a task has been given to him he will be expected to complete it without interruption. But he will also have tasks which are intermittent in time; that is to say, he will work on one for a while, then put it aside, and work on it again, then put it aside, working on other tasks in between times. Emphasize to the manager of a multiple-task role that he leaves discretion to his subordinate to decide when he works on his various tasks and what pressure to apply to their progress, in order to complete them within the specified time.

In short, the characteristic of the single-task role is that the person doing the task is not concerned with priorities. He does not have to worry about organizing the priorities of his own work in the sense of deciding which of his current tasks he ought to be working on at any given time, since he has only one task at a time. In the case of the multiple-task role, the subordinate is always faced with that kind of decision. He has many tasks to do. He must programme his own work so that it gets done when required.

Once you have determined whether the role is a single- or multiple-task role, the analysis takes the course described in sections IV and V. The analysis is different for each of these two types of role, and the technique for each is described separately.

IV

Time-span measurement of multiple-task roles

Level of work in = Time-span of target completion time of
multiple-task role   longest task

The significant time-spans for the measurement of level of work in multiple-task roles are the longest tasks. It is these tasks which set the framework for the planning and priority-setting for all concurrent tasks. They can be borrowed against by being put off or delayed in order to complete concurrent shorter term tasks. But this borrowing against the longest task cannot go on beyond its target completion time.

To measure the time-span of a multiple-task role you have to discover the tasks which have the longest target completion time. Note that the concept here is that of the longest *target* completion time. This target time may differ, and often does differ, from the actual time it eventually takes to complete an extended task. If, once a task is under way, its target completion time is changed by the manager, treat it as though a new task had been allocated.

FINDING THE LONGEST EXTENDED TASKS

Ask manager B which of the tasks he allocates, or will be allocating, into the subordinate role rC have the longest

119

forward completion time targets at the time he allocates the tasks.

Explain to the manager that there are three main areas of work that experience has shown it to be necessary to explore. These are:

1. *Regularly recurring work.* Tasks which regularly come up, such as: getting out monthly and annual accounts in accounting work; regularly visiting certain customers in the case of sales work; carrying out certain repeating scheduled production work in the case of manufacturing; and so on.

2. *Development projects.* Non-recurring tasks of a special kind: for example, an assignment to develop and implement new accounting routines or the use of business machines; or to develop a sales relationship with a new customer; or to introduce a new product; or to introduce and implement certain new manufacturing techniques; or to try out a new personnel selection test; and so on.

3. *Induction and training of new subordinates.* This applies only in the case of managerial roles, and refers to the longest period of time which a manager would allow a managerial subordinate for getting a new green subordinate to the point where he would just be capable of performing at the absolute bottom authorized level of work in the role.

The point of exploring these three areas systematically is that different multiple-task roles may throw up their longest task in different areas. In the case, for instance, of managers in control of machine operators, it is likely that induction and training of new subordinates, particularly supervisory assistants, will throw up the longest task. In the case of higher-level research, it is likely to be the development projects which will throw up the longest tasks. In the case of middle-level accounting, it is likely to be the management of the regularly recurring monthly and annual accounts which will constitute the longest tasks.

TIME FOR INDUCTION AND TRAINING OF SUBORDINATES

How long a manager C would be allowed for the induction and training of new subordinates seems always to be experienced initially as a very difficult question to answer other than in very vague or approximate terms. Discuss it with his manager B, and you will find that it is not such a vague question as it may at first seem.

You will note first of all that the question applies to the level-of-work measurement of managerial roles only. That is to say, if it is the level of work in managerial role rC which is being measured, you are questioning manager B about how long he allows his managerial subordinate C for the induction and training of C's own subordinates.

The question to be posed to manager B is what would be the longest time he would target for C to take a new subordinate who is judged to be potentially capable of doing the work for which he has been appointed, but who at the time of appointment has the least amount of training and experience consistent with being appointed – that is to say, he needs the maximum amount of training.

Such a subordinate will not be much use at first. Gradually, however, with training and experience he will (if he makes the grade) become worth the payment level at the bottom of the payment bracket for the role. That is to say, he will not be one of the best subordinates, or even average. But he will be off probation, and capable of doing just the minimum acceptable level of work in the role. Further development would still be required for him to become acceptable on a permanent basis, and he would have a good way to go before he became capable of performing the higher levels of work available in the role.

The question to be asked of manager B is, what is the longest time he expects his managerial subordinate C to have in mind in connexion with bringing a new subordinate up to his minimum level? Use successive approximation to find out. For example, would he be satisfied if, on questioning C about how his new subordinate was getting along six months after appointment, C were to reply that everything was going fine and that in another six months the new subordinate would be performing mini-mum-level tasks? Is the total of one year thus implied acceptable to B? Would he have allowed C to work on the assumption that he had been allocated a target completion time of up to one year? Or more? Or had he in fact allowed him less?

It is always possible, of course, for B to allocate additional time for C for training a subordinate. The question, however, is what is the initial maximum target completion time beyond which C would have to ask for further time if he felt that, although the subordinate in question had not quite made the grade in the targeted time, he nevertheless was likely to do so given a bit more time?

I have found some quite striking consistencies in the maximum induction and training times allowed to managers for the training of new subordinates. For training shop and office workers for work of up to one-week level, it takes up to a maximum of six weeks; for training manual and office workers for work of up to one-month level it takes up to three months; for training shop floor and office supervisory assistants, up to six months; for training subordinates who in turn are managers of shop and office workers, up to twelve months; for training a new factory manager, up to two years. These times, of course, refer to the time-span of the role of the manager C who is accountable for the training, and not the role of the new appointee.

APPARENT REVIEW PROCEDURES

Tasks are frequently allocated with the proviso that the subordinate C should report, say, monthly or quarterly on his progress. In this way, a task allocated with, say, a twelve-month time-span may appear to be only a series of one-month or three-month tasks. These circumstances must always be carefully investigated.

Just because C has to report monthly to B, it does not necessarily follow that a target completion time of one month has been set. Two different situations must be distinguished from one another.

The first situation is one in which reporting at the end of each month carries with it the instruction to have all the work rounded off at that time so that the manager B can review what has been done; that is to say, a definable end-point has been reached and there are no loose ends or continuing activities. The manager must then issue an instruction with regard to the task he expects his subordinate to complete in the following month, and so on. In other words, the project is allocated in twelve discrete monthly instalments: it constitutes twelve successive one-month tasks.

The second situation is one in which the subordinate C works from the beginning with a twelve-month target completion time in mind. He gets a variety of activities under way, and plans to initiate others only some months later. For example, on a machine tool design project, he gets his draughtsmen working immediately on the design of certain parts which will take many months; other parts which may be standard he leaves aside for the time being, with the idea that he will be able to get them done from time to time during the twelve months as opportunity arises while some of the more complex or unusual designs are being scrutinized, or when other delays occur which give one or other of his draughtsmen some free time. A monthly progress report in these circumstances deals only with those parts of the project which C himself judges to be important. For the rest, he may simply say that the standard parts of the design are proceeding satisfactorily, or there may be no need to say anything at all. This type of organization of work throws up a twelve-month time-span for the task concerned.

In short, a report is a terminal report indicating an end-point to a task if its nature is: 'I have now completed (or have failed to complete) what you gave me to do.' It is a progress report if its nature is: 'Things are going satisfactorily in general on the project, but (at my discretion) here are a few highlights of difficulties I have picked out which I think require discussion.'*

WAITING TIME

The distinction between waiting time in a task which remains under the control of subordinate C, and periods when the task has been taken away from him, also needs to be made clear. A task remains under the control of C if, for example, he has allocated various parts of it to subordinates and is awaiting the results of their work, or if he is awaiting a service or the arrival of some equipment which has been ordered, but he continues to be responsible for keeping his eye on the task,

*The time-span of projects is also discussed in section III, p. 114.

progressing it, chasing delivery if late, or himself deciding just at what points he should take up that particular task; that is to say, the task remains part of C's programme of work which he himself must remain concerned about and take into account in the planning of his own total work load.

Inactive periods on a task are not under the control of C if his manager instructs him to take a task only up to the point where the waiting time begins; for example, to the point where pilot equipment has to be ordered, the task then being handed back to the manager. In such a case, it becomes the manager's task to order the equipment or to get it ordered, to see that it comes in, and to hand to the subordinate what is in effect a new task when the equipment is received.

Or, to take another example, you may have a production controller who is accountable for putting orders into progress and then is no longer accountable for them until they have been completed and are ready for delivery. Even if at the delivery stage he is notified and it becomes his responsibility to progress the delivery of the work, he cannot be said to have had any responsibility in the interim period for ensuring that the work is getting through on time. If, on the other hand, he is accountable during the interim period for watching the work from time to time, as he judges necessary, and assuring himself that delivery is not going to be late, then that period is part of his task.

MEASURING THE LEVEL OF WORK

The time-span of the longest task gives the level of work in a multiple-task role. If you wish to know the level of work currently being allocated, measure the time-span of the longest task for the incumbent of the role. If you wish to find the minimum authorized level of work, measure the time-span of the longest tasks in the absolute lowest level work which the manager is authorized to allocate and yet retain the subordinate in the role. If you wish to find the maximum authorized level of work, measure the time-span of the longest tasks available for allocation to any subordinate C no matter how good he may be.

V

Time-span measurement of single-task roles

$$\text{Level of work in single-task role} = \begin{array}{l}\textit{Time-span of target completion time of}\\\textit{longest task (immediate review), or task}\\\textit{sequence (delayed review)}\end{array}$$

The significant time-spans for the measurement of level of work in single-task roles are the tasks (where immediate review is operating) or the task sequences (where delayed review is operating). It is these tasks or task sequences which give the longest periods during which manager B relies upon his subordinate C to be exercising satisfactory discretion in carrying out his work.

In order to ascertain the tasks and task sequences, you have to be able to distinguish between the discretionary content and the prescribed limits of the work, and to be able to make this distinction clear to manager B whom you are interviewing. You may find it useful to keep the following points in mind.

ASCERTAINING THE ASSIGNED STANDARDS OF DISCRETION

You will find it easiest to identify the assigned discretionary content by inquiring about the effects of marginally sub-standard discretion; that is, inquiring into what the effects would be on the work done, if marginally sub-standard discretion were used in course of doing work.

In examining this question, you must emphasize to the manager that it is marginally sub-standard discretion that you are considering and not gross errors of judgement of an obvious sort; that is to say, discretion that is just sufficiently sub-standard to matter, but not so sub-standard that it would be readily manifest to the casual observation of the manager or others. It must also be emphasized that the effects of failure to conform to prescribed regulations must be excluded: such failure constitutes negligence, not sub-standard discretion. If you put the matter to manager B in this negative manner (namely, in terms of inadequate work, rather than satisfactory work), it makes it possible for him to explore what he relies upon his subordinate's discretion for, by exploring what would happen if the subordinate were just marginally letting him down. It gives him a new and different perspective. It makes it easier for him to organize his experience than if he tries to think what are the things which he relies upon his subordinate to do correctly.

Thus, for example, a manager in charge of a machine operator will ordinarily have no difficulty in describing the deviations from machining tolerances which constitute work which is sub-standard, or in picking out instances of just not good enough finish. Then by the technique of successive approximation, he can be assisted to discover the marginal limits of sub-standard discretion.

In some cases, however, it may not be so easy to get at just what standard of discretion is being expected. For example, in a process like making sand moulds into which metal is poured for the production of castings, the manager may have to leave some discretion about the temperature of the melt, and the rate of pouring, to the moulder. The effects of sub-standard discretion would be too many defects such as gas-holes in the casting. With work of low standard, defects are likely to show up at an early stage, within days of casting, when surplus metal is trimmed off the castings. If the work is not too bad, however, the castings may look right, and yet there may be small gas-holes, which may not show up until the casting is machined weeks or even months later.

In such instances, the manager must make up his mind what he is holding his subordinate accountable for. He may, for instance, be holding the moulder accountable only for a sufficient standard of work to ensure that the casting will be free of the kinds of defect which if present would also show at the rough trimming stage. If, however, he is holding the moulder accountable for the gas-holes which would be revealed only when the casting is machined, then he has increased the standard of work and the responsibility, and this increase will be found to show up in longer time-spans.

There is thus a straight question of fact about responsibility to be decided. If the manager decides to allocate the lesser responsibility, and hold the moulder accountable only for the shorter time-span work reviewed at the trimming stage, then he must hold *himself* accountable for difficulties that may show up at later stages. If he wants to hold the moulder accountable for preventing these later difficulties, then he must recognize that he is giving a higher level of work, and must possibly give him more time for the work to be done. Whichever way he decides to allocate the responsibility, the manager will have to make it clear to the subordinate just where his responsibilities begin and end. Time-span analysis often makes it possible to help the manager to sharpen his perception of the task so as to give his subordinate clearer indications about his responsibilities.

DISCOVERING THE REVIEW POINT

In order to discover the review points for the quality of the discretion exercised, ask manager B when marginally sub-standard discretion would be executively required to show up; that is to say, the point at which, if marginally sub-standard discretion were being continuously exercised, someone would be accountable for noticing it or, if he did not notice it, would himself be doing sub-standard work. 'Someone' might be the manager himself if he is exercising direct review in relation to his subordinate's work; or it may be someone else – an inspector, or an operator doing a succeeding operation – to whom the subordinate's work passes after he has finished it, without the manager himself necessarily seeing the work.

One of the difficulties frequently encountered in discovering review points is that the manager will take just one task out of his subordinate's work, pointing out that if sub-standard discretion were exercised on that task alone, it might not show up for years. It is necessary to explain the assumption that the subordinate is exercising marginally sub-standard discretion in *all* his tasks throughout the full range of his work. This assumption is an extremely important one, since without it the manager would be able to pick and choose which aspects of the subordinate's discretion he thought most important from the time-span point of view. So long as the whole range of activities is taken, then we are dealing with an objectively definable limiting case.

When the manager B is using direct review it is an essential condition that a sufficient review shall have taken place, that is to say a review which relieves subordinate C of further accountability if the result is deemed satisfactory, and which places responsibility back in the hands of the manager.

An example is that of the machine tool fitter who has been given, say, two months to assemble parts into sub-assemblies, and then to fit these together to produce a machine tool which will operate satisfactorily. It may appear that his manager B is in a position to review the quality of his work during those two months. To do so, however, would be a considerable task. For a fitter capable of doing the work would have a general plan in his mind about the relations between the various parts and sub-assemblies, and would have a sense of the minor adjustments and corrections he would be making at the time of his final assembly. Whether or not the way he has set about the task and is progressing with it is sound (from the point of view of the exercise of only marginally sub-standard discretion), cannot be settled until he has done his final assembly and the operation of the machine tool is tested. If the manager B is holding the fitter accountable for this planning and carrying through of the fitting work, he has allocated a two-month task.

IMMEDIATE REVIEW AND THE LONGEST TARGET COMPLETION TIME

For purposes of measurement of level of work in single-task roles under conditions of immediate review (i.e., review – whether direct or indirect – which takes place when each task is completed and before or concurrently with the beginning of the next task), all that is required is to discover the tasks with the longest target completion time, since, on completion, the quality of the work is reviewed and there can be no overlap of one task with another. This point is illustrated in figure 2 which shows the time allocated for a series of single tasks with immediate review. The diagram indicates that it would be task F which would carry the longest unreviewed time-span.

DELAYED REVIEW AND THE LONGEST TASK SEQUENCE

For purposes of measurement of level of work in single-task roles under conditions of delayed review (i.e., review – whether direct or indirect – which takes place after the succeeding task has been commenced), a time-span diagram will usually have to be constructed.

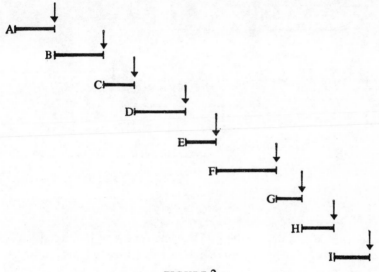

FIGURE 2

To draw up a time-span diagram, take a succession of tasks with their target completion times. Discover how long it takes in practice for each of these tasks to arrive at its review point. It is necessary to discover the actual time to the review points, since manager B may not be completely in control of the work after it leaves his subordinate C and cannot, therefore, target these times.

A simple example of a time-span diagram with delayed review is illustrated in figure 3. It is a diagram of a role into which are allocated regularly recurring tasks of a similar kind, the quality

129

of each task being reviewed at a subsequent stage, the interval being the same in each case.

If you examine the diagram you will note that whatever the task you start with, the same amount of time x-y will have elapsed during which the task sequence of some five and a half tasks has been carried out without any review having taken place. The time x-y gives the time-span of the work. Ordinarily, it would not be necessary to draw a time-span diagram when the

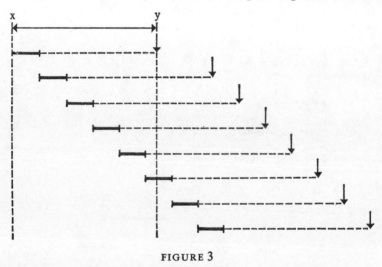

FIGURE 3

data are as regular as these. The time-span can be directly calculated from the beginning of any task to the time it gets through to its review point.

The diagrams become necessary, and more complex, under conditions where the employee is allocated differing successive tasks, which require longer and shorter time for completion, and which then pass by different routes to the review point. Examples of such conditions are commonly found under batch work production, and in offices in roles such as copy-typists not engaged in fixed cycle work.

The type of time-span diagram found in batch work production is illustrated in figure 4. This shows a succession of single tasks which have been allocated and completed. The review points for the single tasks (that is to say, the time they arrive at a point

130

where someone is accountable for discovering marginally sub-standard discretion) are indicated by the vertical arrows*. The review is indirect and delayed.

The problem now is to find the longest task sequence by inspection, beginning with each task in turn. Thus, if we start with task A, it will be noted that tasks A, B, C and nearly all of D have been completed before any of the tasks done has reached

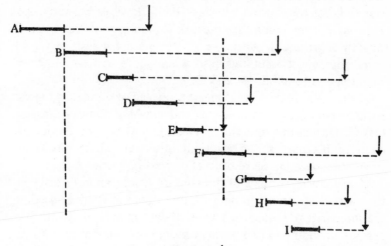

FIGURE 4

a review point. Marginally sub-standard work could have been carried out on all of these tasks without the manager necessarily having had the opportunity to discover it.

If we next start with task B, it will be noted that tasks C, D, E and part of F have all been completed by the turner before the review point – namely, the review of task E – has been reached. The reason that task E reaches the review point before the others is that it had fewer intermediate operations to be done upon it.

If sub-standard discretion turned up on the review point for

* This particular diagram is of turning work allocated in batches, prior to milling, drilling and finish grinding. Marginally sub-standard work will not show up until the grinding stage, at which point it will be discovered if the turner has either taken marginally just too much off so that the grinder cannot do his work, or else has left marginally too much on so that the grinder has an excess of metal to clean off.

task E, it would be the manager's responsibility to decide whether or not to check to make sure that the rest of the work already done during this sequence of tasks was satisfactory. Task B to task F therefore constitutes a task sequence, with its review point that of task E. This sequence is longer than that starting with task A.

It will be further noted that if we started with task C, D or E, the task sequence would end at the review point for task E, as was the case for starting with task B. If, however, we took task F as our starting point, then the task sequence would run to part-way through task I, when the review point for task G would come into effect – but this also would be a shorter sequence than the one beginning at task B.

In short, in figure 4, the longest sequence of unreviewed work is that commencing with task B and finishing midway through task F. During this time the manager is relying upon the judgement of his operator. They both intuitively know this. This time lapse gives the sense of level of work.

Measurement consists of drawing up a succession of tasks in the manner illustrated in figure 4, and discovering by inspection the longest task sequence. I have drawn up such diagrams for periods extending to two years or more for a number of roles. It is striking the way in which the same maximum spans of time recur for task sequence.

ANOTHER EXAMPLE

Here is another example, this time of direct delayed review. It is that of a copy-typist given tasks lasting a few hours to just over two days. Sometimes she is given one task at a time; sometimes she is given a few tasks at once, but is told what order to do them in, finishing one task at a time so that she has no responsibility for deciding priorities. She must exercise discretion with regard to neatness of work, some details of layout, and in spotting what might be inaccuracies or inconsistencies in the original and referring these to her manager.

Her manager directly reviews her work, sometimes immediately it is finished and sometimes delayed for hours or days. A typical sequence of tasks is illustrated in figure 5.

132

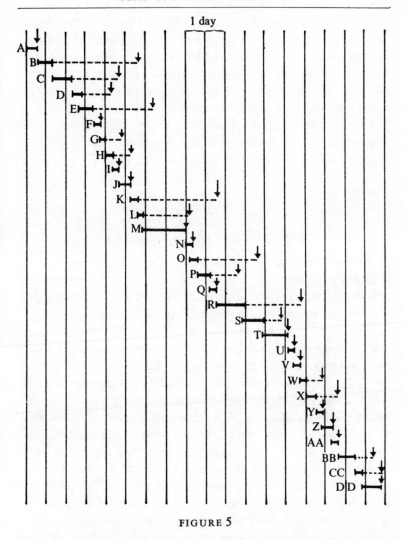

FIGURE 5

Inspection of the task sequences reveals that the longest are sequences of three days, commencing with tasks B, K and R.

MEASURING THE LEVEL OF WORK

The time-span of the longest task sequence gives the level of work in a single-task role. If you wish to know the level of work

133

currently being allocated, measure the time-span of the longest task or task sequence for the incumbent of the role. If you wish to find the minimum authorized level of work, measure the time-span of the longest task or task sequence in the absolute minimum level of tasks which the manager is authorized to allocate and yet retain the subordinate in the role. If you wish to find the maximum authorized level of work, measure the time-span of the longest task sequence available for allocation to any subordinate C no matter how good he may be.

VI

Some questions frequently encountered

There are a number of difficulties and questions which are so frequently encountered in the course of time-span measurement that it may be useful to enumerate them. You can be sure that you will come across all of them at one time or another.

The manager who gives inaccurate or false information. The result will be that he will get an inaccurate or false time-span measurement. The time-span instrument simply measures the level of work in the role by reference to the manager's stated decisions about the tasks he allocates. The butcher's scale cannot be said to be a less accurate instrument just because the butcher puts his thumb upon it. If the manager is not clear about the work he is allocating into his subordinate role, then he cannot expect to get an accurate level-of-work measurement of that role. In short, time-span measurement can be no more reliable than the reliability of the data which it is used to measure.

There is of course an inspection check built into the procedure. That check is in the review of the measurement by the manager-once-removed when he is authorizing the work and payment. An additional check can be obtained by submitting the data and the measurement to the subordinate occupying the role, as well as to the manager-once-removed.

The manager who, without authorization, delegates tasks which he ought requisitely to do himself. The result will be that an improbably high time-span will show up for the subordinate's role; this time-span may be nearly as high or as high as the time-span of the manager's role. This will show up when the measurement is presented to the manager-once-removed for authorization. If the manager tries to conceal that he is allocating tasks which he ought requisitely to do himself, this will show up when the measurement is presented to the subordinate as part of the description of his work; the subordinate then has full opportunity to recognize the incompleteness of material used by his manager in getting out the time-span measurement.

The subordinate who cannot perform work of the time-span level of the established role. In such cases, it is quite easy to get out two measurements. The first is the measurement of the level of work in the established role – that is to say, of the work which the manager is authorized to allocate into the role if he feels that the subordinate is capable of carrying it out. The second is the time-span of the work which the manager is actually allocating into the role, based on his judgement about the limit of the work that his subordinate can carry. By getting out the two time-span measurements it is possible for the manager to assess just how far the performance which he believes his subordinate is capable of achieving departs from the level of work which he needs to get done in the role.

A seeming paradox: that by giving a subordinate more time to carry out a task, instead of making it easier for him you may increase his level of work. It would seem to be common sense that the longer you give someone to carry out a task, the easier you are making it for him. Yet according to time-span measurement, there are some conditions where you would increase his level of work, and pay him more even though you were giving him longer. There is an apparent paradox here, but one which affects only multiple-task roles.

In single-task roles it is possible to give subordinate X longer than you would give subordinate Y to carry out the same task, say because Y is a better operator than X, but this fact alone will not by itself give an enhanced time-span. For this difference in capacity is the same factor which causes you not to give some tasks to X which you do give to Y because they are too difficult for X – and these frequently have longer time-spans which match their difficulty. In addition, the review mechanisms for the more skilled subordinate are usually more extended. Both these factors throw up higher time-spans for the work allocated to more skilled subordinates.

You get the apparent paradox in multiple-task roles, where you do get an increase in time-span if you increase the longest extended tasks significantly (it must be the longest extended tasks for the time-span to be increased). Suppose you increased the longest extended tasks in a role from three months to six months; the subordinate now has to plan the whole of his complex of tasks within a six-month framework, instead of a three-month framework. My evidence is that the longer framework is in fact experienced as a more difficult planning operation at a higher level of work.

If you have a subordinate just capable of working at three-months time-span, see what happens if you increase the longest extended tasks to six months. In my experience, far from finding it easier to have 'more time', he will run into trouble organizing his work.

In short, the longer the periods of time during which you have to plan and organize your own work, using your own discretion, the more difficult you will experience the work to be, and the more capacity you will have to have in order to be able to do it*.

The manager or the subordinate who gets angry or anxious when he feels you are implying that sub-standard work is being done. In the course of time-span measurement it may often happen that the manager or his subordinate feels that their capacities are being adversely criticized when questions about the effects of sub-standard discretion are raised. They may take it as a slight –

---

* See my paper 'Speculations concerning level of capacity' in Wilfred Brown and Elliott Jaques: *Glacier Project Papers*, 1965.

the manager feeling that it is being implied that he is being slack in allowing his subordinate to do sub-standard work, or the subordinate feeling that it is being implied that he is not capable of doing his work properly. I find it useful when talking about time-span measurement to people who have not encountered it previously always to explain that a negative or 'upside-down' approach to work is taken – that it is only by assuming that the work is not being done up to scratch that it is possible to get a picture of the work that the subordinate is being expected to do and, in the ordinary run of events, is in fact doing. It is precisely because work is ordinarily done to standard that review points are not familiar either to the manager or to the subordinate. The existence of a review point becomes apparent only when you ask what would happen if a subordinate had not done his work; looked at negatively in this way, it then becomes possible to see that the manager is relying on his subordinate to avoid trouble.

The individual who feels that time-span does not take sufficiently into account the most important tasks in the role. This criticism comes up mainly in the form of discomfort because in multiple-task roles the longest extended tasks do not always seem to be the most 'important' tasks in the role. Some very 'important' tasks might have comparatively short target completion times.

This type of criticism is a throw-back to the job evaluation outlook. Time-span is neutral with regard to the relative importance of any particular task in a role. What it does do is to give a measure of the maximum time for single-task roles, or scale within which *all* the work in a multiple-task role must be organized, scheduled and progressed. That is all.

It is noticeable that whenever a manager takes steps to increase the responsibilities of a subordinate, he inevitably gives tasks of longer duration as part of the process. The time-span is extended. It is that extension in time which gives the sensation of 'holding a looser rein', or of being 'let off the lead'.

Moreover, it may be useful to point out that the time-span technique is a measuring technique and not a method of role specification. Measuring instruments simply measure what they are asked to measure. They do not pass judgement on all aspects of the data which are measured. The question of whether or not it is useful to know the length of a piece of wood is not answered by a yardstick. Similarly, the question of whether or not time-span measurement is useful is simply a question of whether or not any use can be made of this particular measurement when you have it. The usefulness of the time-span measurement derives not from the instrument itself but from two facts: the fact that time-span measurements of jobs appear to correlate closely with such important matters as the intuitive sense of individuals about fair differential payment for work and for the level or intensity of responsibility carried in a job; and the fact that they give a systematic and comprehensible picture of the time characteristics in the organization of executive work.

Possible discrepancy between the actual wage or salary bracket and the bracket that would be equitable for the level of work as measured in time-span. The application of the equitable payment bracket may throw up discrepancies between those rates and the rates actually being paid. Discrepancies up to 5 per cent are not uncommon, and you may sometimes come across discrepancies as large as 20 per cent or more. All one can do is to ensure that the time-span measurement has been carried out carefully, and that the manager has checked the data that he has presented for measurement. If the real work has been described and an accurate measurement has been carried out, then all you can say is that experience would indicate that, if actual payment conforms to the equitable payment for that level of work, then there is the greatest possibility in the long run that you will have a person of the appropriate personal capacity for the role, and that he will have a sense of fairness in the financial reward for his work.

The apparent anomalies. There are a number of roles which are frequently mentioned which appear to indicate that time-span measurement does not regularly correlate with level of work in the role. One of these, for example, is the role of the *diamond cutter*, which is described as having a time-span of the few seconds it takes to deliver the blow that cleaves the expensive diamond successfully or unsuccessfully. Another example is the *captain of a large ocean liner* who is described as having responsibility extending for only the few days necessary to take his ship from one side of the Atlantic to the other. Or the *higher-level buyer* of goods who sits in his office and within the day makes decisions involving large sums of money – decisions which take only a few minutes to make but which have very great consequence. Or there is the example of the *housepainter* who is seen as having not very high responsibility but a time-span extending into the years that will elapse before it will become apparent that he has not done the undercoating work properly. There are numerous other examples of the same kind.

These examples all suffer in common from one grave shortcoming: the descriptions given are hypothetical. They are descriptions of what the person thinks the work is, but are not necessarily realistic. The real responsibilities in the roles are very different from those quoted. The informant in each case is talking about roles about which he himself does not have first-hand knowledge. If in fact one discusses these roles with the managers in charge of the work – that is to say, with the persons who are actually allocating responsibilities into the roles – then a different picture emerges. Thus, the diamond cutter has many responsibilities other than simply hitting diamonds with a hammer from day to day. He may be involved in buying and selling, and is certainly involved in extensive and time-consuming analysis of crystal structure. The ship's captain is like the manager of a very large on-going business, with responsibility for customer relations, maintenance of the ship, maintenance of a crew of hundreds, and so on, with extended tasks lasting over periods of some years. The high-level buyer may be responsible for, say, development projects involving active support for suppliers by means of enhanced prices or guarantees of purchase for a forward period of (as I have found) up to five years. In the case of the housepainter, the apparently long time-span is not in the discretionary content of his work but in failure to conform to the prescribed content; for example, failure to put on the prescribed number of undercoats, or to use the prescribed cleaning materials, etc. If the prescribed content is conformed to, then any sub-standard quality in the painter's work emerges as he is doing it; the quality of his work can be seen by the foreman or by the client for whom he is doing the work.

The general point that emerges from these considerations is not to allow yourself to be caught in the trap of carrying out time-span measurement of hypothetical roles. The person you must see is the manager in charge of the role, not an individual who thinks he knows what it is about but does not have first-hand contact with it. There can be a very great difference indeed between descriptions of roles by persons who actually know them in the sense of having allocated work into them and been accountable for the results, and descriptions by persons who are onlookers but have not themselves had direct experience either of occupying or of managing the role.

In short, the time-span technique is a measuring technique. If hypothetical or false or inaccurate data, or data suffering from other shortcomings, is fed into the instrument, then it will simply give a measure of the irreality or inaccuracy or phantasy character of the information.

How can a manager's decisions about assigning work be objective facts, since they are only his subjective judgement? The decisions of a manager may be an observable fact, but they are still the product of his subjective judgement and standards. The interviewed manager, if asked on another occasion, or by another interviewer, may say, for example, that the target completion time he is setting is different. How can it be determined what is the correct target time?

This question misses one of the fundamental points about work. The manager's standards of pace and quality, however correct or incorrect, adequate or inadequate, realistic or unrealistic, they may be, nevertheless constitute the real situation within which the subordinate must work. If he is constantly changing those standards, his subordinate will be confused.

From the point of view of measurement, these changes will be reflected in changes in time-span. So, too, would the length of a collapsible telescope be different as you opened it or closed it. In

140

other words, time-span measurement allows you to measure the oscillations in level of work created by a manager who is constantly changing his instructions.

PART THREE

Equity in payment

CHAPTER 6

Norms of equitable payment

I

THE most significant evidence showing that what is experienced by a person as level of work could be measured in terms of time-span, was the totally unexpected finding of a regular connexion between time-span and the sums of money which individuals stated would, in their estimation, constitute fair payment for their work. Regardless of the actual wage or salary they might have been earning, regardless of type of occupation (accounting, engineering, shop management, manual or clerical work, purchasing, research, etc.), regardless of position (from shop floor work to top management), and regardless of income tax paid, individuals in jobs whose range of level of work as measured in time-span was the same, privately stated a very similar wage or salary bracket to be fair for the work they were doing. I now wish to call the pattern of differential payment so derived the *equitable work-payment scale**.

This finding has been described in detail in *Measurement of Responsibility* for results obtained from analyses carried out with members of the Glacier Metal Company. I have since been able to obtain data in respect of over one thousand jobs, with confirmatory findings from a heavy engineering firm, a food factory, a bank, a woodworking concern, and a chemical works.

It is of the utmost importance to note that these analyses (as indeed is all my work) were conducted within a social-analytic relationship†. This relationship gives access to private aspects of

---

*In *Measurement of Responsibility* I used the phrase 'general wage and salary structure' to refer to this scale.

†The social-analytic method is described in *Measurement of Responsibility*, pp. xi–xiii. The essential features of this special type of consultancy work are that: (a) I have no discussions with members of the firm except at the personal request of the member or members concerned; (b) the discussions are confidential; (c) no executive action whatsoever is initiated by me as a result of the discussions, their purpose being to assist members to clarify their own views; and (d) I do not report on members to anyone else, but at the

a person's feelings, judgements and attitudes, which have most likely gone unrecognized by himself. It creates a setting in which a sorting out of these previously unidentified views can take place without any executive action being initiated by me.

I cannot say under what other conditions besides a social-analytic relationship the phenomena I shall describe may be observed. But there are two conditions under which they are pretty unlikely to be observed: discussion between a manager and a subordinate; and ordinary conversation or public discussion between friends, working colleagues, fellow trade unionists, etc. For in such discussions, the deeper-lying personal feelings and views are never able to come to the surface. Even if he has become conscious of these views and verbalized them – a most improbable circumstance – their expression is blocked by stereotypes of what others will expect one's views to be, or by the desire to influence other people's views in some particular direction. I am not here dealing with these manifest social stereotypes, but with the common patterns which characterize the private reactions of individuals – hence my emphasis on the special methods that must be used to make it possible to make contact with these private reactions.

The results suggest the existence of an unrecognized system of norms of fair payment for any given level of work, unconscious knowledge of these norms being shared among the population engaged in employment work. It is because of these intuitive norms that I have had recourse to the concept of equity in describing the scale of felt-fair differential payments. I am using the term equity to express the notion of differentiated treatment rather than equal treatment of individuals, in accord with the differential circumstances affecting those individuals – in this case, differential levels of work or responsibility to which they are called upon to apply themselves. I shall want to return later in the course of our argument to consider how these standards of equity are unconsciously established and carried in the minds of individuals.

---

request of the persons with whom I have had discussions I may include information from these discussions, in general terms, in comprehensive reports – a process which has been gone through in clearing the present data for publication.

II

The character of the equitable work-payment scale is shown in figure 6*. A number of features of this graph require comment and explication.

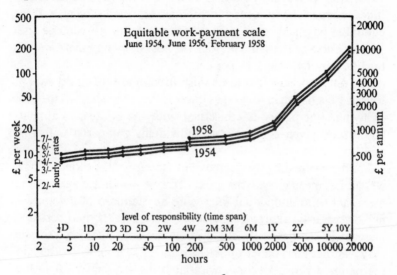

FIGURE 6

A. The earnings refer to total emoluments; that is to say the wage or salary plus any other fringe benefits such as, for example, use of car, assistance with purchase of house, provision of canteen meals, etc.

B. There is an artifact in the horizontal scale of time-span. In order to get a continuous scale from hours to days to weeks to years, I have taken one day to comprise eight working hours, a week to comprise five working days, a month to comprise four working weeks, and a year to comprise twelve working months.

C. During the five years I have been collecting data about felt-fair payment and level of work, the standards of what constitutes

*The curves on this graph have been made by plotting the time-span felt-fair pay data from just over 1,000 analyses. For any given time-span, the deviations between individual statements of felt-fair pay range are of the order of ±5 per cent, with standard deviations of the order of 2 to 3 per cent.

equitable payment have moved upwards. Percentage-wise this upward movement has conformed closely to upward movements in the wages index*. This finding is illustrated in figure 6 by the three curves showing the equitable levels as they were in June 1954, June 1956, and February 1958. In these periods the wages index moved 1.10 per cent and 1.07 per cent respectively, and the equitable payment levels took a corresponding percentage rise. In the course of the same periods the cost of living index† moved by 1.06 per cent and 1.11 per cent.

It is not surprising that these shifts in standards of equity should follow movements in the wages index rather than shifts in the cost of living. For equity is concerned with the relative treatment, within any given economy, of individuals compared with one another, rather than with any absolute standard of living – a factor determined by the degree of prosperity of the economy as a whole. Let me elaborate this point. In an expanding economy the mere fact of an individual increasing his standard of living does not necessarily represent personal progress. If his personal increase is identical with the average national increase, then he may feel that he is better off in the sense of sharing with others in the national prosperity, but without being any better off in the sense of having made personal progress in his career relative to others. *Per contra*, in a period of economic contraction or depression, an individual's standard of living may be decreasing and yet at the same time he may be making individual progress in his career, in the sense of receiving merit increases which cancel out some of what would otherwise be a bigger drop in living standard.

We may note, therefore, that our findings are suggestive of the fact that the standards of what constitutes equitable differential payment tend to move in unison throughout the population, in terms of percentage proportional movement. The effect is that the differential pattern of payment for different levels of work has

---

*The Ministry of Labour wages index derived from the current average of negotiated and standard minimum wage rates for manual work: it is an index of the average national minimum wage for a normal working week.

†The cost of living index (the retail prices index) is derived from the current average prices of a standard list of consumer goods.

remained fixed. It is important to note, of course, that my data have been obtained during a few years only. A much longer time will be required to discover whether in fact there has been any genuine shift in the differential pattern, i.e., a closing or opening of the gap.

D. The norms of equity are independent of the amount of income tax paid by individuals. The independence of these norms from income tax probably reflects the commonly held view that it is unsatisfactory for employers to have to decide upon the relative needs of different employees and their families. These are matters for society as a whole to decide, and to express through government. Equitable payment levels can be maintained regardless of an employee's family and other commitments or absence of such commitments, leaving it for taxation policy, national insurance, and welfare legislation to regulate how much of that income a person shall keep.

E. The discontinuity in the curves at the four-week time-span level has to do with the effect on norms of equity of whether or not a person is paid for doing overtime work. A very consistent and striking reaction has been observed. In 1958, for any given time-span level, a person who was paid for overtime work stated an equitable rate some 25s. per week below that stated by a person who was not paid for overtime work. For example, the equitable rate for one-month time-span level of work stated by a man paid for overtime was £14 per week, and by a man not paid for overtime, £15 5s. per week. (In 1955, a difference of 20s. was pretty consistently stated.)

It is noteworthy that this consistently stated difference is given regardless of the actual amount of money being earned on overtime work. The most likely explanation would appear to be that employees who receive overtime pay count upon this pay to provide a supplement to their wage or salary of 25s. per week. Anything over and above this amount – and in some periods the amount may be considerably larger – is considered as a perquisite, and not to be counted upon in the sense of budgeting for ordinary home expenditure.

That this differential amount comes into the norms of equity about payment is not surprising. A certain amount of overtime is a relatively common feature of employment work, the difference between different grades of personnel being whether or not they get paid for it. In considering a fair and equitable weekly wage or salary, therefore, for a standard working week, individuals automatically take into account the meaning of these wages or salaries in terms of the total earnings likely to be involved. This effect will be familiar to anyone who has had experience of firms where promotion from the shop floor staff, or from one grade of staff to another, involved the giving up of payment for overtime work. The universal reaction is the expectation that with the promotion there should go an increase of at least about £50 to £75 per annum merely to compensate for the loss of basic overtime earnings.

In connexion with this overtime effect, I have found repeatedly that as individuals approach or surpass the one-month time-span level of work in their jobs, they begin to think in terms of having a flat weekly salary and of forgoing payment for overtime work. This is a finding which I shall consider at greater length in a succeeding section when I turn to the question of individual progress: I have used this finding in choosing the particular point at which to break the graphs showing the equitable work-payment scale. This break is not intended to indicate that all payment for overtime ceases at the one-month time-span level. I have data on individuals whose jobs range up to the two-month and three-month time-span level who continue in receipt of overtime pay. More properly, therefore, the two segments of the graph should be drawn as overlapping. I have not so far come across any jobs whose level of work bracket extends above the three-month time-span level for which payment for overtime is given at the top end of the bracket. Nor have I found any jobs whose bracket extends below the one-month time-span level for which payment for overtime is not given at the lower end of the bracket.

F. A particular problem arises in equating hourly-rated wages with weekly wages and salaries, because of the different length of working week which is often involved. The working week for the hourly-paid workers with whom I have dealt has been 44 hours; for the non-hourly-rated the working week has varied – 38 hours for some, 40 hours for others, and 44 for supervision in charge of hourly-rated workers*. The problem is this. How does one equate the norms of equity of a manual worker who states, say, 5s. 6d. to 6s. an hour as a felt-fair pay bracket for his job, with those of a salaried staff member who states, say, £12 to £13 per week for a job with the same time-span bracket, but whose normal working week is 40 hours as compared with the manual worker's 44 hours: to turn 5s. 6d. into a weekly figure for purposes of comparison, should one multiply it by 44 hours or 40? I have used the following assumptions in dealing with this problem.

The value to an hourly-rated worker of his pay is his hourly rate times the number of hours in his working week. I have accepted this fact in making my comparisons. The vertical scale of figure 6 comprises a number of different weekly hours of work – 44 hours a week for the hourly-rated, and various lengths of working week for the non-hourly-rated. The significant thing to note is that the norms of equity for all hourly- and non-hourly-rated workers are the same regardless of the length of their normal working week. It would appear that length of working week and pay are kept as separate issues where norms of equity in payment are concerned, just as they are kept separate in negotiations. Moreover, it is of some importance to note that the 40-hour (or less) week for the higher levels of staff is in any case something of a myth: it simply states the minimum required attendance geographically on the job, but omits the additional hours usually put in either on the job or at home. The fact that norms of equity in payment are not affected by hours worked – except for the special case of the standard correction for overtime described above – strengthens the conclusion that these norms are related solely to the level of work carried.

G. There is one particular feature of the scales used in plotting the graph in figure 6 which must be recognized if false interpretation of the graph is to be avoided. The particular shape of the curves – the increased steepness after the one-year time-span level – has occasionally invited the observation that it would seem that those in higher-level roles fare much better salary-wise when they are promoted than those in lower-level roles: if they are promoted

* These hours of work refer to the standard working week before the decrease in the working week negotiated in the spring of 1960.

from one rank to the next, equitable treatment in their pay seems to call for it to rise at a very considerably more rapid rate than for those in lower ranks. Why should this apparent disparity in treatment be equitable?

This observation is not a correct one. The graph simply shows the relationships between time-span and felt-fair pay, and does not give any information about levels of executive responsibility and promotion. While the evidence points to the fact that the higher the time-span the higher the responsibility, this fact does not necessarily imply that the same increment in time-span will be found to occur with each step up in executive level or rank. Indeed, as I indicated in *Measurement of Responsibility* (page 47), the relationship between time-span and rank is a complex one, and constitutes a problem requiring further analysis and understanding.*

* I have now discussed this problem in *Time-Span Handbook* and *Glacier Project Papers*.

CHAPTER 7

Actual and equitable payment

I

A POINT which calls for the most emphatic enunciation is that I have so far been talking about norms of *equitable differential* payment – of felt-fair payment – and have not said anything about the *actual* payment received, other than to report that the earnings considered to be fair were independent of the actual wage or salary being earned by the person concerned. Norms of equitable payment are connected with level of work as measured by time-span. They appear to be uninfluenced by the fact that a person might never have received actual earnings which conformed to equity.

If individuals engaged in employment work do possess these shared norms of what constitutes fair pay for any given level of work, we may then ask whether these norms of equity influence a person's feelings about his actual pay. There is strong evidence to show that this influence does in fact exist. A person's attitude towards the wage or salary bracket paid for his work appears to be fundamentally influenced by the extent to which that bracket is consistent with what would be equitable for the range of level of work in his job, or deviates from equity either upwards or downwards. The following findings were obtained.

II

The results of individual discussions about actual pay in the course of the social-analytic work to which I have referred have been illuminating. A degree of consistency has emerged that has made it possible to predict individual feelings about actual payment brackets, if the actual and the equitable payment brackets are known. And conversely, it is possible to guess a person's actual payment bracket within a five per cent degree of accuracy, if the equitable payment bracket and his feelings about his actual payment bracket are both known. These results can be briefly summarized.

Individuals react to conformity or non-conformity between their actual earnings and equitable payment in a characteristic manner. If the actual salary bracket for a person's role coincides with equity, he expresses himself as being in a reasonably paid role. If his actual payment bracket has fallen below the equitable bracket, he expresses himself as dissatisfied with the financial recognition for his role. If, on the other hand, his actual payment bracket has risen above the equitable bracket, then he reacts with a sense of being paid within a rather higher range than he can ever hope to maintain. The intensity of his reaction varies with the size of the discrepancy between the actual and equitable brackets.

More specifically, this trend of reactions of individuals to deviations between actual and equitable earnings is as follows. Individuals whose actual payment bracket remains within ±3 per cent of equity, tend to express themselves as feeling that their role is being reasonably paid relative to others. They may be dissatisfied for other reasons – they may not like that type of work, or their general working conditions, or they may think they could carry higher responsibility either within the same bracket or in another role, or they may just be dissatisfied with life in general – but they will, nevertheless, state that their pay is within a bracket that is reasonable enough for their work.

A person whose actual payment bracket falls 5 per cent below equity feels moderately retarded, and states that the employing organization is treating him to some degree unfairly. If his actual payment bracket is 10 per cent below equity, he feels he is definitely being treated unfairly; he may appeal to his manager; or if he does not feel his security of employment is strong enough to allow him to appeal, he will harbour ill-will. A fall in payment bracket greater than 10 per cent below equity is accompanied by an employee's beginning to consider the possibility of getting satisfactory financial progress by seeking another job. If the employment situation in his occupation and his personal circumstances are such as to permit a change of employment, he will tend towards seeking such a change if the deviation reaches 15 per cent, and the likelihood of his making the change becomes high if the deviation moves towards a 20 per cent discrepancy. If the employment conditions in his occupation, or his personal circumstances, are such as to make a change of job impossible, then at the 10–20 per cent discrepancy range he will tend towards a state of mind in which he swallows his resentment and carries on with his job, but in what I can best describe as a depressed way: that is to say, he will tend to do his job more or less competently, but with an absence of that zest and enthusiasm which makes for high efficiency and personal satisfaction in work. Even under the conditions of full employment that have obtained in recent years, these latter circumstances have occurred in some types of employment, as, for example, in roles within some types of manual work and within the lower levels of accounting and general office work.

If a person's actual payment bracket moves to more than 5 per cent above equity, he considers that he is getting more than a fair deal in his role as compared with his fellows in other roles. At the 10 per cent level, compulsive elements begin to enter into his attitude. He may often have some anxiety about being able to maintain the high level of earnings; this anxiety increases with the length of time the earnings are received, the extra earnings themselves being treated as not secure and not to be counted upon. He experiences feelings of guilt with regard to others who are not doing so well. But guilt may be warded off by a devil-take-the-hindmost attitude. He may express resistance to change in the content of his work, to the introduction of new methods, or to transfer to other jobs. Greed and avarice may be stimulated, with a resulting anti-social grasping for further relative gain regardless of the consequences for the common good.

It may be useful to add that the reactions I have described apply equally at all executive levels. They are not confined to any particular group of people – high income, medium income, or low income.

III

When a group of individuals who compose a socially connected network – such as members of the same department, or the same trade union, or the same professional group, or the same specialist occupation such as chemists or mathematicians – are all subject to disparities between actual and equitable payment levels in their roles, there is a cumulative effect. One such instance was characterized by lowered group morale due to actual payment levels that were lower than equity would demand. It showed in one company in the form of complaints about the physical conditions of work and lack of opportunity, which were formally placed before management by elected representatives of the members affected. Employment in the particular occupation was readily available elsewhere, and the company was hit by unwanted labour turnover, losing members who were extremely difficult to replace. The managers concerned were most anxious to come to grips with the problem, but found it extremely difficult to get to the heart of the matter so that effective action could be taken. They accepted the complaint about the physical conditions and improved the situation. But no change in morale occurred. They were unclear on what further steps to take, for there appeared to them to be plenty of opportunity for most of the members of the group to advance, and, furthermore, they considered that the payment levels were adequate.

An analysis instigated jointly by the department managers and representatives, revealed that the top of the payment bracket for these jobs was about 15 per cent under equity. Those members working at the top of the bracket felt underpaid. This feeling had spread through the whole group, each of the others intuitively feeling that he would become underpaid as he progressed towards the top. Hence the feeling expressed as a sense of lack of opportunity. The problems were eventually resolved in depth by a number of management actions, including not only an adjustment of the payment bracket, but the working out of a career plan for each individual. It was explicitly recognized by all concerned that there could not be promotion opportunities for everyone, and members who eventually decided to leave did so in an open way, their search for employment being facilitated by the firm.

Another instance was that of an office in which salary brackets were in line with market values, since there were no outstanding problems in filling vacancies. But these brackets and market values proved to be between 10 and 20 per cent under equity. This disparity reflected a state of some unemployment in the occupational field, and there was little opportunity for the members to find alternative employment. An attitude composed of feelings of regard for the firm mixed with chronic feelings of disaffection held sway in the office – and while work was done satisfactorily, the managers concerned were left with the uneasy feeling that morale was not all it could be. Analysis indicated that were it not for the fact that their subordinates were in an occupation in which there was little hope of getting better conditions elsewhere, they would be having more serious and manifest morale difficulties in the department. The firm gradually moved in the direction of bringing the salary pattern for this occupation into line with the equitable scale. This step brought the salaries above current market levels for that work. But the potential gain obtained by getting rid of the underlying disaffection, and by being able to move towards a systematic salary structure, was judged by them to outweigh the additional cost.

The cumulative effects of payment of whole occupational groups at levels above those dictated by equity-payment for their roles, may be illustrated in one factory where, as far as the available evidence went, rates of pay for manual workers obtained which were some 15 to 20 per cent higher than was equitable for the level of work in the roles. The purpose of these rates of pay was to attract scarce labour from neighbouring areas. One effect of these rates of pay was a disturbance of the local economy, with local prices – particularly for lodgings – rising, and other firms having to increase their wage levels. These increases were never, however, nearly as great as the first firm's, the other local firms keeping to levels more in line with their judgement of the current market levels. A second effect was the stirring up of rivalry and disaffection within the non-manual sectors of the firm, and strong pressures from these sectors to have salaries brought into line with wages. A third effect was that an intransigent attitude was encountered when the firm ran into economic difficulties and found it difficult to maintain its inflated wages policy and necessary to reduce the number of its employees. Although there was plenty of alternative employment locally, the official trade union attitude was that there was no 'equivalent' employment available, and a severe industrial disturbance occurred.

157

Another instance of the effects of over-equity payment was that of a research laboratory in which the employing organization had maintained a policy of paying relatively high salaries to attract recent university graduates and scientists from industry. By high rates of pay, I mean rates of pay which were shown by analysis to be above equity for the level of work allocated to all except a few very mature and capable individuals who were early on appointed into positions of responsibility equivalent to their payment, either as group leaders or as scientists carrying out longish time-span projects.

The over-equity payment tended to encourage and reinforce unrealistic attitudes among those who received it. Four individuals whom I saw, for example, had been repeatedly striving for projects and positions which they had begun to believe they could carry, despite a great deal of evidence which they themselves were able to adduce to the contrary. There was a great deal of envy and rivalry towards others who were growing into positions of responsibility in which they would be able to maintain their rate of earning even though it might no longer be over-equity pay. They felt they were being victimized. Their best chance of recovering their reality sense in an effective way lay in seeking and finding employment in other companies where their feelings of victimization could no longer be maintained.

Over-equity payment did not bring genuine satisfaction to anyone. The ones who had the ability to carry the responsibility that would be consistent with the payment were disturbed because they did not have that responsibility. The less capable were disturbed because they wanted to hang on to the money but did not feel secure. In encouraging dissatisfaction, rivalry and envy, over-equity payment weakened group cohesion. The general effect was one of an unsettled atmosphere in the laboratory.

IV

If these findings about the reactions to consistency and disparity between actual and equitable payment apply generally, then what of the chronic unrest over wages which bedevils industrial relations? Are we to conclude that the manual and clerical workers represented by the trade unions are all under-equity paid and striving for equity; and that all other employed persons – managers, technologists, directors, scientists, and other professional and technical personnel – are paid either at equity levels or above for their work, and hence are out to protect a favoured position?

The main significance of my findings is that the problem simply cannot be tackled in such general terms as whether manual workers, or professional workers, or physicists, or the working classes, or the middle classes, are over- or under-paid. The view here put forward is that whether or not payment is equitable can be decided only in relation to the level of work in particular roles, and the payment brackets for that work, and not in terms of generalized groups of roles. Even where there may be pockets of under- or over-equity paid roles (by pockets I mean either occupational or geographical regions), the pattern is never a simple one. Thus, for example, if a particular trade union succeeds in negotiating generally favourable rates of pay for its members, both over- and under-equity paid roles will be found within that very occupational group. The same holds true for physicists, or young mathematicians, or senior managers, or skilled toolmakers. Conversely, some over-equity paid roles are always likely to be found within pockets of under-equity paid roles.

The real issue has to do with the *distribution* of over- and under-equity paid roles. My findings would lead me to expect a distribution mainly around equity, with some over-equity payment among the roles occupied by younger men of high potential ability in technical and professional occupations; scarce technological personnel; highly organized occupational groupings of manual workers; manual workers attracted to geographical areas where there is a labour shortage; certain high-level managerial personnel. These groups of employed persons bear the familiar stamp of rates of pay inflated by scarcity value or by organized group action. On the other hand, I think a skew towards under-equity payment will be found in the distribution of payment among groups in some areas of manual and clerical work. The view that I am expressing can be roughly illustrated in the accompanying diagram (figure 7).

Given the current methods of wage negotiations, the patterns

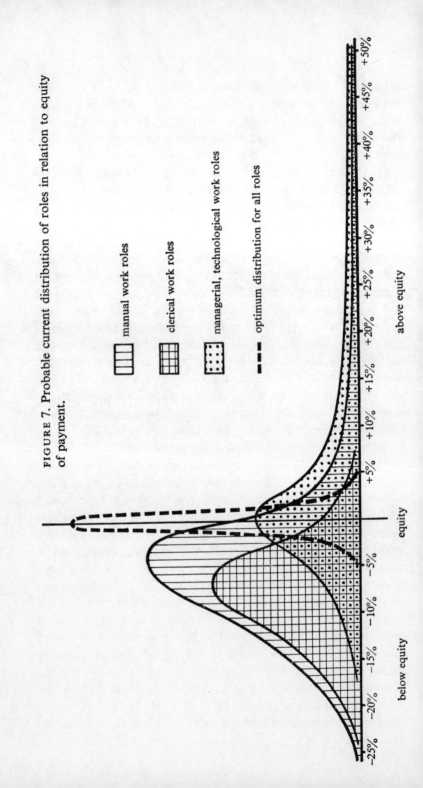

FIGURE 7. Probable current distribution of roles in relation to equity of payment.

manual work roles

clerical work roles

managerial, technological work roles

optimum distribution for all roles

-25% -20% -15% -10% -5% equity +5% +10% +15% +20% +25% +30% +35% +40% +45% +50%

below equity   above equity

depicted would be consistent with the chronic instability which characterizes the wage structure. For, in the absence of any objective criteria or regulations for dealing with questions of differential payment distribution, organized labour acts within a general policy of improving the conditions of all manual and clerical workers, regardless of whether they are in equity, under-equity, or over-equity paid roles. In other words, these improvements are not differentially directed to bringing about a situation in which the under-equity paid roles are brought into line with equity, while over-equity paid roles – whatever the occupation – are relatively held back. The increases are won for whole occupational groups, or for all the members of large unions, usually leaving the pattern of the differential payment distribution within the occupation or union quite unchanged.

Moreover, an increase for one section produces demands elsewhere. And not only from groups comprising predominantly under-equity paid roles. Favoured groups comprising largely those in equity or over-equity paid roles struggle just as hard to retain their favoured position or to improve it still further, whether by organized trade union action, or by the private bargains driven by individuals who possess the particular managerial or technological or manual skills or potential avidly sought by large organizations and by small ones as well.

There is little enough chance, therefore, that a stabilizing of payment relationships at equity will come about by means of existing negotiation and bargaining methods. The situation is unstable, not unlike the surface of a choppy sea. As certain roles gain towards equity or over-equity, wages inflation occurs, and other roles drop down. These depressed roles are then pulled up and others, relatively, are pushed down. And so the surface never becomes calm.

What is required is a system which can ensure that payment for all roles is within ± 5 per cent of equity, so that the distribution of payment in roles in relation to equity will be a normal distribution pattern as shown in figure 7*.

* May I re-emphasize here that I am not referring to the distribution of equitable earnings – that distribution is shown in the equitable

For equity thus to be served and greater stability to be realized, appropriate differential gains in payment would have to be granted to those roles which are under-equity paid, which will probably include a large number amongst manual and clerical roles. Payment for those roles – whether manual, managerial, technological, or other – which are over-equity paid would have to suffer a differential loss to be brought into line with equity.

I shall return in chapter 14 to some aspects of how these problems of adjusting payment and arranging equity all round might be tackled, after I have brought considerations of the progress of individuals into this analysis. In general, a levelling-up process would probably have to be used. The strongest resistance is, of course, likely to be aroused even at the merest mention of the possibility of groups of individuals in favoured roles relinquishing differentially favoured positions*. Neither organized workers, nor executives, nor professional or technological personnel have in my experience shown any greater signs of adaptability in practice in this respect. There is a profound conflict here to be faced up to in society and resolved. The decision will have to be made either in favour of equity all round with no one in a differentially favoured position; or in favour of continuing payment instability, inflation and industrial stress, but with the opportunity to seize bargaining advantages to capture or maintain favoured over-equity positions.

Even if the desire is for equity, the absence of an established externally operating equitable framework makes it extremely difficult – indeed, if not impossible – to express a decision in favour of manifestly equitable behaviour, even where individuals might be driven by the best of intentions towards their fellows. Thus, for example, even where a manager has the strongest desire to work out fair and reasonable rewards for his subordinates, he

---

work-payment scale in figure 6. I am referring to the extent to which the actual payment in individual roles is in line with equity; that is, the pattern of distribution of equity, over-equity and under-equity paid roles.

*As one spokesman of a favoured group receiving over-equity payment in their roles put it: 'The trouble with time-span is that it measures downwards as well as upwards!'

will nevertheless be more likely to find himself confronted by the desires of individuals and groups to see to their own welfare and protect their own interests, than he will be aware of the operation of impulses of equity. The familiar manifest pattern is that of individuals claiming what appear to be unreasonable increases; or of an organized occupational group seeking to prevent another occupational group which by tradition has had lower negotiated earnings, from reversing the position; or of groups clinging to equal increases for everyone or none at all, rather than accept an increase which might apply differentially to the apparent relative advantage of some over others or to the giving up of a relative advantage.

Whatever the system for achieving equity, there is likely to be experienced the greatest difficulty in the first instance in getting all-round agreement to begin the process of differential sorting out. These difficulties can be illustrated in the situation in the Glacier Metal Company, a company which is more than ordinarily sophisticated about matters of differential payment. The Works Council has not so far accepted, even on an exploratory basis, the notion of the time-span yardstick and the associated equitable work-payment scale whose development it initiated. The Managing Director and the representatives of the lower levels of staff have argued in favour of slow advance to try out and test the instruments, in order to examine the problems of executive implementation and to discover whether the measuring instrument and payment method are likely to work out in practice. The representatives of the higher levels of staff have, however, adopted the view that more work needs to be done to establish the time-span instrument in generally understandable form before it is tested further; and the Works Committee representatives, while not wanting to stand in the way of staff members, have opted out of any participation in the use of these notions in connexion with hourly-rated roles. In the absence of all-round agreement in the Company, it has not been possible to make open comparison of level of work measured in time-span as between all types of role within the Company*.

* The lack of use of time-span measurement in the Company for purposes of systematically regulating payment does not mean, however, that the

This experience in the Glacier Metal Company I think represents in microcosm the more general industrial situation. The best-willed attempts to achieve equity run foul of existing anxieties and suspicions, and the resistance against giving up bargaining. In assessing, therefore, my findings and conclusions about there being strong impulses of equity in individuals, it will have to be kept in mind that these impulses are unlikely to gain any very extensively open expression in the existing bargaining market which is the hallmark of payment matters. Their easy recognition and expression may need the support of a regulated equitable payment system. I shall now consider the hypothesis that these forces of equity do, nonetheless, have important effects – even though they act in a hidden manner.

V

To recapitulate my findings, the reactions of individuals to conformity and to deviations between the actual payment levels for their work and equitable payment for that work suggest that:

(1) a state of equilibrium* with regard to payment is encouraged inside each person when these two levels are in balance;

(2) this equilibrium is disturbed by disparities between the two payment levels, the disequilibrium becoming more intense the greater the disparity;

(3) under-equity payment of more than 10 per cent brings about disequilibrium sufficient to cause individuals to want to take action to get their actual payment levels raised more into

---

measuring instrument has not been used at all. The sorting out of a large number of staff roles in terms of time-span has given a foundation for establishing a staff grading structure based on salary brackets. The exploratory use of time-span measurement has led to the resolution of a number of disagreements between managers and subordinates about payment and progress. All job specifications are now set out in terms of prescribed and discretionary content of work, this procedure having been found useful for selection purposes. The training of managers to specify jobs in this way has helped to sharpen their appreciation of the work content of their subordinate roles.

*See J. M. M. Hill: 'A note on time-span and economic theory'.

line with equity, so as to achieve a state of internal equilibrium; and disparities which approach 20 per cent produce an explosive disequilibrium;

(4) over-equity payment brings about disequilibrium in the form of an insecure non-reliance upon the continuation of the earnings, provokes fear of rivalry in others who are not favoured, and stimulates an anxious and selfish desire further to improve the favoured position;

(5) when whole groups are affected, the individuals concerned may resort to action at the social level and, through representatives acting for the whole group, exert pressure – depending on the circumstance – to get their payment either increased to equity level or brought into line with other groups who may be favoured by over-equity payment;

(6) the more widespread in a population are the roles whose payment deviates either above or below equity, the more unsettled will be the social climate.

The picture which emerges is one in which forces tending to drive the payment structure towards an equitable distribution are opposed by forces tending to favour payment for the roles in some types of occupation or in some geographical areas, and to provoke disequilibrium. The ordinary assumption, therefore, that workers simply strive to drive their wages and salaries as high as possible without regard for differential capacity, while employers simply strive to prevent or hold back increases as much as possible without regard for fair reward for their employees, is seen to be a misleading over-simplification. Although reality may sometimes appear to conform exactly to either or both sides of this stereotype, my analysis suggests that it would be grossly inaccurate to conclude that these are the dominant opposing forces whose resultant determines the distribution of real wage and salary levels. Let me therefore consider more systematically this question of the relationship between real and equitable payment levels.

The hypothesis I would suggest with regard to the determinants of actual wage and salary levels is this. There are two powerful and opposing sets of forces inside each of us which determine our behaviour with regard to differential payment: a socially cohesive sense of economic fairness; and a socially disruptive greed and envy and anxiety about position*. The forces of fairness cause us to act both individually and collectively to keep our own earnings and those of others in line with an equitable differential distribution. The forces of anxiety, greed and envy cause us to seek individually and collectively for personal security or economic advantage regardless of others.

There are two main external factors (apart from the internal ones) which influence the strength of these forces among the members of a society: the state of the labour market, and the policies and procedures for regulating payment and ensuring some degree of equity. In the absence of manifest and explicit equitable regulating mechanisms, the forces of anxiety, greed and envy are strengthened, and attempts to guarantee personal security and to achieve and maintain a favoured position over others may be rife. Opportunity to gain favoured positions occurs as a result of advantages given by the state of the labour market. For, when the labour market is in equilibrium, under conditions of perfect competition, then the actual distribution of wages and salaries will conform to the equitable work-payment scale. Under such conditions any deviation from equity would be self-correcting: it would produce a strong increase in the restraining forces exerted by the losing party, simultaneously with some decrease in single-mindedness in the drive for greater gain by the gaining party, so that the actual payment distribution would return to equity.

In the real-life situation of imperfect competition and unevenness in the labour supply and demand situation – whether through labour scarcity or surplus, or collective action or restrictive practices, or other factors – the favoured groups of employers or employees are able to procure or sell labour at rates which depart from equity levels. The actual wage and salary levels will settle out at that point where the excess of bargaining strength and its release of greedy self-seeking is balanced by the two restraining

*A brief consideration of the nature of these forces is undertaken in chapter 15. A more thorough-going consideration requires reference to the work of Freud and of Melanie Klein on the life and death instincts, quoted in the bibliography. See also Jaques (1958d and 1960).

forces of feelings of inequity in the losing party and feelings of social cohesion in the group with the upper hand.

Regardless, however, of the degree of unevenness in the labour supply and demand situation, inequity in wage and salary distribution cannot be pushed beyond a certain limit. Once the balance of bargaining strength is such as to force actual wage and salary levels towards a 15 to 20 per cent deviation from equity, an explosive situation ensues due to the intensity of disturbance of individual equilibrium, and the likely results are difficult to predict. Not that deviations from equity greater than this extreme never occur. I have no doubt that they do. But where they continue as a permanent condition, they require either a police state to maintain them by force, or else the operation of strong and deeply ingrained social and cultural *mores* supporting the existence of economically favoured groups of elites side by side with economically dispossessed groups or strata.

The picture which I am presenting may appear unfamiliar because, in negotiations, the representatives of employees and employers accept the socially disruptive bargaining method of demands and rejection of demands. When this mode of bargaining is used, there appears to be justification solely for the view that there is no end to the demands that would be made – that employees' representatives are out to get as much as they can, while employers' representatives are out to give as little as possible. The forces connected with the sense of equitable differentials remain hidden in individuals – but exert a nonetheless powerful influence on the negotiations by establishing the intensity of the demand and the resistance to it. It would require explicit and open recognition in society of an equitable differential pattern of payment for this split-mindedness which occurs in the negotiation situation to be eliminated, and for the socially cohesive sense of economic equity to be openly manifested.

If this hypothesis about payment levels proves correct (and part of my justification in putting forward this and other hypotheses is that the instruments I have described make it possible to test them), we may note that our conception of equity payment levels does not necessarily conflict with current conceptions about the determinants of payment levels. It does, however, state that these current conceptions are in a major respect incomplete. The relative strength of the opposing negotiating groups and the forces they exert – as influenced by the supply and demand situation – certainly play an important part in determining the level of actual wages and salaries. But these forces interact with the forces produced by the disequilibria caused inside individuals by the experience of disparity between actual and equitable payment. These forces automatically come into play immediately the state of the labour market causes payment deviating from equitable payment to be offered for given types of work. In other words, the law of supply and demand always operates within the harness of restraining forces produced by individual and group reactions to deviations from equity in payment. The present theory, therefore, supplements and frames current conceptions by providing a quantitative base-line for them, and by stating the limits within which they operate.

VI

One of the implications of this analysis is that many of the reasons advanced for the granting of special payment may often turn out to be unfounded. For example, extra payment is offered in a given job or jobs because they require outstanding honesty, as in a cashier; or because a high degree of confidentiality is called for, as in a private secretary doing minutes for a top management committee. The meaning of such statements is that the salaries paid in these jobs are higher than the salaries paid for jobs which are 'equivalent' except for the special characteristic in question.

My experience has been that when time-span analyses are carried out, the jobs with the special characteristic turn out to be organized differently and may have a higher level of work than the so-called equivalent jobs. In other words they are not really equivalent at all. It is of the utmost importance in industry to be clear upon this point, for the most invidious comparisons begin and trouble arises just as soon as additional payment for special characteristics is publicly allowed. If the cashier is paid extra for honesty, what about the nightwatchman who looks after stocks of precious metals? And what about the confidentiality that must be exercised by accounts clerks? And the versatility that must be exercised in this job just as much as in that one? Or the hardship, or the physical exertion, or pleasantness to customers, or the hundred and one other qualities that are used to justify the payment of a supplement, which can be called into question as justifying special payments in other jobs as well? In those cases where in fact what is occurring is that an unrealistic reason is being used to express a realistic intuitive judgement about level of work, then a great deal of trouble may be saved if level of work is used as the rationale for the increase, and unrealistic reasons eschewed.

The matter of supplemental payment for scarcity value in the case of technologists and skilled personnel perhaps requires special comment. Let me reformulate the problem more precisely. Payment for scarcity value would imply that payment levels above equity are offered for given levels of work in order to attract scarce personnel, while payment levels at equity or below are being offered for other positions with the same level of work.

Applying this criterion of comparisons of level of work, my experience has been that payment for scarcity value may easily be confused with situations where the true level of work in a role is higher than has been recognized, false comparisons having been made with other jobs at a lower time-span level.

I can illustrate this point by the example of the firm which introduces a new technology – employing for the first time, say, mathematicians or electronic engineers, or physicists. Simplifying the example by taking one person rather than a department, the firm is fortunate in its initial appointment, and takes on a bright young man at a starting salary of £1,000 per annum, and he does extremely well. The responsibilities allocated to that section are increased, and the man's salary is stepped up, first to £1,150, then to £1,300, and then to £1,400, in a period of less than two years. What is not recognized, however, is that the rate of increase of level of work in the job has outstripped the salary increases, a part of the latter having merely compensated for an upward movement in the wages index.

The original occupant of the job then unexpectedly leaves (unexpectedly to the firm but not to him, for he has been seeking alternative employment for some time, feeling that there is little scope for him in that firm since it is slow to recognize the real value of his type of work and seems to him to be unprogressive), going to a new post in which he gets a starting salary of £1,800 with good prospects. He is said to have been 'bought' by his new employer.

The vacant post is then advertised. It is not expected that a new man will necessarily be able to start in at the level of the previous occupant of the job, so a starting salary of £1,150 to £1,200 is stated. The first crop of applicants is disappointing. It does not contain any candidates who appear likely to be able to do the job. The job is re-advertised, now with a starting salary of up to £1,400, because there appears to be a scarcity of suitable personnel and some financial inducement seems to be necessary. The previous experience is repeated, and the post is once again re-advertised at a starting salary of up to £1,550. The firm is desperate to find a suitable person, and is willing to pay a premium for 'scarcity value'. A youngish man is found who, with training and experience, it is thought will eventually be able to carry the job, and so he is appointed.

That a great deal of trouble might have been avoided is indicated when, on analysis of the level of work in the job, it turns out that the £1,550 per annum was not in fact excessive as was thought to be the case, but was equitable for the level of work in the job as it had been authorized to grow under the first occupant. Recognition of this fact might have prevented the departure of the first occupant of the role. It would certainly have prevented the costly process of advertising the job three times, at new salary levels each time.

A further lesson to be drawn from this example of a more or less typical occurrence is that it is easy, in the absence of measurement, to under-estimate the level of responsibility which is usually to be found in newly-introduced technologies – and just as easy to over-estimate it. Such under- or over-estimation becomes a very serious matter in a nation which is engaged in trying to increase its rate of technological development and its use of technologists.

VII

The findings and hypotheses I have outlined may be at variance with common expectation and stereotype, but they have the support of common sense and common observation. For example, when labour is extremely short, wages and salaries may rise, but what usually happens also is that work is reorganized. Processes are eliminated. New methods are developed. Or products are simply dropped from the market. The aim of these procedures may be either to get by without the unavailable personnel, or to raise levels of work in roles to bring them more into line with the payment offered. And if, with a subsequent influx of new personnel into the field, wages rapidly drop to a lower level, what may have occurred is routinization and standardization of method to encompass the newly available labour, and hence an equivalent fall in level of work. This total process is concealed behind the simplest possible disguise: that of keeping the same job title to refer to the work, regardless of the fact that the level of work has altered so greatly as to make a nonsense of behaving as though the jobs had remained unchanged throughout the fluctuations in payment levels.

The point to be emphasized is that it is a fallacious mode of thought and expression to compare jobs and job values – as is done in such a widespread manner – in the absence of any yard-stick for comparing these jobs, and to behave as though the most important aspect of the discussion – that of level of work – can simply be taken for granted. The confusion is increased when the jobs have the same job title. When we say that this job is worth more than that, we usually mean that in our opinion it has a higher level of work than the other. When we say that the rates of payment for this type of work have increased because of shortage of labour, or argue that an unfair decrease has occurred because of surplus of labour, we assume, without ever giving the matter a second thought, that the level of work has remained unchanged. Any such assumption about level of work cannot be upheld without measurement to determine the degree of the effect on payment of the scarcity or surplus.

The theory outlined thus leads us to a new frame of reference

171

within which to arrange wage and salary levels. Briefly, it suggests a policy of payment for level of work carried in each specific job at any given time. Custom and practice, advantageous position gained through scarcity, social stereotypes about manual as against non-manual types of work – all such criteria would have to be abandoned. Questions of socially necessary income – such as the requirements of those with large families or the needs of men as compared with those of women – would be matters of government policy, to be dealt with by such mechanisms as taxation and insurance.

This type of policy has two essential features. It rests upon a foundation of the explicit recognition and institutionalized acceptance of objectively discoverable norms of payment in relation to level of work; and it subjects everyone in industry – senior executive and unskilled worker alike – to the same scale of value for the work he does. Under such a policy the burdens of an under-abundant economy would be equitably shared; and increases in national productivity would be reflected in an upward shifting of the whole scale of payment. Individual progress in earnings relative to others could be obtained only by a person's attaining and carrying out higher levels of work.

Before we can be too positive about any such policy there are many questions which must be considered. How could such a programme be administered? How could the necessary time-span analyses be carried out? Would the cost not be prohibitive? What would happen to industries which were finding it difficult to compete, and which might find it impossible to pay equitable rates and continue to survive? What would happen in geographical or occupational regions where, either through union organization or through rivalry between firms to attract scarce personnel, there was a high incidence of roles with over-equity payment?

Moreover, how could the equitable work-payment scale be agreed nationally? How could changes in distribution of wealth be dealt with? And even if equitable rates were paid for work, what guarantee is there that individuals could be employed in work at that level – and hence at that rate of income – which fully occupied their capacity and hence gave them a financial reward consistent with their capacity?

These are all weighty questions. They indicate firmly and sharply that other dimensions must be added to our analysis before we can presume to speak too definitely about a national wage and salary policy and its administration. I shall direct our discussion, therefore, to some of these questions, and consider first some of the more fundamental properties of the equitable work-payment scale.

CHAPTER 8

Determinants of the norms of equity

I

THERE are many questions to which we must devote our attention if we are to understand the particular character of the differential payment distribution which our findings have led us to conclude is experienced as equitable by those engaged in employment work. Why, in the first place, are norms of equity experienced in terms of a differential payment structure rather than in terms of complete equality? How general are the norms we have described? Do they apply equally to any society? In any epoch? How stable are these norms: do they shift and change with changes in social outlook, custom and fashion? Or are they relatively independent of external social conditions? Why does it turn out that equity in payment is related to level of work? Why, given a differential distribution, does the distribution take the form we have described – or more generally, what are the forces which would cause it to assume any particular form? Are there any limits to the size of income likely to be experienced as equitable? Would the character of the distribution experienced as equitable vary with the state of the economy? What kinds of distribution would be experienced as equitable under conditions of extreme national poverty or, conversely, of extreme national wealth?

In considering these questions, we shall for the time being have to leave the more objective realm of conclusions built upon a foundation of empirical data for the realm of hypothesis and speculation. My justification for so doing lies in the demands made by the importance of the questions themselves: they force themselves upon our interest. And if theoretical speculation cannot provide the definitive answers it would be desirable to have, it may help to deepen our analysis. It may also help to clear away some of the emotional impedimenta which hinder observation of the data which are necessary to the systematic resolution of these issues.

II

It may seem self-evident that individuals engaged in employment work expect differential reward for differential responsibility carried. The notion of a fair return for work done, a 'rate for the job' notion, is certainly widely held. In my experience, even those who publicly profess an economically egalitarian political credo privately profess themselves in favour of the more 'realistic' notion of some differentials in reward, so that the worth of a man's work may be recognized. Economic egalitarianism seems to be more of an idealistic credo, a credo for a time in the future when the nature of man shall have undergone a profound change as a result either of a radical social and economic transformation, or of an equally radical spiritual one.

The self-evident quality of the notion of differential reward may possibly stem from the fact that those engaged in employment work are employed in organizations where products and services are the creation of many hands. Differential payment stems from the circumstance of men having to be brought together to produce something. Because of differences in capacity, not everyone can make an equal contribution to the final result. Not everyone should share equally in the rewards. There is a conception of each man reaping the just rewards of his own labour which is deep-seated in the mind.

It may prove useful at this stage to re-emphasize the fact that the differential payment we are considering is payment for employment work. If this point is not kept firmly in mind, it will assuredly leave unnecessary obscurity and confusion in the way of the line of thought I wish to pursue, a path which may in itself prove sufficiently difficult to traverse as to justify the most meticulous clearing of the way.

Our argument has to do with the attitudes shown towards their money earnings by persons – the vast majority of the working population – engaged to do work by an enterprise – public or private – whose purpose is to produce economic goods and services. The employees of an economic concern are not engaged in a personal vocation. They are not, for example, tending the spiritual welfare of their fellows; they are not engaged in artistic creativity. The enterprise for which they work is producing material wealth – goods or services which are real and tangible, as is the financial return received by the enterprise for its goods or services. The question of the apportionment of the accruing wealth is a real and tangible question. It exists because the material wealth resulting from the work of the enterprise (and all other economic enterprises which employ people to work for them) exists. The wealth is there. It has resulted from the organized efforts of people, carried out within the unifying force of an employing organization constructed by the enterprise. How is that wealth to be shared? No amount of ascetic or puritanical or embarrassed recoil from money questions can alter the fact that the question arises.

It may, of course, be argued that there is a satisfaction to be gained from work over and above that of mere financial gain. I have no doubt whatever that this is perfectly true, and that the most profound human needs are satisfied by work. To recognize this personally satisfying content of work is not at all the same thing, however, as saying that payment is of less importance than other psychological satisfactions in work. This latter is the theme of some managers and industrial psychologists who, in their lists of factors of incentives to work, seem to be able to show that such factors as person-centred supervision, or letting subordinates know where they stand, or good leadership, or democratic participation in decisions, or the elimination of boredom, are of more importance than money in establishing good morale and motivating employees to work with zest and efficiency.

The fallacy in this line of reasoning is to have separated the question of payment from these other issues. Leadership, recognition of good work, interest in subordinates – these and many other social or psychological factors in the employment work situation – are inextricably tied up with payment. Payment is the practical and concrete means of expressing the evaluation and recognition of the relative value of a man's work – and in precise quantitative terms. This is not to say that these other psychological factors are not important. It is to say that if good psychological conditions of work are not matched by equity in pay, they are to a greater or lesser extent negated.

It is this appreciation of the value of his work which is of such very great importance to the individual. The essence of a vocation is that external appreciation is not of primary importance. The evaluation and recognition come from an inner feeling of personal worth. But such feelings cannot be matched in the employment situation in an economic enterprise. The employed person is one element in a larger whole, and does not set himself his own task. As far as the consumer's appreciation of the goods he helps to produce is concerned, he is totally anonymous. His appreciation must come from his recognition within the enterprise, and the money he earns is a factor of central importance in the constellation of factors which go to create this feeling of worth and recognition. Differential financial reward is an integral part of differential, and therefore of discriminating, recognition and is not separable from it.

III

Our discussion so far has, of course, assumed that we are talking about an economy capable of providing not only for basic needs but for some degree of abundance in life. It is only under such conditions that there is any realism in the niceties of arranging for appropriate differential financial recognition in work. Under harsh economic conditions where the problem is that of how to remain alive, questions of fairness in differential economic recognition take on a very pale hue indeed – although symbolic recognition and honours may become important. Where life is not at stake, however, then questions of differential recognition do obtrude in a most definite way. It still remains to discover, therefore, what is the general pattern of differential reward which might satisfy the members of a society under conditions of abundance. Or perhaps different patterns are called for under different conditions.

We may get a better perspective, and hence a better grip on our problem if we consider it negatively for a moment, and ask whether there are any conditions in which differential reward might be experienced as inequitable. Consider for instance the attitude in Great Britain during the Second World War. Under conditions of grave economic distress an attitude quickly developed in

177

favour of fair sharing of commodities which were in short supply – and special conditions for children, the ill, and the fighting troops. Suppose a situation of even greater impoverishment arose – one in which there were literally just sufficient material goods to provide a mere subsistence level of income per head of population. It is not at all unlikely that in such circumstances the notion of differential reward would be forgone, and would be supplanted by an economic egalitarian outlook for the duration of the crisis. Equity would dictate that the available goods should be distributed in such a manner as to provide subsistence for all, rather than that some should live – and starve – at a below-subsistence level while others had more than subsistence required.

But we may also note that this equitable attitude which we might readily assume for Great Britain in wartime, is not an inevitable or a necessary one. It cannot be counted upon. It did not exist in Great Britain in the depression during the decade preceding the war. And the more common experience in nations which have never known anything other than economies which by modern industrial standards are impoverished, is that of starvation for some existing side-by-side with great wealth in the hands of a few. An egalitarian economic outlook cannot by any means be considered an automatic consequence of economic conditions which cannot provide subsistence for all. There are other impulses in man than that of fairness, especially when economic power and security are concerned. But even when economic inequity is maintained either by the exploitation of ignorance and inflexible culture patterns, or by force, the inequity itself is nevertheless felt. A widespread sense of the unfairness in life may be expected, even though these sentiments may not inevitably lead to action to change the situation, or may even be obscured as, for example, by narrow religious beliefs in the rightness of suffering for some, at least in this world.

Where economic inequity exists, the fact of the feelings of unfairness which exist with it will be revealed just so soon as greater social and political awareness is awakened and freedom achieved. Thus with the spread of education, modern democratic thought, and the means of raising standards of living throughout the world, failure to distribute goods so as to wipe out starvation and sub-human modes of existence leads more rapidly to organized discontent and radical or revolutionary change. Wealth is often expropriated and a more nearly egalitarian distribution instituted, until the economy is rich enough to provide something more than mere subsistence for a nation as a whole.

At the same time, it should be noted that egalitarian forms of distribution appear to have a temporary rather than a stable character. It is the type of distribution which is tolerated under conditions of economic distress, when fairness demands an equal chance of life for each one. The national striving, however, is to overcome this situation of distress, to produce greater wealth, and to give something more than a subsistence level of existence as the material reward for one's work. Utopian communist communities which become economically prosperous and which nevertheless continue to distribute goods equally are rare, if they exist at all. Some communities which appear to approximate to such a state seem pretty generally to require rigorous conformance to a strong and restrictive religious outlook in order to maintain the system intact.

The experience in the U.S.S.R. is instructive in this respect. Immediately after the revolution a strong wave of egalitarian feeling took hold, and all incomes were nearly levelled. Increasingly, however, the system appeared unworkable, and in 1928 a decision was taken to shift the emphasis in the direction of differential rewards. This policy was pursued until, by 1934, the differential distribution of income from the lowest to the highest earners was similar to that which obtained in the United States, a pattern which appears to have continued to the present time*.

We begin to suspect, therefore, that although an egalitarian form of distribution is most consistent with the demands of equity under a subsistence economy, it is nevertheless a temporary and unstable form of distribution – a holding action until greater prosperity is achieved, rather than a form of distribution which fulfils in any lasting way a permanent human need. We are still left, therefore, with the question of why fairness in a prosperous

*See, for example, David Granick: *Management of the Industrial Firm in the U.S.S.R.*, 1954.

economy appears to be subserved by a man's being rewarded for his work differentially, and in a manner which accords in some way with the level of work he carries.

IV

There are deep-seated needs in human nature which dictate the ideas of fairness which influence economic customs and *mores*. We may get nearer to the heart of our problem if we try to examine the nature of these needs. It might prove useful to ask, in connexion with earnings, the simple question: 'What does a person need to spend?' Could, for example, each one spend as much money as he could get? In one sense, perhaps, he could. But he would most likely have to squander his money in order to do so. The idea of spending, then, is a complex conception, comprising very different kinds of activity – two of which may be distinguished as spending which is characterized by squandering, and spending which is not. If we are to proceed with an analysis of the concept of spending, we shall first have to sharpen its definition.

The fact that we speak both of spending money and of squandering it suggests that we are dealing with some sort of series, with a conception of degree of spending. Consideration of the opposite to squandering reinforces this notion of a series of types of spending: we find at this opposite extreme the conception of undue parsimony and miserliness, or if a person does not possess sufficient money, the concept of poverty and impoverished spending. Somewhere between, there seems to be a point of equilibrium, a point of normal spending, of spending that is neither impoverished nor careless. The wealthy man who does not foolishly spend his money – does not throw it away – is not necessarily considered miserly. The poor man who spends all his money as he earns it is most unlikely to be squandering it.

There is some particular quality – or perhaps qualities – of expenditure which we must ferret out and define, which give spending the characteristic of being normal, balanced, sound. Without as yet having pursued the subject of that quality, it will be useful to affix some tentative labels to allow us to distinguish this optimum level of spending from foolhardiness and impoverished spending. I propose to use the phrase *discriminating expenditure.* I shall distinguish it from *constrained expenditure,* by which I shall refer to all types of spending in which it would be possible for a person to spend more without squandering; and from *indiscriminate expenditure,* by which I shall refer to fool-hardy, squandering behaviour.

Looked at from the point of view of consumption, these three types of expenditure correspond to what I propose to term *satisfaction, under-satisfaction,* and *over-satisfaction consumption.* I shall use the conceptions of *abundant, under-abundant,* and *over-abundant* incomes, to refer to the extent to which a person's income provides him with the opportunity for discriminating expenditure and satisfaction consumption; and *abundant, under-abundant,* and *over-abundant economies,* by which I shall refer to the state of a country's economy in terms of the extent of abun-dance of income which is provided to the citizens of that country by its economy.

Finally, I propose to use the phrase *level of capacity for discriminating expenditure* to denote the amount of money a person could spend in obtaining a satisfaction level of goods and services for his own personal use (and that of his dependants, if any), avoiding both over-satisfaction and under-satisfaction consumption.

V

What then are the characteristics of discriminating, constrained, and indiscriminate expenditure? As with so many human characteristics, it may prove easier to define negative qualities than to define positive ones. It may therefore be prudent to begin our exploration from the extremes and work in towards the normal: to attempt to define the characteristics of foolhardiness and impoverishment and thus to provide ourselves with a starting point of a negative definition of what reasonable expenditure is not, rather than to try from the outset to define it in a positive way.

Indiscriminate spending is careless and thoughtless, uncritical and unimaginative. It is often spur-of-the-moment spending, driven by whims and fancies. It may be imitative, moved by impulses to keep up with others and to have what they have. It

181

will tend to be coarse and ugly, and to conform to externally established rather than personally felt values, on the grounds that whatever is more expensive must be better. It will rarely and only accidentally produce anything of lasting beauty. Moreover, for all these reasons, it leads to over-satisfaction consumption and is always to some extent wasteful. Whims and fancies disappear as quickly as they appeared. Imitative buying tends to be compulsive, and doubles upon itself – two cars, and two or more of this and that being more indicative of affluence than one. Because it is undiscriminating it does not lead to lasting satisfaction, interest tending to be lost in the object of the expenditure, and new objects sought – sometimes provoking a revulsion for a time against spending at all.

In short, indiscriminate expenditure is promiscuous spending, in the fullest and deepest meaning of that word. It is spending *pro-miscere* – that is to say, mixed before, thoughtless, without prior reflection. It is not to be confused with Thorstein Veblen's conception of conspicuous expenditure, which may or may not be undiscriminating. Conspicuous expenditure (*con-specere* – seen together, visible) is expenditure which is intended to be seen. But in a person of high capacity with a corresponding income, conspicuous expenditure may manifest itself in the form, for example, of a beautiful home which gives him delight and aesthetic satisfaction, and enriches the physical environment of his community. Conspicuous expenditure becomes ugly when it becomes indiscriminate and reflects a state of over-satisfaction for the individual.

Constrained expenditure is characterized by excessive concern over each item of expenditure. It may become compulsively and obsessionally discriminating. It is insecure and dogged by inhibition and indecisiveness, and often by regrets that more time could not be or had not been taken, because a better bargain might have been driven or a better article found. It is unhappy and unsatisfying expenditure because it gives under-satisfaction consumption. There are always things which are seen, which are desired, and which could be put to good use if only the money were available. It is anxiety-ridden, ungratifying and unfulfilling, and leaves quantities of unused capacity for discriminating spending. It is resentful when it exists in the midst of satisfaction consumption, and becomes hate-ridden when it co-exists with over-satisfaction.

Miserliness differs from constrained expenditure mainly in the fact that although the necessary money is available, the miser maintains an under-satisfaction mode of consumption as though he were more impoverished than he actually is. The type of expenditure is constrained; but the motive is avarice arising out of psychic inhibition, rather than true poverty.

By contrast, therefore, we may state some of the characteristics of discriminating expenditure and satisfaction consumption. They are neither wasteful nor insufficient. They are not blown by whim, nor are they compulsively restrictive and inhibited. They are neither promiscuously unsatisfying nor poverty-stricken. They are free from the guilt of excess and the anxiety of insufficiency. They absorb a person's full capacity for imaginative buying for his own needs and those of his dependants as determined by himself rather than as determined by imitation or dire necessity to subsist. They call forth his full capacity for judgement and discretion, in assessing his and his family's personal needs and requirements and in choosing and selecting what will meet those requirements and fulfil those needs. They will not lead to coarse or ugly buying; and at their best, they may lead to the creation of beauty.

The essence of such expenditure is that it requires genuine psychological work. A person considers what he is buying and chooses what he needs or wants. He chooses what suits him. In exercising choice, he examines the details of what he is buying, at least sufficiently to understand its relevance to his own needs. He must, therefore, possess sufficient intuitive and worked-out insight to understand his wants. He thus has a sufficient idea in advance of spending – or, for example, in building a house, in the course of spending – of what will be suitable. His expenditure will prove to be less satisfactory, or possibly wasted, only as a result of inadequate discretion, and not for want of trying. In its net effect, if his income is just large enough his spending will be experienced as sufficient – neither too much nor too little. It will give him a sense of abundance, of having enough but not too much. His rate of consumption will lead to satisfaction free from guilt.

In short, discriminating expenditure and satisfaction consumption are gratifying in a permanent and stable sense to the non-neurotic areas of the personality.

VI

This short descriptive discourse on expenditure will have contributed little that is not already familiar, or at least contained in the dictionary definitions of the terms which have been used. It is not at all a part of my intention, however, merely to go over familiar ground. I wish to draw attention to two particular features embedded in the familiar, but which ordinarily are left unidentified. Our everyday common-sense ideas about spending and consumption contain the implicit concepts, first, that wise spending requires skill, discretion, and work, and, second, that individuals differ in their capacity for spending and in their level of satisfaction consumption. That is to say, it is a part of our ordinary way of thinking about these matters – even though not an explicit part – to assume that the level and rate of what constitutes reasonable spending and satisfaction consumption will differ for different individuals. And I do not refer only to the commonly recognized difference that the larger a man's family then obviously the larger the economic requirements of that family. I accept that difference, but wish to add to it the fact that over and above these differences, individuals themselves differ in their capacity for exercising discretion in their spending and in the level of consumption which gives satisfaction.

Thus it may already have been noticed that certain very familiar themes have appeared in our consideration of spending and consumption: those of discrimination, judgement, selection, discretion – some of the characteristics concerned with level of work. This fact may immediately attract our interest. If indeed it should prove that the qualities which determine a man's capacity to carry a given level of work are in some manner connected with the level of his capacity for discriminating expenditure, then we may rightly feel that we may be proceeding along a useful path towards the resolution of some of our problems.

A possibility which strongly presents itself is that what constitutes a satisfaction level of consumption for any given individual is associated with his capacity to carry responsibility in his work, in that both are associated with his capacity for discriminating expenditure. The link between level-of-work capacity, and capacity for discriminating expenditure reveals itself in that both are characterized by the psychological work of scrutiny, discrimination, selection, and decision. Discriminating expenditure is genuinely discretionary expenditure; and more, it utilizes a person's full capacity for the exercise of discretion. By contrast, indiscriminate expenditure is that which does not result from genuine psychological work, because the rate and level of expenditure exceeds the person's capacity to exercise discretion; hence the promiscuity and the over-satisfaction and wastefulness of the resulting consumption. Constrained expenditure is that in which the rate and level of expenditure do not call upon the full deployment of a person's capacity to exercise discretion, but leave him with unused capacity and unsatisfied needs.

Before proceeding further, there are two residual questions which we ought not to overlook. If a person has more money than his capacity for discriminating spending can cope with, might he not avoid the pitfalls of promiscuous spending either by saving or investing his money, or by hiring others to help him with his spending? Saving and investing can be considered together. They represent a giving up of immediate expenditure in favour of expenditure at some unspecified date. There are two kinds of such saving and investment. The first is saving and investment maintained at a level to ensure against unforeseeable heavy demands; i.e. precautionary measures. The second is the putting away of excess income and simply letting it lie fallow; i.e. accumulation and hoarding. The first type – precaution – we must include in our concept of discriminating use of assets. The notion of discriminating expenditure must be widened to include the notion of fair and reasonable precaution. This extension of the concept of expenditure is justified by the fact that genuine precaution is nothing more than a means of guaranteeing the availability of funds for expenditure at a later date.

If, however, in order to absorb excess income, saving and

investment have to be carried farther than reasonable insurance level would dictate, then a situation of disequilibrium has occurred. Promiscuous spending may be avoided, but uncreative hoarding takes its place. I would broaden my analysis, therefore, and say that over-abundant incomes must inevitably encourage either promiscuous spending or hoarding.

The use of expert advice and service in spending is of course common enough; for example, in decorating, building, purchasing of pictures, planning of holidays – the list could become a very long one. One feature, however, characterizes every kind of advice and service of this kind. If the person buying the assistance is not of greater calibre than the person who provides it, then excessive spending once again takes on the character of promiscuous spending, because it is no easier to use discrimination in the choice of experts than in the choice of whatever it is the expert is hired to buy or provide. Charlatans and inadequates abound in this field of expertise. It takes great capacity to sort the wheat from the chaff. The use of experts for this purpose is not unlike the hiring of employees in production work. It extends the potential range and quantity of activity, so long as the person who employs the expert is in control of the situation by virtue of his capacity critically to assess the result. Without such capacity, the employer of experts to help with spending is in the same position as the employer of labour for production whose subordinates are of greater capacity than himself; he is in their hands; disrespect, disregard and unscrupulousness are always close at hand; the relationship is a potentially unstable one.

VII

Two sets of ideas await our further scrutiny. The first is that the character of a person's spending will be coloured in a most important way by the degree and quality of the discretion or psychological work which enter into his spending, and that spending behaviour may be connected with the use of discretion in work. The second, which is implicit in the conception of doing psychological work, is that different individuals will differ in their capacity to spend and in their level of satisfaction consumption; that is to say, they will differ in their level of capacity for discriminating expenditure. It will readily be apparent that contained within this conception is the view that a rate and level of expenditure that leads to satisfaction consumption for one person and his family, may not do so for another – it may lead either to over-satisfaction or to under-satisfaction according to the capacity of the person for discriminating expenditure. That the needs of one man differ from those of another will be experienced as no new idea, and may be regarded as self-evident. What will require more positive demonstration is the proposition that these differences in need are not simply a question of fortuitous differences in individual requirements and circumstances, but are related to differences in individual capacity. In brief, the level of a man's economic needs can be stated in terms of capacity and, so stated, can be quantified, his capacity to spend and his level of satisfaction consumption being commensurate with his capacity to produce.

I can exemplify the conception of level of satisfaction consumption which I wish to discuss by reference to the epigram of Karl Marx, 'from each according to his abilities and to each according to his needs'. This epigram may prove to contain, if our analysis is correct, a social and psychological principle that was not perhaps intended. For if the principle of the congruence of capacities and needs is correct, then genuine economic equity can be served by a social conception of reward in accord with capacity – from each according to his capacities and to each according to those capacities. Individual human needs and the demands of social balance and stability may prove to be well served by such a principle.

VIII

It will not be within our achievable goal to resolve within the scope of our present analysis this hypothesis that a person's economic needs are congruent with his level of capacity to spend and to work. It appears to me to be a justifiable hypothesis, and one worth testing. But at this stage, with the data at present available, it will have to remain a hypothesis; one which could go far towards helping to explain the character of the equitable work-payment scale. Here, systematically presented, is the hypothesis.

For each person at a given age there is a given level and rate of consumption which will provide him with a sense of true satisfaction in his standard of living. The rate of expenditure which provides this satisfaction state will be in equilibrium with his capacity for discriminating expenditure. A rate of expenditure above or below a person's capacity for discriminating expenditure will provoke in him a state of disequilibrium. If it is below his capacity, he will suffer the dissatisfaction of containing unused and unexpressed capacity. If it is above his capacity, he will suffer the disturbance of forced activity out of control because it is beyond his capacity. These two trends of disequilibrium above and below equilibrium level will be accompanied by states of experience of under-satisfaction and over-satisfaction consumption.

The hypothesis of individual differences in capacity for discriminating expenditure – and changes in this capacity with age – contains the secondary hypothesis of individual differences with respect to what constitutes a satisfaction standard of living. The greater the capacity for discriminating expenditure, the greater the level and rate of expenditure that will be required for the satisfaction of the sense of abundance. The capacity for discriminating expenditure, being a derivative of the individual's capacity to exercise discretion, is directly correlated with capacity for production work as measured in time-span.

In short, I am postulating an equilibrium level of expenditure and consumption for each individual, related to his time-span capacity. I am at the same time postulating forces in the non-neurotic parts of the personality which actively spur the individual to achieve this level of expenditure: deviations towards the under-satisfaction side will lead him to strive for a higher standard of living; deviations towards the over-satisfaction side will lead to a feeling of satiation, and a diminution of active expenditure, and possibly an increase in saving or in philanthropy. His ambition will also be critically influenced. Normal ambition – in contrast to lethargy or greed – may be stated as a drive to achieve that level of work and of income which will constitute a state of equilibrium in the non-neurotic part of a man's personality with regard to the exercise of his full capacity for production and for spending. Regarding ambition in this manner, we may note that a goal which might rightly be regarded as a sign of greed and excessive ambition in one man, could be normal and reasonable in another man of higher capacity. It makes ambition, greed and lethargy into relative rather than absolute conceptions, dependent upon the level of capacity of the individual.

IX

We are now in a position to present our main hypothesis to explain the shape of the equitable work-payment scale. It is this. An equitable distribution of income in an abundant economy is that in which there is a match between the payment for any given level of work and the capacity for discriminating expenditure (and satisfaction consumption level) of an individual whose capacity is consistent with that level of work. In an over-abundant or under-abundant economy, it is that in which the payment at all levels of work exceeds or falls short of satisfaction by the same psychologically proportionate amount; that is to say, by an amount that would produce the same degree of disequilibrium of either over-satisfaction or under-satisfaction in all individuals whose capacity was consistent with their level of work.

In accord with this hypothesis, I would explain the particular shape of the equitable work-payment scale which I have described, as follows. It represents that distribution of earnings in employment work which would give relatively the same experience of satisfaction throughout the whole scale of levels of work, and the individual capacities corresponding to those levels of work, under the conditions of the British economy at the present time.

What then of the general shape of the equitable work-payment distributions which would be found in accord with this hypothesis? Their construction, and the testing of the validity of the hypothesis, are matters for empirical research and observation. It might be possible, however, even in the absence of such data, to go some way towards a hypothetical pre-construction of what such an array of distributions might prove to be like.

First, I believe we know one of the equitable distributions – the one which obtains for the British economy at the present time. Moreover, I think there can be little doubt that the British economy is an under-abundant economy, and hence the equitable work-payment scale described represents one pattern of equity in under-abundant conditions. It may be thought that the patterns of spending in Great Britain during the past few years contradict this assumption of under-abundance, because of the apparently widespread indiscriminate expenditure which there has been. It must be realized, however, that higher incomes have been experienced for the first time, with a resulting burst of catching up on the purchase of previously desired but economically unavailable goods. The existence of both under- and over-equity payment, and the lack of assurance of continued higher incomes, add an element of compulsion to the spending. Discriminating expenditure requires confidence in the continuance of economic equity and abundance.

Second, we have considered the proposition that in an economy that was under-abundant to the point of being a mere subsistence level economy, equity would be served by everyone's receiving broadly the same return, with variations to allow for individual differences in the physical requirements for mere subsistence.

We may find that these two distributions in fact manifest a general characteristic of the array of equitable distributions; namely, that as the economic conditions obtaining become increasingly abundant, an increasingly steep differential pattern of payment will be found to be experienced as equitable. The array would look something like figure 8; all incomes would be found to increase with increases in the national abundance, but the higher the level of work, the greater the rate of increase of income that would be found.

To put the matter in other words, I think that the quasi-political issue of egalitarian versus differential distribution of income is debated in an over-simplified manner. The genuine issue is that of the degree and pattern of differentiation of income that is equitable under given economic conditions. And it need not be a matter for debate; it might be resolved by the empirical investigation of underlying human norms of what constitutes equity.

I have said that the present-day British economy is probably under-abundant. A higher level of personal expenditure, as well as corporate and public expenditure, could readily be absorbed. But at what level does abundance obtain? It is an hypothesis, but I would conceive of it at a level akin to (or perhaps slightly below) those industrially prosperous areas in the United States where genuine and widespread affluence can be said to exist. The abundant distribution curve which I have drawn is thus something of the order of twice the present rate and level of expenditure in Great Britain.

This assumption about abundance level – as in the case of my assumption about under-abundance in Great Britain – is open

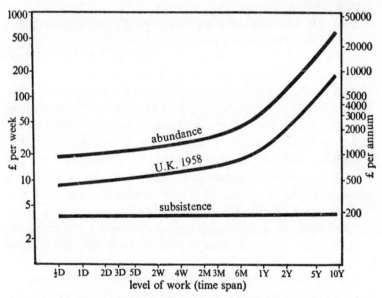

FIGURE 8. Array of equitable income distributions

to criticism on the grounds of the promiscuous and compulsive expenditure and conspicuous waste which characterizes so much of the consumption pattern in the affluent areas of the United States. I am inclined to believe, however, that these negative features are the product of three main factors: first, pockets of gross over-equity payment, with resulting promiscuous consumption; second, anxiety and insecurity, connected with lack of assured continuity of economic abundance; third, guilty expenditure due to the lack of assurance of widespread equity in the

United States, and the knowledge of gross poverty elsewhere in the world. Given an equitable distribution of payment throughout the United States, the social picture would be radically altered. The fact must not be overlooked that large sections of the population are able to employ abundance of income in a discriminating manner and without promiscuous consumption.

In short, economic abundance is not the sole factor necessary for discriminating expenditure and satisfaction consumption. There must be an accompanying assurance of equity all round, and of the continuation of the abundance so far as society can control its own destiny (that is to say, natural catastrophes excepted). For reasoned individual behaviour to predominate in a society, a reasoned society is essential.

In the modern world, forged into one world by the dramatic change in communications, the assurance of equity all round implies equity at the international level. Isolated economically abundant nations are unlikely to achieve a state of genuine socio-economic equilibrium internally. To the extent to which manifest economic equity exists within such a nation, the achievement of equilibrium will be facilitated. But the international tensions arising over gross differences in economic abundance preclude a stable equilibrium. Whereas at the national level economic inequity produces industrial and political strife, at the international level the tensions arising out of inequity and economic disequilibrium are reflected in social upheavals and ultimately in war.

In the face of international under-abundance, therefore, the achievement of socio-economic equilibrium in relatively prosperous nations requires that they give aid to underdeveloped nations – the nearer the nation to a state of economic abundance, the greater the amount of aid. In the absence of giving such aid, the symptoms to be found in over-equity paid groups may be expected to be magnified into the gross expressions of social pathology by their reflection in social processes on a national scale. Given an operating conception of economic equity at international level, inter-group tension within nations, and tension and instability between nations, may be reduced.

To put each citizen in possession of more money than he has

the capacity to spend in a discriminating manner would be tantamount to social collusion to encourage economic foolhardiness. Contrariwise, however, to provide each citizen with an abundant income in return for the exercise of his true level of capacity in his work, is an aspiration worthy of any mentally healthy state. It is the intention of this analysis to suggest that abundance has a finite limit. There is little evidence to suggest that men really are striving after the economic infinity of Eldorado, except in infantile phantasy or in psychotic omnipotence. In terms of a world economy, there is a finite level of production which can give satisfaction all round, and which once achieved need not be surpassed.

X

It may also now be noted that our line of reasoning has put us in possession of a conclusion which must always have been obvious but which consistently tends to be overlooked. This conclusion is that payment dissatisfaction may arise from two important different sources (and there may be others besides) which require to be distinguished from each other: dissatisfaction due to inequity, and dissatisfaction due to under-abundance of the economy as a whole. They might be expressed as: 'Regardless of the state of the economy, I am not getting enough in comparison with others'; and, 'We are each getting our fair and proper share, but our economy is not providing any of us with a satisfying standard of living.'

This distinction between inequitable distribution and under-abundance with equity is important to recognize, because it is only the former which in itself carries the seeds of dispute. To take a very practical example, a governmental policy (and such policies are not confined to any one type of political party) which says, in respect of chronic wages dissatisfaction, that a greater national output must be achieved before wages can go up, begs a most fundamental question: to what extent is the dissatisfaction due to feelings of inequity? For to the extent that it is – and as we have noted in the first chapter, all payment disputes are fundamentally differentials disputes – then to wait for greater output to provide a higher standard of living for all still leaves the problem of the currently existing inequity unresolved. (Although, be it noted, the inequity might disappear due to the greater differentials which might be experienced as equitable the more abundant the national economy.) Meanwhile, one of the greatest spurs to increased national productivity is lost; that of the social cohesion which is stimulated by an equitable sharing of the burden of an under-abundant national economy. Moreover, inequity in income distribution is probably the strongest force contributing to wage and salary inflation, which in turn disrupts the economy and weakens national morale.

Hence the possible significance in the current economic situation in Great Britain of the propositions (a) that the British economy is an under-abundant economy; and (b) that actual wages and salaries are not equitably distributed. The effect of this double impoverishment in some areas of lower-paid jobs is to produce industrial dispute and disruption because of the inequity in the situation, and thus to weaken the capacity of the country to overcome the lack of abundance in the economy as a whole. And although political parties may argue differently about the problem, there is a noteworthy incapacity in practice to deal with the situation, because the blunderbuss quality of the policies of all parties (e.g., raise all workers' wages at the expense of the middle classes; introduce profit-sharing; benefit pensioners; etc.) makes them far too crude as instruments to deal effectively with the day-to-day realities of the actual work and payment relationship in a vast and complex multitude of jobs and occupations.

National and individual self-interest would be best served by the continual discovery and rediscovery of the equitable pattern of differential distribution of payment in relation to level of work at each successive change in the abundance of a national economy. Greater individual satisfaction and a tightening of social cohesion would result. Before such a social gain could be achieved, however, it would be necessary to be able to provide opportunity for employment of each person at a level of work consistent with his capacity. I now propose to consider this matter in detail. I shall return to a foundation of empirical data as my starting point. It is an issue of great importance, without which our theory would be most incomplete. For an equitable work-payment distribution is of no great significance to the individual who is blocked from obtaining a level of work consistent with his capacity, and hence from a level of income which would satisfy that capacity.

At stake in this question is the issue of full employment in its deepest sense. Full employment, to do justice to the term, must be defined not merely as available work for everyone who wants to work. It must include available work in line with a person's interests and capacities, and work which gives him the possibility of movement through jobs – in short a career opportunity – in such a manner as to cater for individual growth and development. I propose to use the phrase *abundant employment* to refer to this special definition of full employment. It is the state of affairs which obtains in a healthy and expanding economy.

We may turn now to consider what social mechanisms may be needed and constructed to cater for the progress of individuals in their work at a rate consistent with their progress in capacity.

PART FOUR

Individual progress in work

CHAPTER 9

Growth of individual capacity

I

WHEN a person complains that he is not being fairly paid, he may mean that he is not being paid fairly for the work he is doing as compared with what others may be receiving for similar types of work. Or he may mean that he is dissatisfied with his own standard of living regardless of whether or not others may be finding it equally difficult to make ends meet. These two conditions we have already considered. A third possibility exists, however. Even if he is receiving differentially fair pay in an abundant economy for the work he is doing, he may yet feel underpaid if he is capable of doing a higher level job than the one he is in, and hence of earning higher pay given a proper job. Such a person, although he feels underpaid, is in fact being under-employed. Arguments about the fairness of pay are commonly bedevilled by the failure to distinguish between these three different situations which can and do vary quite independently of each other. In practice, in considering questions of fair payment, it is essential that we separate sharply and unequivocally those feelings which are genuinely about payment, and those which are really complaints about under-employment.

Failure to separate these issues leads to blockage of attempts to resolve the complaint (even with the best will on the part of a manager and his subordinate), or to unrealistic action. I have been present at many arguments, for example, where a disagreement that arose about payment has led to inaction and festering trouble, both the manager and the subordinate (or in some instances a whole group of subordinates) having failed to recognize that the central and presenting problem was one of a damming up of routes of progress, so that the individuals concerned – although equitably paid for the work they were doing – were barred from advancement into jobs whose level of work, and hence payment, would be more in line with individual capacity.

It is clear, therefore, that although we have considered questions

199

of equity and of economic abundance, we shall not have established a sound basis for our analysis of payment patterns until we look more closely at this problem of individual progress. This question has, of course, followed us from the very earliest chapters. We then put it aside, with the comment that in considering the issue of equity in payment, we would carry out the analysis on the basis of the equitable rate for the job, explicitly leaving out of account all matters having to do with individual capacity, such as the quantity or level of skill, experience, knowledge, training, initiative, dexterity, honesty, reliability, reasoning power, intelligence, neatness, and a multitude of capacities besides. In so doing, we arrived at a mode for determining the level of work bracket in a job, and the equitable salary bracket for that job. We have not considered, however, who should get any given job, nor have we considered where within a salary bracket any particular individual ought to be paid.

These questions of the individual and his capacity can no longer be ignored. If a person is under-employed, to receive equitable payment for that work is only partially satisfactory to him. Full satisfaction demands not only the opportunity to work, but the opportunity to work in a job which is consistent with one's capacity, and to progress within the job bracket in a manner consistent with progress in one's capacity. In making this statement, I do not mean to imply responsibility on the individual firm to provide work at the advancing level of capacity of each of its employees. No single firm can hope to do so. I shall return to this particular problem later.

II

In *Measurement of Responsibility** I put forward the view that there is a regular pattern of progression in the development of individual capacity in work. I further suggested that each person exerts a strong force towards obtaining work of a level consistent with his level of capacity – that a kind of Archimedes principle operates according to which each of us seeks his equilibrium level of work.

If these suggestions are valid, one can postulate further that
*pp. 93 to 106.

individuals who (a) are employed at a level of work consistent with their capacity; (b) have the opportunity to progress in level of work in accord with their growth of capacity; and (c) are getting payment and progress in payment that is equitable for their level of work, might be expected to experience a sense of harmony or balance with regard to their work, payment, and progress, and ought to show signs of this psychic equilibrium. Those for whom the above circumstances do not operate ought to manifest signs of psychic disequilibrium, such as dissatisfaction, uncertainty, or masochistic gratification.

I had at the time of writing that book some evidence for these assumptions about progress in level of work. This evidence derived from analyses that I had carried out upon the career progressions in successive jobs of six persons, in terms of the progress in their level of work as measured in time-span. The results did indeed suggest, as would ordinary common sense, that individuals became unsettled if their level of work was too high or too low for their capacity. The idea then occurred that if individuals were not receiving payment that was equitable for the level of work that they were capable of carrying, then they would show signs of disequilibrium, and that this relationship between payment (and progress in payment) and the capacity (and progress in capacity) of the individual could be studied in its own right. One of the potential results from the examination and study of this relationship might be the establishment of a systematic basis for considering questions of individual progress, and perhaps of developing better techniques for the administration of wage and salary increases.

I had the opportunity to test these assumptions in discussions with the shop stewards at the Glacier Metal Company. Difficulties had arisen over 'merit' reviews for them, because many of them had to spend so much time away from their normal work. The details of the project itself need not concern us here. It is sufficient to say that we decided to examine the character of the actual earning progression of each individual. In order to form a clear picture of genuine 'merit' progress, as distinct from the increases which simply corrected for conditions of economic inflation, it was necessary to devise a rough method to eliminate the effect of inflation. The wages index was chosen for this purpose, and all the earning data were corrected to a chosen base period by the use of this index.

When these progressions were drawn for each person, I discovered in individual discussions that each person reacted to upward and downward movements in his earnings as though they were movements towards or away from some inner personal standard of what constituted an expected or desired progress for himself. Empirically, by trial-and-error method, a smoothed curve could be drawn that represented the quasi-stationary equilibrium for each one: deviations downwards in actual earnings from this smoothed curve being reacted to with dissatisfaction; and deviations above the curve (rare in an inflationary situation) being sensed as a kind of temporary phase of being relatively better off than one expected, it being taken for granted that one's earnings might soon level out again.

III

This experience led me to the conclusion that there might possibly be a smoothed curve of progression in earnings for each person which coincided with his development in capacity, and hence represented the equilibrium situation with regard to his economic progress. It also seemed likely to me, since this was concerned with an aspect of human development, that these individual equilibrium curves might order themselves into a continuous family of curves according to a common underlying pattern of biological growth, like a visually observable, regular pattern in which iron filings array themselves in response to a magnetic field of force. In order to check these notions, and to see whether I could construct some kind of approximation to an orderly pattern of equilibrium progressions, I decided to plot the actual earnings over time of a number of individuals. The wages index was again used as the basis of correcting the earnings, even though a very high proportion of my data now referred to salaried staff. In the absence of a salaries index, and within the rough limits of accuracy employed, the use of the wages index appeared a reasonable method of removing the major effects of inflation from the data.

Accordingly, the achieved earning data of some 250 persons were obtained in this way and set out in graphic form*. These total emoluments comprised wage or salary, established bonuses, and that proportion of other forms of facility, such as a house or a car, as might be of recognized personal value to the individual. The data were set out on semi-logarithmic graph paper to facilitate plotting, and to enable percentage changes in earnings to be read directly from the charts by simple arithmetic measurement. The purpose of the study was to ascertain career movement, and therefore the earnings were plotted against age. All earnings were corrected to the value they would have had in June 1955, for the simple reason that the plotting was first done at that time and it was easier for those who were taking part in the study to think in terms of their earnings as they were currently. I have continued to use June 1955 as the base period in all subsequent work, as a matter of convenience. In practice, I have found that it has been sufficient to use a correction factor which takes into account the average movement of the wages index in six-monthly periods. The June figure takes into account the wage index

---

*It may be worth noting that there is a very considerable difference between plotting the earning histories of individuals, and the more usual practice of plotting either the averaged earnings of groups – the progress in average earnings of, say, hourly-rated workers, or doctors, or engineers – or the current earnings of a group – the distribution by age, say, or by number of years following qualification, of the earnings of doctors, or engineers, or accountants. I think that neither of these usual practices is of much practical value. They rely upon job title and thus cannot take into account changes in the content and level of work. And they fail to take into account the distribution in capacity of the individuals comprising the groups. Thus, for example, while the average earnings of engineers may seem to be progressing 'satisfactorily' or 'unsatisfactorily' relative to other group averages, there is no way of knowing what has been happening to the differentials in work level. The fact that the average engineer is earning, say, £2,000 per annum twenty years after qualification, or that the averages reach a peak at age fifty and then fall away, tells very little about the career opportunities of engineers. These averages are the resultant of the particular groups analysed – with the possibility of considerable variation in the composition of those groups. They cannot be used to conclude what is the likely career pattern for the average engineer, nor does the averaging of, say, the upper twenty-five per cent tell much about the higher-level career opportunities.

movements from April to September; the December figure, the movements from October to March. The correction factors for the six-monthly periods from December 1946 to December 1959 – taking June 1955 as 1.00 – are given in the following table.

CORRECTION FACTORS

1946–1960, *taking June* 1955 *as* 1.00

Dec. 1946	1.55	Dec. 1953	1.10
June 1947	1.52	June 1954	1.07
Dec. 1947	1.48	Dec. 1954	1.06
June 1948	1.43	June 1955	1.00
Dec. 1948	1.42	Dec. 1955	0.99
June 1949	1.39	June 1956	0.92
Dec. 1949	1.39	Dec. 1956	0.92
June 1950	1.38	June 1957	0.87
Dec. 1950	1.33	Dec. 1957	0.87
June 1951	1.28	June 1958	0.87
Deo. 1951	1.21	Dec. 1958	0.84
June 1952	1.18	June 1959	0.84
Dec. 1952	1.13	Dec. 1959	0.84
June 1953	1.13	June 1960	0.81

The results of plotting the data are shown in figure 9.

Each of the discrete progressions in this graph is the achieved progression in earnings of one person up to June 1955, corrected to the June 1955 level of the wages index. The figures include all changes in total emolument, whether negotiated awards or individual merit increases. It will be noted that practically all the progressions show downward movements at one or more points. Each of these downward movements represents a phase during which the wages index was increasing, and an individual's increases in total emoluments were not as great as the upward movement in the index*. There are few instances where there was any

* The progressions in figure 9 use an early form of plotting. The corrected earning levels were calculated, and a point plotted, on each occasion when a person received an increase in payment. These points were then joined, to give the progression shown, the downward movements in the progression reflecting a situation where successive increases in payment did not overcome the drop in relative earnings due to rises in the wages index. My

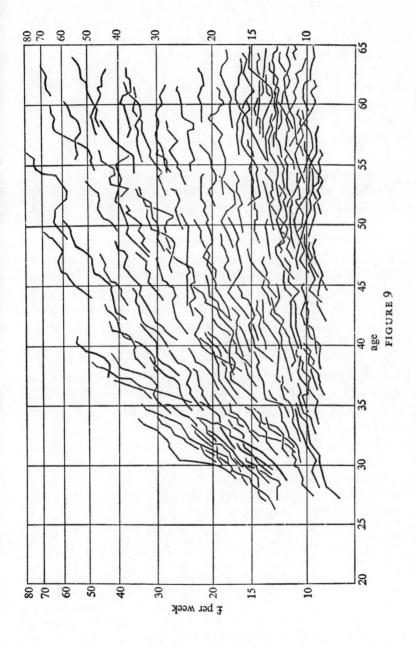

£ per week

age

FIGURE 9

decrease in money earnings. The data were obtained from individuals in five different companies. They were selected so as to include as far as possible progressions for all ages from 20 to 65, and earnings ranging from £8 per week up to £4,000 per annum. Women were excluded from the sample because of the complications in equating the value of men's and women's salaries owing to the undefined male-female pay differential.

If figure 9 is examined, a very decided patterning of curves may be noted. There is a fanning of the curves upwards from the lower left-hand corner. The general direction of the trend is that of a faster acceleration in the younger age group, slowing down at older age, but a higher rate of progress maintained throughout, the higher the earning level.

I drew through this population of individual progressions a number of smoothed continuous curves shown in figure 10, representing to me the general trend of movement of the individual curves, discounting both the non-uniformity within individual progressions, and the deviations of individual curves, some of them gross deviations from what appeared to me to be the general trend. In drawing these trend lines by inspection, I took into account as much information as I had about the form I expected these equilibrium curves to take. Thus, for example, the most rapid rate of progress is made in early working life, and slows down with years. Those engaged in jobs providing the lowest pay tend to drop in level of work, and thus to lose in relative economic status in old age. Those engaged, at the other extreme, in work requiring the highest skill and knowledge and commanding the highest incomes, tend to move into positions of greater responsibility, as, for example, directors, statesmen, judges, and can be described as making continued progress in

---

present method of plotting, shown in figures 12 to 17, is to plot two points on the occasion of each increase in payment: one is the corrected value of the person's earnings at the time of the increase; the other, the corrected value of his newly-increased earnings. By this method, a step type of progression is obtained, which shows both the size of each increase and the change, if any, in the relative level of a person's earnings between increases on account of movements in the wages index.

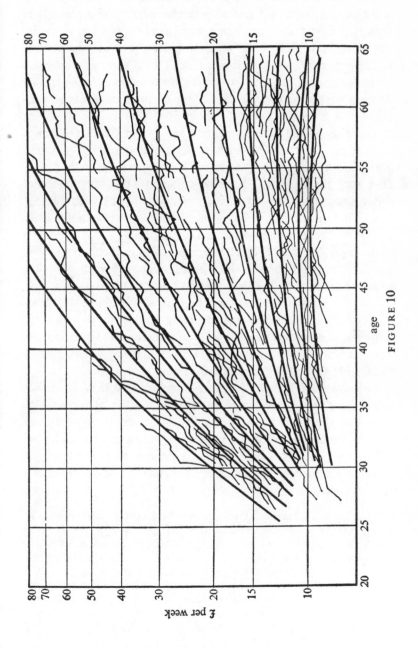

FIGURE 10

their careers well beyond the common retiring age of 65. Although some of the higher progressions tended to fall off rather more rapidly towards older age, sometimes as early as 40 or 45, I did not reflect this falling away in my smoothed curves, because this phenomenon is quite possibly a reflection of the fact that some individuals begin to age earlier than others; in other words, I decided to try to exclude the effect of premature decay processes.

These smoothed curves, which I shall term *Capacity Growth Curves*, are illustrated in a more elaborated form in figure 11* (see pages 210–11). The pattern of these capacity growth curves, drawn by the method I have described, follows the sigmoidal progression characteristic of biological growth, although this fact does not in itself prove that we are dealing with a biologically determined general pattern. It had, nevertheless, proved possible to draw, in the manner described, a set of smoothed curves – the capacity growth curves – which in a rough-and-ready way did some justice both to the very general trend of the actual earning progressions and to the assumptions I had made about the direction these smoothed curves were likely to follow. It remained, however, to demonstrate whether or not the standard progressions were anything more than a neat but meaningless construction. I shall now turn to my findings from the use of these standard progressions which have led me to conclude that they do in fact represent a close approximation to a description of the lines of growth of time-span capacity in individuals, and therefore of the lines of equilibrium for actual earning progressions for those individuals in terms of the current equitable rates for levels of work consistent with their capacity†, hence the phrase, capacity growth curves.

*The Earning Progression Data Sheets as illustrated for income levels up to £10,000 per annum, are obtainable in blocks of fifty sheets from the Glacier Institute of Management (G.I.M.), Ruislip, London, England. A Conversion Rule is also available for convenience in converting wages and salaries to the June 1955 level, for plotting on the Data Sheets.

†Data have now become available which indicate that the capacity growth curves apply for the United States precisely as for Great Britain. This finding serves to reinforce the assumption that the curves reflect a very general characteristic of human development; it also makes the curves

Before doing so, it will be necessary for me to define a few conventions and concepts which I shall use. A person's *earnings* refer to the total emoluments (as defined earlier) he receives in connexion with his work. His *achieved earning progression* refers to his progress in earnings corrected to the 1955 level of the wages index. The *potential progression* of an individual refers to the progress in level of work he would achieve if he were continuously employed at the full level of his capacity. It would require a psychological assessment of capacity. Since, in the absence of an objective measure of capacity, it is not possible to be sure whether a person is in fact exercising his full capacity, this capacity progression must be distinguished from a *potential progress assessment* (P.P.A.), which is a managerial assessment of the level of work an individual is likely to achieve in practice. Both these progressions can be expressed in terms of that earning progression which he would achieve were he to receive the equitable rate of payment for his work.

The capacity growth curves can be labelled in terms of the time-span level at the point at which they cut the vertical scale at age 55. These points, stated as a scale of index numbers, are shown in figure 11.

IV

If (a) there is any connexion between the pattern of the course of the capacity growth curves and that of the normal rate of development of capacity in individuals*; (b) it is true that each person seeks a level of work consistent with his capacity; and (c) it is true that each person seeks that rate of payment which is equitable for his work; then, evidence should be obtainable that each person strives to attain to a progress in his earnings which will conform to a capacity growth curve. Conversely, if such evidence could be obtained, it would support the conclusion that

---

available for use in the United States. See the appendix to this chapter, p. 321.

*That is to say, if the potential capacity progression of an individual conforms to one of the capacity growth curves, his development not being impeded either by psychological or physical illness, or by lack of opportunity and use through adverse socio-economic conditions.

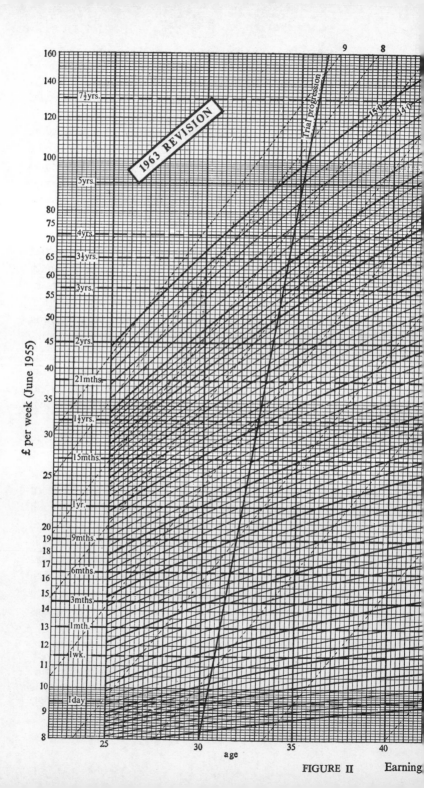

FIGURE II   Earning

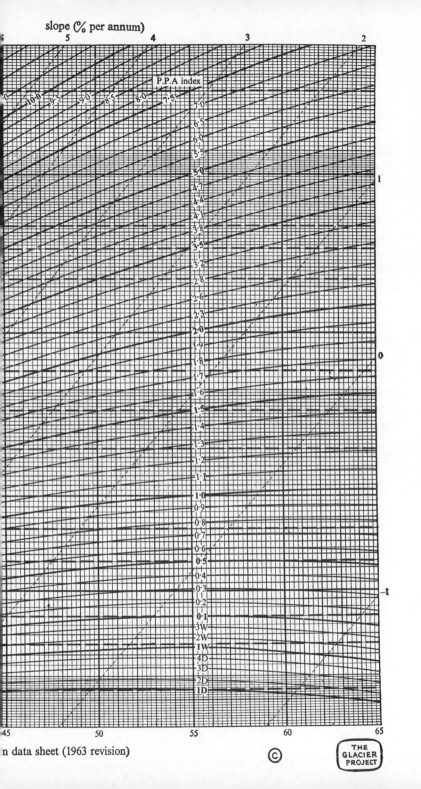

slope (% per annum)

P.P.A index

n data sheet (1963 revision)

THE GLACIER PROJECT

the array of curves depicts the pattern of normal development of capacity, even though it would not necessarily be definite proof of such a connexion.

To put this derived assumption in another way: if a person's achieved progress in earning did conform to a capacity growth curve, he ought to show evidence either (a) of being satisfied that, whatever else might be happening, he was at least achieving a rate of financial progress that matched his rate of development in capacity, or (b) of having a sense that his financial progress was maintaining a steady and unvarying level above or below satisfaction level; if his achieved earning progression deviated downwards in relation to the capacity growth pattern, he should experience a sense of retardation in his rate of progress in earning; if it deviated upwards in relation to the capacity growth pattern, he should experience a sense of acceleration in his rate of financial progress.

Lying behind the derived assumption is a hypothesis that I should like to emphasize by more detailed elaboration. It is that a person's primary drive with respect to his work is towards a level of work that can absorb his capacity: towards a job in which he can use his capacities to the full. His drive for money follows from this prime urge to employ his skill and talent in his work – and is a drive for a rate of reward that is equitable and gives him a relative economic status coinciding with his capacity. The notion that individuals strive in the first place to get all the money they can is, in my experience, a seriously oversimplified and unnecessarily nihilistic account of human behaviour. The present account assumes that a person's attitude towards his earnings is strongly influenced by norms of equity and to be inter-related with a primary striving for a level of work consistent with his capacity. It thereby posits that conditions can be found which allow of equilibrium in the individual coincident with equilibrium in the economic sector of society.

There is, of course, one obvious difficulty that we shall encounter immediately we turn to consider what evidence there may be to support the foregoing assumptions: a firm conclusion would require the possibility of determining a person's level of capacity to carry responsibility in work, and the rate of development of that capacity. This capacity is something more than that which is measured by intelligence tests, as has been demonstrated repeatedly in studies of the relationship between intelligence and successful discharge of responsibility both in industry and in the Services. A rough working definition would be that it is the capacity of individuals to carry responsibility by exercising discretion on their own account for lesser or greater periods of time: in short, the time-span capacity of the individual.

But naming a concept does not constitute a method of measuring what the concept is about*. In the absence of an objective measure, to ascertain a person's time-span capacity is not a straightforward task. We shall have to be satisfied, therefore, with something less than the objective measure it would be so desirable to have.

As an intermediate step, it would have been extremely useful if, when a person's achieved earning progression happened to conform to one of the array of capacity growth curves, it could have been taken to mean that his earning progression was a true reflection of his growth in capacity. But as we have seen, any such interpretation would beg the whole question. It could just as readily have been a result of having progressed in payment at a rate consistently either above or below that warranted by his capacity. For example, the expression of this capacity might have been inhibited either through illness or through chronic lack of opportunity. The impossibility of drawing any conclusions about a person's capacity from his achieved earning progression is a matter of considerable importance. There is always the possibility of temptation, when a person's achieved progression conforms

* Work is presently in hand to discover means for measuring the time-span capacity of individuals. A first break-through has, I think, been made, in the definition of discrete levels of abstraction in mental work which correspond to discrete time-span ranks. If such a measure is forthcoming it will add incomparably greater flexibility to our analysis, since it will make it far easier to deal with level of work, individual capacity, and payment, as three independently measurable variables. This separation would make it a simpler matter, for example, to give separate consideration to a person's work in relation to his capacity, to his payment in relation to his work, and to his achieved earning progress in relation to his rate of development in capacity. See, for example, 'Speculations concerning level of capacity' in *Glacier Project Papers.*

exactly to the pattern of one of the array of capacity growth curves, to assume that he has been making good progress. This type of conclusion is not justified, and it is of the greatest practical importance to remain consciously aware of this fact.

V

In practice, however, it has turned out not to be too difficult to establish a working datum line for the individual and his growth in capacity; that is, tentatively to establish an estimate of his likely progression in level of work, an estimate which may be modified upwards or downwards in the light of further experience of his actual progress in performance. It is the datum line I have defined above as the potential progress assessment. The tentative fixing of this potential progress assessment is achieved by combining time-span analysis with the assessment of performance in work, in the following manner.

It is usually possible to find at least one point in an individual's career where his level of work, and the equitable payment for that work, can be determined. The conditions I seek are conditions where a person has felt himself to be fully occupied in his work, his manager judged him capable of doing it, and he was making progress in it that was requiring him to exercise his full capacity – even though he may have felt that his payment had not been keeping pace. Thus, for example, he may have been appointed at the age of 35 to a position with a range of level of work of 6 months to 1 year, and a June 1955 equitable salary range of £775 to £1,150. He himself felt just ready for his new job, and his manager confirmed him after three months, say, as being just satisfactory, and likely to develop well. Or, another person may have reached the top level of a job with a time-span range of 3 months to 6 months, and an equitable salary range of £700 to £775, again, say, at the age of 35. He would know he had reached a ceiling because no further opportunity for new types of work or extension of responsibility presented itself. This experience of there being no further scope, of having encompassed the job, can usually be confirmed by the manager, who, finding that his subordinate has come to know every aspect of the job, can see no way of offering him more scope. In both these cases, for the different reasons described, I would make the assumption that they had reached the six-month time-span level, or the £775 equitable payment level, at the age of 35 years. Reference to the data sheet shows a P.P.A. of 1.2 – i.e., the points described are on the capacity growth curve which cuts the vertical scale (age 55) at index number 1.2.

The greater the number of such assessments of performance level and age that can be made for a person, the farther it is possible to go towards constructing a potential progress assessment for him. But even the estimation of one such point in a person's career will often suffice for our purposes. For one such point will allow that capacity growth curve to be selected which, according to our assumptions, ought to conform to the normal rate of progress in performance level.

In the absence of time-span data, a rough guide to a person's potential progress assessment may be obtained if he has progressed through a job or jobs which have known salary brackets. His achieved progress, in terms of the age at which he reached various bracket limits, may be treated in the same manner as that described for time-span brackets. The potential progress assessment thus obtained will, of course, be limited in its accuracy by the accuracy of the salary brackets themselves; that is to say, by how closely they conform to the equitable rates for the range of level of work in the jobs concerned. Without some form of measurement of level of work, the accuracy of this conformance between the salary brackets and the range of level of work cannot be known.

A manager can cross-check his judgement of the potential progress assessment of a subordinate by considering his judgement of the subordinate's future. For example, the P.P.A. of 1.2 for the two individuals mentioned above leads to the prediction that they will reach the one-year time-span (rank 3*) level at about 45 years of age. This datum gives the manager a base-line against which to consider his judgement. A more detailed description of this cross-checking procedure will be found in chapter 13, and in the appendix describing the practical application of these conceptions in the Glacier Metal Company.

* The concept of ranks is described in my paper 'A preliminary sketch of a general structure of executive ranks' in *Glacier Project Papers*.

In trying to establish a potential progress assessment, it is of the greatest importance to keep in mind the point, emphasized above, that these assessments cannot be based upon the pattern of progress of a person's actual earnings. Thus, for example, Mr R was a man of high intelligence, a refugee from a foreign country, who had been an apprentice engineer before he came to England. He took a job as a clerical worker, being ineligible for any other work because of his lack of experience in British industry. During the first two years of his employment he showed evidence of high ability in suggestions which he put forward. He was accorded what his manager considered good financial progress. After some three years in his first job, he applied for an administrative post in the same firm, and was successful in being appointed to it. Once in that job he showed himself outstandingly capable of organizing work, and within a year was given a number of additional responsibilities to carry. Within another year he was promoted into a mid-level administrative post, and since that time has continued to show a steady development in performance as he gained greater confidence from a growing familiarity with the English ways of business.

Analysis of the level of work in R's successive jobs shows an increase at a rate that cuts across the capacity growth curves, and this rate of increase in level of work is reflected in his achieved earning progression (see figure 12). What then is his potential progress assessment? He was undoubtedly employed at a level well below his capacity as originally manifested in his home country, and has been steadily recovering lost ground as he becomes familiar with the new language and culture. The level of work consistent with his capacity is probably still somewhere above his present work. That is to say, he has yet to find his own level. The sensible policy is to continue to progress him in work at an accelerated rate (if the work situation allows) so as to absorb his unused capacity in work that will allow him to exercise his full potential, and at that stage to establish a definitive potential progress assessment. My experience with the capacity growth curves leads me to predict that R's progress – should he find employment in which he can exercise his full capacity – will take the form of an eventual falling off of the present steep rate of progress, and will subsequently follow a course represented by the capacity growth curve which he reaches.

Thus the fact that R's progress in achieved earnings for the first two years conformed to a standard earning curve, cannot by itself be taken as proving that he was receiving sound reward and

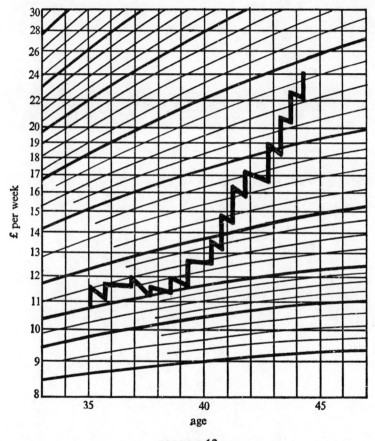

FIGURE 12

recognition for his ability. As his subsequent progress demonstrated, although he was at that time being equitably paid, he was nevertheless under-employed because of the special circumstance of adjusting to a new culture. Satisfactory potential progress assessment could not be made from his achieved earning curve. To assess potential performance from payment is no more than saying that, because you judge a person's performance to be worth £x, therefore – since you are paying him £x – his performance is at that level. Assessment of potential must stem directly from the assessment of performance in jobs of known level of work. Payment then follows.

CHAPTER 10

Individual progression studies

I

THE findings described in the foregoing chapter may be illus-trated by a few typical case studies, the progressions for which are shown in figure 13.

Mr A (see curve A, figure 13) was a 46-year-old man, who at the time of interview had been in a new job with a new firm for about 1½ years. He had left his previous firm because, after making good progress for some years, he felt that he had reached the ceiling in his job, and his career had hung fire for three or four years, until he decided to move on because he could get no definite information from his manager either about the upper limit of his job or about his future prospects. He felt that he came into his present job three or more years later than he need have done. He was satisfied with his current salary progress, and stated that he expected to reach the equivalent of £70 per week by the time he was 50.

A time-span analysis of his current job showed a range of level of work from 2 years to 4 years. He was judged by his manager to have picked up the job very quickly, and to have progressed half-way up the bracket, this progress being the reason for the very considerable increases in pay which he had been granted. His manager also confirmed Mr A's own view that he would have been capable of doing the job some years before (in Mr A's judgement between the ages of 41 and 42), when he felt he had reached the ceiling in his previous job – a job which on recon-struction appeared to have a maximum time-span of 2 years, that is to say coincided with the starting level of his present job. Taking these data together, the tentative conclusion is warranted that he crossed the 2-year time-span level at about the age of 42, from which a P.P.A. of 4.6 is obtained. This progression coincides closely with his predicted future earning of £70 at age 50. The limits of accuracy of this P.P.A. of about ±5 per cent are shown as the darkened band in curve A, in figures 13 and 14.

This example illustrates many of the features in an individual's

219

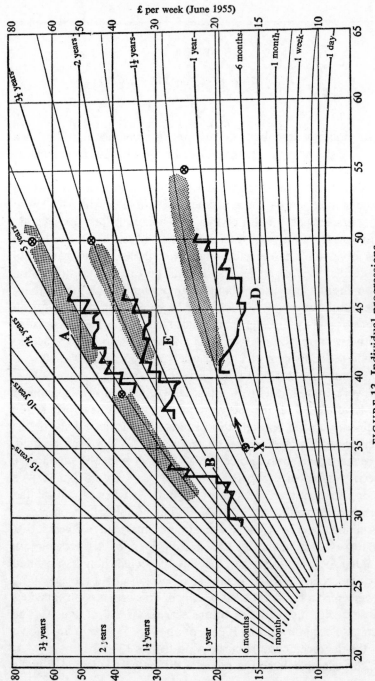

FIGURE 13. Individual progressions

progress. Mr A reacted to reaching a ceiling in his job, which blocked his way to progressing at his own normal rate. He persisted in his job until his achieved rate dropped to some 15 per cent below his normal. During this period he became increasingly restless, feeling that he had come to a dead end in his current job. By the time he had dropped to over 15 per cent below his estimated earning capacity progression, he had bounced for nearly 3 years against the ceiling. He sought other work, both in the factory and outside it, and obtained his present job with his new firm. At the time of the analysis he felt settled, with plenty of scope for progress.

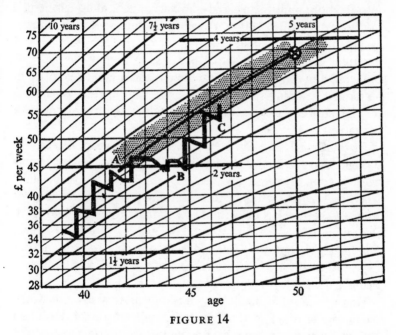

FIGURE 14

If one now examines the enlarged drawing of his achieved earning progression in figure 14, it may be noted that it hits the minimum level in his current job between the ages of 41 and 42, at point A. It may be noted that his earning progression then clings to the 2-year time-span between the ages of 42 and nearly 45, between A and B. It is at point B that he finally decided to change his job. He went into his new job with a fair increase in

221

payment. After a year in that job he had another sizeable increase at point C. It was at this stage that he felt that he had regained a proper level of earnings.

II

If we now turn to the case of Mr B (see curve B, figure 13), a younger man, we may note certain other characteristics of these progression phenomena. Mr B went into his current job – which time-span analysis showed to have a range of level of work of one year to 18 months – when he was just 33 years of age. He said that he had had a very sizeable increase in payment when he went into this job, and this pleased him very much, although he had not been dissatisfied before. His previous job, he said, had interested him greatly. He had been in it for nearly four years. He did not think he had made actual progress in it, but this had not bothered him too much because the job had a great deal of what he termed 'training value'. It had given him just the experience that he had been seeking, and he now felt ready to move on with his career.

At the time I saw him he was just over 34 years of age. He thought that his salary was just about right, and he looked forward to good future progress. He thought that in five years' time, when he was 39, he ought to be earning at a corrected level of some £40 per week. Furthermore, he thought that he would reach the ceiling of his present job in about two to three years' time. His manager confirmed this judgement, saying that he did not expect to retain Mr B for more than two years, and that he was being groomed for a higher post.

On the basis of available data, it is difficult to assign other than a tentative or trial P.P.A. to Mr B; the main reason for this is that he obviously did not enter his present job as soon as his capacities might have allowed. He would appear to have remained in his previous job rather longer than might have been necessary, in order to take advantage of certain training opportunities it gave him.

If one takes his achieved earning progression, however (see figure 15), one notes that there is a consistency between his feelings of fairness about his present earnings, his judgement that he

ought to reach the top level of his present job in two to three
years' time, and his estimated earning in five years' time, all confirmed by his manager's judgement. These three data put together

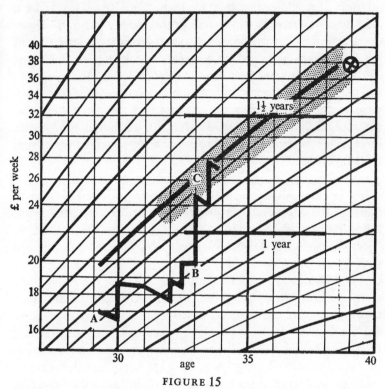

FIGURE 15

combine to give a trial P.P.A. of 4.7. Given such an interpretation,
there is a consistency in the total picture. Between points A and B
on this curve we see him in his previous job not making very great
financial progress but, as he described it, satisfied with his
training. At B, however, he moves into his new job with a salary
boost to C, and from there on begins to pick up his estimated
earning capacity progression.

This phenomenon of younger men – particularly younger men
who are going along fairly high-level career progressions – seeking
jobs and staying in them for some years because they have a high
training component, is one that is not uncommon in my experience. One of the difficulties that arises from just this practice is

that managers frequently tend to underpay them as they begin to move into their full-scale work. One commonly hears the argument that you cannot pay very young men such very high salaries – it would not be good for them. Thus, for example, for a man who was moving along one of the steeper progressions on the data sheet – say the progression that is moving up the 10-year time-span line – it would be necessary to take him from £24 per week to £40 per week between the ages of 27 and 32 in order to keep him on this progression. At the same time, young men may be given an inflated and excessively rapid progression if they show any sign of high-level potential. All in all, it is not an easy matter to arrange a sound payment progression for younger men of very high capacity*.

III

Some of the effects of over-progression can be illustrated in the following example.

Mr C was a 45-year-old manager of a branch in a chain of stores, employing some 35 people. He had two assistants who carried managerial responsibility, one for the goods handling staff, and one for the selling staff. Before being appointed branch manager, he had been an excellent administrator in the accounting department of the head office, where he had shown a keen interest in human relations and management. The circumstances of his appointment as branch manager were that the regional manager in charge of six branches which included the branch in question, wanted a good administrative type to fill the position. His desire to make such an appointment stemmed in part from the fact that this branch was by far the largest, and he wanted to develop it into a model showpiece of good human relations.

Mr C's appointment was accompanied by a sharp increase in salary, as shown at point A in figure 16. This increase represented a jump from a P.P.A. of 1.5 to one of 1.9. That this jump in his progression reflected over-promotion from a progression that had probably been about correct for his capacity, was revealed by his performance in his new role. His tenure of the role proved to be a

*A more detailed discussion of the progressions for younger employees of high capacity will be found in chapter 14.

very troubled one. He did not have the direct business experience necessary to run the business side of the branch, nor did he have the necessary capacity to cope in practice with the problems of managing his extended command. As a result of recurring difficulties, the regional manager himself had to step in very frequently and take over decision-making which was requisitely in Mr C's role, with respect both to business matters and to the management

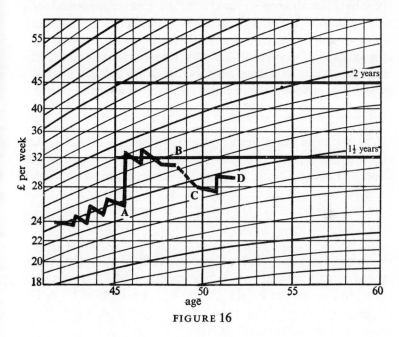

FIGURE 16

of staff. This type of action in the early stages of his appointment would have been understandable, for it was realized that he would need training for his new post. But by the end of two years, his subordinates had lost confidence in him, for they found themselves still dealing with Mr C's manager rather than with Mr C when they wanted to take up any matters with regard, say, to payment or to conditions in the shop.

Mr C's manager then found himself increasingly in one of the most difficult positions which managers have to face. He had a subordinate whom he knew was not capable of making the grade. Analysis of the level of work in the role showed a time-span of 18 months to 2 years. It began to be pretty clear that Mr C had been on a sound progression before he was promoted. This P.P.A. might just have taken him eventually into the level of work called for in his branch manager role. But Mr C was a popular person. He was liked by everyone, including the customers and the subordinates who did not have confidence in him. And Mr C's manager enjoyed to some extent his participation in Mr C's work. It enabled him to keep his hand in at the direct management of a shop, and gave him the opportunity for direct experimentation with new methods. The combination of these circumstances, among others, prevented Mr C's manager from taking the necessary action to replace Mr C. Without his being consciously aware of it, however, the increases in payment which he awarded to him were not quite sufficient to make up for movement in the wages index.

The problem solved itself towards the end of the third year (B on figure 16). Mr C became ill. He had become increasingly depressed about his job, but could not face the prospect (which he had consciously contemplated) of asking for a change, perhaps back to his previous job. His illness lasted for some months during which he was away from work. On his return (at point C) to work, he was put on to light duties in an office job which turned out to suit him very well. It was tacitly accepted all round that he should remain in that role. His subsequent salary progression (C–D) follows on remarkably closely from the trend of his earlier progression, considering that earning progression curves were unknown to that company at the time.

This case is fairly typical in my experience where over-promotion, and accompanying over-payment, have occurred. Payment that was equitable for the branch manager role as requisitely established became over-equity pay for the level of work in the role as eventually carried by Mr C, with his manager taking the major decisions and maintaining shorter-term review of discretion. In such cases the problem continues to fester. The occupant of the role hangs on. The manager wants to avoid doing irreparable damage to his subordinate's confidence and self-esteem. So for a long time after the situation has become clear to everyone, nothing is done about it. It is probably pretty consistently the case, however, that the earlier action is taken to relieve the situation by transferring the individual out of the role, the better off everyone will be. The circumstances are rare where a valued employee cannot be found temporary – and eventually permanent ⊸ employment in a satisfactory role, if there exists the will to face and resolve the problem.

In the case of young men of high potential ability, most firms, without necessarily recognizing it, employ a systematic policy of over-progression of a number of individuals in order to be sure of catching the one or two who will turn out to be capable of progressing to high responsibility. One large commercial institution, for example, progresses its managerial training group by annual increments between 25 and 31 years of age, at a rate which corresponds precisely to the P.P.A. 1.9*. At 31 years, the training group is divided quite explicitly into A, B and C streams. From then until 37 years, the A stream get annual increments which continue them along a P.P.A. of 1.9. The B stream increments fall away to P.P.A. 1.5. And the C stream increments flatten off to P.P.A. 1.0. The individuals who are dropped away from their original higher-level progression know about it. They were on trial until 31, and have not made the grade in the same way as the A stream group. The explicitness of the policy, and the fact that the progression until the age of 31 was a trial progression, facilitates adjustment to the drop.

These trial progressions are necessary with young men of unproven ability. Over-progression for most of the group during the trial period is an inevitable consequence, since the general level must be pitched to that of the highest capacity sought. Non-explicit recognition of this fact stimulates omnipotent phantasies and increases the difficulties of the eventual adjustment of the less capable.

---

*This correspondence between the firm's payment scale and one of the capacity growth curves was quite fortuitous. A similar correspondence has occurred in the annual incremental scales for management trainees in some half-dozen other large organizations which I have analysed. These data suggest that these firms are using an intuitive sense of the normal rate of progress in capacity, at the age range in question, of young men who will develop into the higher-rank managers being sought.

IV

It might be assumed from these notes so far that no individual is ever satisfied if his achieved earning progression fails to conform to his estimated capacity growth. It is not my intention to give any such impression; there are many circumstances that may prevent an individual from achieving progress in his work and payment consistent with probable growth in his capacity. Among such factors are: long periods of physical illness, or long periods of emotional disturbance or emotional illness. Either of these chronic conditions may lead an individual to rest content with a progress in work and salary below the level of his capacity growth. Or, in the case of emotional illness, his capacities may be inhibited in such a way that he cannot make full use of them, a fact of which he is ordinarily aware. The neurotic individual commonly knows of the discrepancy between his actual capacity and the level at which he is operating at any given time. Indeed, inhibition of the ability to apply one's capacity in work is one of the common complaints in neurotic disturbance.

Some of these points can be illustrated in the case of Mr D (curve D, figure 13). He was just over 51 when I first saw him, and described himself as having just got back to what he thought was his real level after what he described as a period of about five to ten years during which he had never really been able to achieve any success in work. During that period, he said, he had been very disturbed both in himself and in his home circumstances. He had received psychological treatment for some years during this phase of his life. He had reached a crisis in his life when he was about 45. Many of his difficulties had been resolved. His children having grown up, he had settled his home difficulties by obtaining an agreed divorce from his wife, and had then remarried; he now felt very much more settled in his new life. From that point on he had found his interest in his work picking up once again, and he felt that he had begun to work himself up into a proper position. This phase of rehabilitation of himself in his work had been going on, he thought, for about three to four years before the time I saw him, and he considered he had made fairly good progress during that time. He felt he was now nearing a satisfactory level of income, and hoped that by the time he was 55 he would be earning at the maximum level in his current job, which he thought would probably be at the corrected level of £25 per week.

He had gone into his present job when he was just over 40. He had done well for the first year or so, and his manager had rated him as performing in the job at about the level of the bottom of the bracket. Taking this finding as a base (see point A of figure 17), it indicates that he is on a P.P.A. of 1.1. Between points A

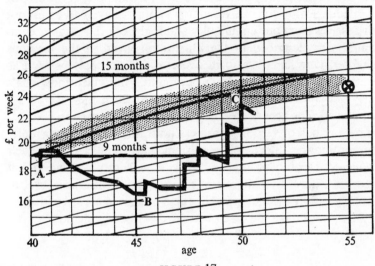

FIGURE 17

and B, which is the furthest back we can take his earning progression, his achieved earning progression moves downwards, and corresponds with the period when he thought that, so far as his work was concerned, he was feeling the full effects of his disturbed state. At B, a couple of years after the crisis and to some extent the straightening out of his life, his achieved progression begins to climb towards the estimated range of level of work in his current job, which turned out to be between 9 months and 15 months. It will be noted, therefore, that up until his achieved earning progression crossed back into the level-of-work bracket of his job, he had really been carried along in his work. When I put this point to him, he agreed that this was so. During this period, although his achieved earning progression had been far

229

below his P.P.A. (at point B, for example, his achieved progression was fully 30 or 40 per cent below his P.P.A.), he felt, nevertheless, that he had been receiving very fair treatment because the management had recognized his disturbed home and personal conditions and had allowed him to carry on at his job at a reduced level of activity and pay.

The kind of steep-climbing achieved earning progression that we see in Mr D between points B and C on his curve is one that I have not infrequently met. One sees it, for example, in the case of individuals who, for one reason or another, have had to uproot themselves from one community and find work in a strange community, as described in the illustration given in the previous chapter. One finds it also in overcrowded occupations such as some types of office work and accounting in which individuals may get stuck for some years in jobs in which they are under-employed. The achieved earning progressions of such individuals show periods of very flat progress until they get an opportunity for promotion into a job consistent with their capacity. Their achieved earning progression may then climb steeply until it reaches a level that more nearly conforms to the new level of work, possibly thereafter picking up a pattern in accord with their P.P.A., not unlike the case of Mr R described in chapter 9.

V

The notion that each one reacts, and reacts strongly, to his achieved progress as though he possesses an intuitively known internal standard of development of his capacity, is strongly reinforced by the following evidence of an almost unerring ability of individuals to forecast their likely or desired future earnings in terms of their own intuitive estimate of the rate of development of their capacity.

If you were to ask a number of people what they hoped to be earning at some date in the future – where their ambitions lay – it might be thought that some rather unreasonable answers, or at least unrealistic ones, would be given. The opposite turned out to be the case when just such a question was asked of various individuals under the social-analytic conditions under which I work.

I phrased my question in terms of what level (given that general economic conditions remained constant) they would wish to achieve in a given period of time – what level of salary they would hope to have, were they able to progress freely at their own chosen pace in work and salary. The point of time in the future I left to their own choice. They generally chose periods three to five years away.

Some answer to such questions quite readily and freely, as though they have their plans clearly in mind. A typical comment would be: 'If I am not getting such and such a salary by the time I am 35, I will be looking for another job.' Others, apparently less concerned about money than about a job which holds their interest, may have trouble in replying. If encouraged a bit, however, a reply might be given to the effect that: 'Well, I find it difficult to think in terms of money, but I suppose if I were earning such and such when I am 45, I should be quite content – so long as my work remained interesting.'

Irrespective, however, of professed interest in money, or in work, or both, each one states a figure which falls within the extrapolation forward of his intuitively estimated P.P.A. I have data now on some 650 discussions in which this question of future earnings was raised, and in which, at the time the question was asked, the individual knew nothing about capacity growth curves. In every case but three, the stated future earning fell within the estimated earning capacity band*. The replies of A, B and D to such a question are shown at X in figures 14, 15 and 17.

Nearly everyone reacted in a typical manner to the discovery that he had extrapolated his intuitively estimated P.P.A. At first he was surprised momentarily, recovered, and then made a comment like: 'It's all right for someone with my income to be reasonable in my demands, but surely all the people there (pointing to the lower-level curves) would say that they were expecting to get a salary like mine.' Each person appears to see those below him in the economic hierarchy to be dissatisfied with their lot and thus aspiring to his own income level – and presumably envious

*I would re-emphasize that these data were obtained within the social-analytic relationship referred to on p. 145.

231

of him if they cannot get there. No-one, however, has as yet noticed that one implication of this depreciatory view of those whose earning capacity is lower than his own is that he himself ought by the same token to be envious of those of a higher-level earning progression. But each one characteristically chooses to leave out of account those earning more than himself. Envy is a quality much more readily attributed to others than perceived in oneself; so too the possible effects of envy tend to be assumed in others.

VI

The consistency between these individual feelings and judgements about capacity and progress, and the predictions to be derived from a potential progress assessment, shows in its most clear-cut form in the reconstructions that I find it is possible to make of a person's achieved earning progression, by taking account of his feelings about his progress. The following example may illustrate my meaning.

Mr E (curve E, figure 13) was 45 years of age when he and his manager jointly requested me to carry out an analysis of his job and his earnings, because he had begun to feel that his progress had become unsatisfactory. As is my usual practice under such circumstances, I saw each of them individually, with a view to reporting back to them together the material they each agreed I should use.

Mr E described himself as being quite happy about his work; he felt it gave him full scope for the use of his capacity. But he was not satisfied with his financial reward, and was thinking of leaving. He was uncertain about making any such change, however, because of his age.

A time-span analysis of his job, based on data given independently both by himself and by his manager, showed a range of level of work from 18 months to 2 years. He had been promoted into this job 4 years before, at the age of 41; he had felt just ready for the job at the time, and this had been the judgement of the manager who had appointed him – a judgement confirmed by his manager's assessment of his performance during the course of his first year in the position.

On the basis of this information I took his P.P.A. as 2.0 (see figure 18). The converted earning to which he most likely aspired when I saw him at 45, therefore, I assessed as about £38 per week; and in view of his desire to change positions, I took him to have an actual earning of some 15 per cent below this figure, that is, about £32 per week.

Further discussion elicited the following information. He had been satisfied with his payment on taking up his current position,

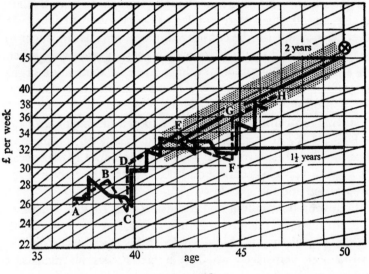

FIGURE 18

but then felt that he had gradually been dropped back to his current level. This progression is shown in figure 18 between E and F. Going back further, he remembered a very happy year in a new job which he took up when he was 37. During this phase (A-B) I assumed his achieved progress to conform to the P.P.A. He remembered that following this phase he had a strong feeling of being let down by a newly appointed manager in charge of him, until a particular time – which turned out to be a few months before his fortieth birthday – when he sought and found a job with another firm. When he told his manager of his intended leaving, there was a great stir. Apologies were made for his having been overlooked, and he was offered a very considerable increase and asked to stay on. Because the increase was very satisfactory, and because he liked the firm and wanted to stay with it, he agreed to remain. He was then given satisfactory progress until he took up his current job at 41 years of age. This sequence of events I interpreted as his having dropped 15 to 20 per cent below his P.P.A. just before he was 40, and of his being brought back to the estimated level, and progressed along it until age 41 – shown in B-C-D-E.

In considering his future, he thought he ought to be at a salary level at age 50 which corresponded to £46 per week at June 1955 level (X in figure 18); he considered, moreover, that he ought to be ready by about that time, or even perhaps a year or so earlier, for a promotion into a job at a higher level. Examination of the diagram shows these aspirations of his to conform to the extrapolation of his estimated progression.

Having reconstructed a predicted achieved earning progression A-B-C-D-E-F, we then plotted his actual achieved earning progression. This is shown in the solid curve in figure 18. There can be noted a very close correspondence between the reconstructed progression and the actual one.

Following this analysis and reconstruction, I had a discussion with Mr E and his manager together, to report to them the results. During the discussion, Mr E spoke to his manager of his dissatisfaction, and asked whether in fact it was his manager's judgement that he was worth no more then than he had been worth when just appointed to the job four years before. His manager, who was genuinely concerned to clear the matter up, explained directly to Mr E what he had told me – that he assessed him to be competent, that he had been correctly appointed at 41, and had progressed well since. He judged that Mr E had moved well into the job – and that he was doing the job at a level perhaps halfway up the bracket. He thought Mr E might reach the top ceiling of the job in 5 to 8 years' time. In connexion with the range of level of work in the job, the manager said he accepted the time-span analysis which had already been carried out, and his own intuitive judgement of a salary range (the company had no explicit salary structure) was in line with the equitable salary range obtained from the time-span analysis.

The manager then told how disconcerted he had been to discover that although he had increased Mr E's salary from £1,300 to £1,700 during the four years he had been in the job, this increase had served only to keep Mr E at relatively the same level he had been at when he began the job. It had been his conscious intention to give Mr E genuine financial progress, but obviously the increases he had granted had been insufficient to correct for inflation.

Following this discussion, the manager got sanction to increase Mr E's salary by 15 per cent, and just under a year later gave him another increase of about 10 per cent. These increases are shown in sequence F-G-H in the figure. It will be noted that these increases have brought Mr E just within his P.P.A. band. He is currently earning £2,300 per annum. His manager has arranged this progress quite consciously using the Data Sheet, and states that he intended to progress Mr E in accord with his P.P.A. so long as Mr E continued to discharge his duties competently and to show signs of progress in his work at the same rate as he had shown up until then. Both he and Mr E expressed themselves privately in discussion with me to be satisfied with the result; the manager because he felt he had a rationally settled plan that had allowed him to have very frank discussions with Mr E about his work; and Mr E because he felt satisfied with his work and payment, and could see prospects of reasonable progress for some years ahead. With regard to the longer-term future, neither Mr E nor his manager could quite see whether or what higher-level employment might be likely to be available. They agreed to keep the matter under review for a few years however, and if each was in the same position, to consider at some appropriate time with the manager-once-removed, and with the personnel department, what prospects there might be of a continuing career for Mr E within the firm. Examination of his P.P.A. suggests that this next job would be likely to be the highest that Mr E will achieve, and that it is the one in which he will eventually retire.

I have had the opportunity now to carry out some fifty reconstructions in this manner, including cases where over-payment occurred at several points, with similar results. The conformity between the reconstructed and the actual achieved earning progression in this particular example is perhaps closer than in most, but is by no means unusual. I have chosen the example because it also illustrates the possible executive use of this type of progression analysis for conducting salary reviews and for future manpower planning. The theme of the possible development of procedures for salary administration and coordination is a very broad one, however, and I shall deal with it separately in the following chapters.

VII

I cannot finish this chapter without adding a short comment on differences between the attitudes and self-evaluations of individuals which I have described from within a social-analytic relationship, and the everyday behaviour of individuals in the employment situation – particularly in the manager-subordinate relationship.

Just because individuals have a realistic intuitive assessment of themselves and their work, there is no guarantee that this assessment will dominate their behaviour when they are discussing their progress with their managers. As with individual and collective negotiation of payment where the lack of an objective yardstick inhibits the play of reality, so with individual progression the lack of a long-term datum line for each individual allows for the free play of ideas of what a person would like to be, and inhibits the play of his awareness of what his capacity and potential really are.

I have frequently enough encountered situations where an individual, in discussion with his manager about his salary progress within the payment bracket for his role, argued for a higher rate of progress than he himself had considered he warranted when he discussed his career progress with me. The accompanying attitude in such cases is that there is nothing to lose in so doing; and it is better to pitch high, since you can always come down. After all, that is the essential step always to be taken where bargaining is the main mode of human relationship or an underlying component of it.

In the face of such attitudes managers are in a very difficult position. There is no available measure of capacity. You can never be absolutely sure of your judgement of a subordinate's capacity or of his future potential. How then are you to distinguish between a subordinate who may be actively pushing for high progress, and one who does not say very much about his feelings but who may leave if he becomes inwardly dissatisfied? Subordinates in turn know about these difficulties in which their managers are placed (and, indeed, many subordinates are themselves managers). If, then, for example, relations are a bit strained between a manager and his subordinate, it is easy enough for the subordinate to imagine that the manager's judgement is distorted – for even under the best of circumstances the manager's judgement may be inaccurate, erring on the high side as well as on the low.

Subordinates and managers are thus inevitably in a difficult and unenviable position over the question of the subordinate's progress. The problem is made worse in periods of active inflation, when it becomes harder to get merit increases into proper perspective. These difficulties are well known. They are mainly kept in check by goodwill and good working relationships. But the problem is there, nevertheless: not continuously; but periodically manifesting itself over the years, if not every time a wage or salary review takes place.

The significance, therefore, of the existence of the capacity which I have tried to demonstrate in individuals intuitively to assess their level of ability and their potential capacity progress, is that if this intuitive judgement can be tapped by systematic progression procedures, some of the disconcerting and unsettling vagaries may be taken out of the wage and salary progress and review situation. A bargaining frame of reference is unlikely to do so. What is needed is a breakaway from bargaining to an agreed and more objective framework. This framework must be one which allows for the accumulation of judgements from year to year, so that the progress of the individual can be followed without having to make a fresh start at assessment every time a member's wage or salary, or his progress, has to be reviewed. I shall describe in the final part of the book how the capacity growth curves may be used for this purpose.

PART FIVE

Conditions for psycho-economic equilibrium

CHAPTER 11

The work-payment-capacity nexus

I

TAKING my experience as a whole with the use of the time-span of discretion, the equitable work-payment scale, and the capacity growth curves, and with due regard for the data which have been described, a number of assumptions seem to me to be warranted, some of which I have already stated:

A. We each have an accurate unconscious awareness of the level of work we are capable of doing, the level of work in the role we occupy, and the equitable payment level for both the level of work we are carrying and the level which we are capable of carrying (if these are different).

B. We are each aware of any discrepancies which may exist between our capacity and our level of work, and between our actual payment and the payment which would be equitable for our work.

C. We each have an accurate unconscious awareness of our level of capacity for discriminating expenditure and of our level of satisfaction consumption, and we are aware of the extent to which our actual income may deviate – either above or below – from that which would provide abundance.

D. The development of our potential capacity follows a regular course which can be described by one of the capacity growth curves representing the earnings which would be equitable for work consistent with our capacity at any given age.

E. We are each motivated towards a level of work that is consistent with our capacity, and a rate of progress in our work that conforms to our rate of progress in capacity.

F. We are each motivated towards equitable payment for our work.

G. Each of us will be stimulated towards the maximum psychological equilibrium of which we are capable, by a level of work consistent with our capacity, and equitable payment for that work within an economy of abundance.

These assumptions about our unconscious awareness of the degree of consistency between our capacity, work, earnings and consumption, and of the sense of balance and of peace of mind with respect to them which we tend to experience when we judge all to be in line with each other, may be at variance with everyday notions and with customary ways of talking about these matters. Work and money are so commonly the source of phantasies and daydreams of wealth and creativity, comfort and security, greatness and power – or, in contrast, of masochistic phantasies of failure, impotence, and destructiveness. Our conscious self-evaluation and ambitions may be subject to gross fluctuation from depressed self-contempt to omnipotent aggrandizement, according to our mood as affected by our unconscious phantasies. We may all have had experience of individuals whose thinking was thus dominated by irrational phantasies – consciously and unconsciously – for greater or shorter periods in their careers, and who became failures because of them.

There is an apparent paradox in this outlook. Our unconscious awareness seems on the one hand to be unexpectedly realistic, and on the other hand and at the same time, to be irrational and emotionally unstable. This paradox is resolved once it is recognized that both processes – reality-tested awareness and phantasy-dominated wish-fulfilment – may go on simultaneously in different parts of the unconscious mind. In the neurotic parts of our unconscious minds – and indeed in the psychotic pockets which are a part of the mental make-up of even the most normal persons* – the picture we may have of ourselves and our economic condition may be totally at variance with that outlined in the foregoing assumptions.

It is likely that anyone who is capable of earning his own living has developed a sufficient degree of inner reality to be able to make the unconscious judgements about himself and his work of which I am speaking. But the existence of an unconscious assessment of our real capacity does not necessarily mean that

---

*I refer here to the profoundly important work of Melanie Klein (e.g., 1948, 1957, 1959) in exploring the very deepest layers of the human mind. Her work relating to the existence of psychotic pockets in the normal mind has been further elaborated by Bion (1957), Segal (1957) and Jaques (1960).

this assessment is consciously accepted. Quite the contrary. Very few of us are capable of consciously sustaining an accurate and stable self-appraisal of our capacities and limitations. Some of our deepest unconscious defences against anxiety would be threatened – phantasy gratification, omnipotence, self-efface-ment. We repress our knowledge of our true capacity, and retain it repressed in our unconscious mind. This repression makes for emotional oscillations in our conscious self-evaluation, while at the same time we may maintain our unconscious awareness of our adjustment to work reality. It is only in the exceptional mature and integrated person that the unconscious awareness of work and capacity becomes the sole or even the major determinant of conscious self-appraisal.

At the same time, just because our conscious picture of our-selves and our capacities may be heavily influenced by unrealistic unconscious phantasies, this does not necessarily imply that we will behave unrealistically in our work and economic life. The un-conscious reality sense is an extremely powerful controller of be-haviour in the real world, particularly in that area of the real world where behaviour is reality-tested by economic satisfaction or dissatisfaction and, in the final analysis, by economic survival. We are always dealing, therefore, with a typically human situa-tion of conflict in each person between the demands of phantasy satisfaction and the demands of the reality sense*, as influenced by the character of the social and economic environment within which he lives and to which he must adapt.

I do not propose, however, to consider in this book – other than in general terms – the dynamics and structure of inner psychic conflicts in the individual in connexion with work, capacity, and economic rewards and consumption†. My present concern is more with the economic and work environment and with how these conditions affect individual and group behaviour, either reinforcing the reality sense or stimulating and encouraging

---

* This theme is one of the cornerstones of the psycho-analytic theories of Sigmund Freud, and is vividly presented in his book, *Beyond the Pleasure Principle*, 1922.

† I have sketched in certain aspects of these complex inner psychological processes in 'Disturbances in the capacity to work'.

the operation of unrealistic components of thought and judgement. The effects of these outside circumstances on any specific person will be influenced by the conflicting tendencies within him towards both realistic and unrealistic attitudes and behaviour. The specific contents and amounts of these conflicting tendencies will of course differ from person to person, as I indicated at the end of the previous chapter. But these individual differences need not concern us for the moment. The effects common to everyone can be considered in their own right. By so doing, we shall be able to get closer to the type of behaviour which could be encouraged by equitable payment and sound progress.

II

In exploring the work-payment-capacity nexus, I am fully aware that a person's payment and his level of work are not the only factors which make for his satisfaction or dissatisfaction in his job. There are other important factors: the interest which the type of work has for him; the physical and geographical surroundings; the congruence of the social atmosphere and the temperament of managers and colleagues with his own temperament and general psychological make-up; and many other factors besides.

But just because these other factors exist, it does not necessarily mean that it is not useful to treat of work, payment and capacity apart. There are in fact some weighty reasons for doing so. The provision of work consistent with a person's capacity, and of equitable payment for that work, may be regarded as fundamental responsibilities of an industrial society to itself and to its individual members. These factors are essential to the optimization of the production of wealth for the society, and to the maintenance of individual health and satisfaction. Direct personal interest in the job, or an equable geographical surround, or congenial colleagues, however desirable in themselves, cannot be considered to be the responsibility of society in the same way that equitable payment and opportunity for full use of capacity may be. This is not to say that these factors are unimportant, but to claim for them an importance as secondary factors compared with the prime significance of the work-payment-capacity trio.

All the various possible combinations of level of work, level of payment, and level of capacity, can be described in terms of thirteen fundamental patterns (the three variables are indicated by W, P and C in the schematic illustration for each pattern):

(a) The individual occupies a position whose range of level of work is consistent with his capacity, $\boxed{\text{C-W}}$, and receives:

1. equitable payment for the level of work: $\boxed{\text{C-W}}$ -P

2. payment higher than equity: $\overset{\text{P}}{\underset{}{\boxed{\text{C-W}}}}$

3. payment below equity: $\underset{\text{P}}{\boxed{\text{C-W}}}$

(b) The individual occupies a position whose range of level of work is greater than his capacity: $\boxed{\begin{matrix}\text{W}\\\text{C}\end{matrix}}$, and receives:

4. payment above equity: $\overset{\text{P}}{\boxed{\begin{matrix}\text{W}\\\text{C}\end{matrix}}}$

5. equitable payment: $\boxed{\begin{matrix}\text{W}\\\text{C}\end{matrix}}$ -P

6. payment below equity, but higher than would be equitable for the work consistent with his capacity: $\boxed{\begin{matrix}\text{W}\\\text{C}\end{matrix}}$ -P

7. payment that would be equitable for the work consistent with his capacity: $\boxed{\begin{matrix}\text{W}\\\text{C}\end{matrix}}$ -P

8. payment that is below equity for work that would be consistent with his capacity: $\underset{\text{P}}{\boxed{\begin{matrix}\text{W}\\\text{C}\end{matrix}}}$

(c) The individual occupies a position whose range of level of work is less than he is capable of carrying, $\boxed{\begin{matrix}\text{C}\\\text{W}\end{matrix}}$, and receives:

9. payment above equity for the work level consistent with his capacity: $\overset{\text{P}}{\boxed{\begin{matrix}\text{C}\\\text{W}\end{matrix}}}$

10. payment that is equitable for the work level consistent with his capacity: $\boxed{\begin{matrix}\text{C}\\\text{W}\end{matrix}}$ -P

11. payment that is below equity for the work level consistent with his capacity, but above equity for his current work level: $\boxed{\begin{smallmatrix} C \\ \dot{W} \end{smallmatrix}}$-P

12. payment that is equitable for his current work level: $\boxed{\begin{smallmatrix} C \\ \dot{W} \end{smallmatrix}}$-P

13. payment below equity for his current work level: $\boxed{\begin{smallmatrix} C \\ W \end{smallmatrix}}$
$\dot{P}$

These thirteen patterns can be schematically summarized in this manner. I shall use this schematic shorthand to identify the particular pattern I am discussing:

$$\overset{\dot{P}}{\boxed{C\text{-}W}}\text{-P} \qquad \overset{\dot{P}}{\boxed{\begin{smallmatrix} W \\ C \end{smallmatrix}}}\begin{smallmatrix} \text{-P} \\ \text{-P} \\ \text{-P} \end{smallmatrix} \qquad \overset{\dot{P}}{\boxed{\begin{smallmatrix} C \\ W \end{smallmatrix}}}\begin{smallmatrix} \text{-P} \\ \text{-P} \\ \text{-P} \end{smallmatrix}$$
$$\dot{P} \qquad\qquad \dot{P} \qquad\qquad\quad \dot{P}$$

III

There is a general reaction pattern to each one of the thirteen C-W-P situations which is common to us all. Of course there are individual differences within each of these general reaction patterns. But despite these individual differences, there are fundamental similarities in the way we respond to each of these situations, in our feelings about them, in our descriptions of them, irrespective of what we might do about these feelings, of how we might express them in action, or indeed of how we might adjust within ourselves to our reaction. The experience of each of the thirteen C-W-P situations acts as a force stimulating particular feelings and attitudes.

It will be appreciated that each of the C-W-P patterns is dynamic in content. Each of the patterns must be conceived as occurring in time. Individual capacity, level of work in the job, and wage or salary (or the value of money), are each in a state of more or less rapid change. For purposes of description, therefore, I shall assume that all three factors, although undergoing change, are nevertheless changing at the same rate and hence the pattern of the factors is remaining unchanged. I shall assume also that an abundant economy is operating. In an over-abundant or an under-abundant economy we may expect additional reactions according to the extent of the over- or under-abundance.

A. The first pattern, and the most important of all, is the $\boxed{\text{C-W}}$-P pattern. This is the pattern which stimulates in us the maximum psychological equilibrium which we are capable of experiencing with regard to our work and payment. Our work is just matched to our capacity, and there is opportunity for our level of work to increase at a rate nicely attuned to the growth and development of our capacity. Our payment is equitable for the work we are doing, and we can make realistic plans for the future because we have a good intuitive idea of the rate of increase of our earning power.

Just how much any particular person can achieve a sense of balance in his economic life under such circumstances will depend to a certain extent on how balanced he is in his emotional life in general. The more well-balanced and stable we are and the more able we are to apply our capacities, the greater the peace of mind we will be able to achieve for ourselves. Contrariwise, the more neurotically insecure we may be, the less will we be able to take advantage of our position to help us towards peace of mind. But deep within ourselves we will be aware that our insecurity is a personal matter, and that there is little or nothing that our employer, or society at large, can do by way of underpinning our economic security.

B. Correct work level, and over-equity payment: $\dfrac{P}{\boxed{\text{C-W}}}$. This pattern gives the possibility of manifest great satisfaction with the employing concern in the early stages. Then some uneasiness and guilt develop, but these feelings remain largely unconscious. There is the fear of envy from less well-placed groups, and of retaliation by them, as well as of the possibility of the favoured payment attracting personnel of greater capacity than ourselves. In the long term, personal selfishness and insensitivity – or their opposite, a feeling of surfeit – are aroused. We are likely under these conditions to try various techniques of evasion of the fact that we are receiving relatively better financial treatment than colleagues or other groups.

C. Correct work level, and under-equity payment: $\dfrac{\boxed{\text{C-W}}}{P}$. This pattern provokes gradually increasing psychic conflict and dis-affection. The rightness of the fit of the work to our capacity is a strong attraction. It binds us to the job. But our payment remains unsatisfactory. We feel unfairly treated as compared with others. Our zest and enthusiasm for our work will be less than it would otherwise be. If our interest in the job was high, it will be lessened; if it was low, we will be stimulated to change jobs. If, however, the circumstances in our occupation, or our personal circum-stances, preclude the likelihood of our being able to obtain equitably paid work, we may say and do nothing, but the under-mining of our morale will be greater. We fall in, in a veiled fashion, with group protest and criticism of the institution.

D. Too high a level of work, and payment at or above equity:

$$\overset{P}{\boxed{\begin{smallmatrix}W\\I\\C\end{smallmatrix}}}\ \boxed{\begin{smallmatrix}W\\I\\C\end{smallmatrix}}\text{-P.}$$ These are patterns which are often likely to be associated with the so-called stress disorders of executives. An individual who strives to hang on to a job whose level of work is too high for his capacity is the prey of excessively neurotic am-bition and drive – under the dominance of unconscious des-tructive impulses, of envy, hate, jealousy and greed. Greed for financial reward above that consistent with our capacity, and for the enhanced status, drive us to hang on. Mental conflict and strain result. The impact may be lessened for a time by un-conscious collusion with our manager to protect us. But the in-evitable break will come in due course – either through personal breakdown (which may give rise to psycho-somatic illness), or change in job, or through being taken out of our job (whether by open dismissal or transfer or 'promotion').

E. Too high level of work, and payment below equity:

$$\boxed{\begin{smallmatrix}W\\I\\C\end{smallmatrix}}\text{-P}\ \boxed{\begin{smallmatrix}W\\I\\C\end{smallmatrix}}\text{-P}\ \underset{P}{\boxed{\begin{smallmatrix}W\\I\\C\end{smallmatrix}}}.$$ These patterns are manifestly very unstable.

We have the attraction of employment with enhanced status. But we are confronted by the personal strain of work beyond our capacity; and the financial return is not worth the candle. Very scarce employment or strong neuroticism must be at work if we try to stay in a job in these circumstances. These comments apply the more strongly the more the earnings fall towards or below a level that would be equitable for work consistent with our capacity. The few instances I have come across have been embedded in strong personal disturbance in both the individual and his manager, and have ended (if not worked through) in bad industrial relations and personal breakdown.

F. Too low a level of work, and payment at or above the level consistent with capacity:
$$\begin{array}{c} P \\ \boxed{\begin{array}{c} C \\ \hline W \end{array}} \quad \boxed{\begin{array}{c} C \\ \hline W \end{array}}\text{-P} . \end{array}$$

These patterns may give equilibrium on a temporary basis, where the organization wishes to retain the services of the individual but does not at that moment have a job in which it can utilize his full capacity. With the agreement of the individual, the above-equity payment may represent a kind of retainer fee designed to keep him in the enterprise until a suitable vacancy (or a planned vacancy) occurs.

In the absence of this very special condition, these patterns are calculated to induce disorganization. In effect you have an under-employed and over-paid individual. He tries to take on other people's work, and gets into trouble with them. Conscious or unconscious contempt will inevitably arise for the employer who pays for value not received. Insecurity is equally inevitable: over-payment is never experienced as secure (unless of course one is dealing with a favoured family member in a family business). The seeking after windfalls and easy gain is satisfied, with consequent appeal to the weaker areas of character.

G. Too low a level of work, and payment at or below equity:
$$\boxed{\begin{array}{c} C \\ \hline W \end{array}}\text{-P} \quad \boxed{\begin{array}{c} C \\ \hline W \end{array}}\text{-P} \quad \boxed{\begin{array}{c} C \\ \hline W \end{array}} . \atop P$$
These patterns are inclined to induce dissatisfaction, the degree of the dissatisfaction becoming severe at the lower levels of payment. At the extreme, where payment is below equity, our work is doubly unrewarding: not only is our capacity being under-employed, but we are not even getting equitable payment for this unsatisfying level of work. Given reasonable employment opportunities, we will probably seek other employment, and labour turnover is practically assured.

It is only under conditions either of severe personal disturbance or of unemployment in a person's occupation that he is likely to continue in such a job. The case 'C' in chapter 10 illustrates the former point; that of a person suffering a nervous breakdown who is glad to be under-employed for a period of some years until he manages to get over the breakdown.

Apart from such catastrophe, it is during periods of unemployment that large numbers of individuals suffer subjection to these unrewarding work conditions. Those who are unemployed are exposed to total dejection. And of those who continue to be employed, a large proportion will be under-employed and under-equity paid. So that even being lucky enough to be employed in a situation of widespread unemployment may nevertheless be to be degraded and demoralized in work. Added to which is the general effect of the fall in individual standard of living accompanying the decline in the abundance of the economy under such conditions.

The main point is that these demoralizing effects which stand out so dramatically in times of economic depression can quite readily occur in times of relative prosperity and full employment in localized regions, in sections of an industry, or in sections of an organization. These are the conditions for boredom and human waste. These patterns obtain for many university graduates in their first experience in industry in management training groups. They are equally the patterns for bright craftsmen who have grown in capacity beyond craft jobs, but cannot get up the ladder. It is of the utmost importance for both efficiency and the well-being of the individual that each person should have the opportunity to work under conditions such that the level of work in his job matches his capacity, and he receives equitable payment for that work.

IV

The judgement we possess about ourselves, our work, and our earnings, implied by these patterns of response to the various W-C-P patterns, is judgement based upon unconscious intuitive awareness, the awareness of experience. The processes by which norms are built up in our minds occur unconsciously. We have feelings about these things – deep inner awareness, or ideas-in-feeling – a sense of things either being in balance or out of balance, and a sense of striving for something more or a sense of ease and peace of mind and satisfaction. We do not have explicit knowledge in the sense that we can put forward valid reasons for our judgements of our level of capacity, level of work, and level of equitable pay. And although equitable pay can be talked about in terms of money, there has been no language at all with which to speak about level of capacity and level of work.

If these assumptions are correct, we are faced by the question of how the intuitive awareness I have described comes about. In what form is it carried in the mind and made available for use? This problem is one aspect of the very general problem of how any sort of social norm is formed, how that norm becomes established in individuals, and how the individual reacts to these norms and uses them.

Intuitive awareness is built up from small increments of experience in which non-verbalized awareness and ideas – ideas-in-feeling – are repeatedly subjected to the testing of reality and modified bit by bit until a moderately realistic set of internal standards is established. At work especially, the requirements of reality have to be subserved – continued employment and survival depend on it. If anyone takes on work at a level above his capacity, he eventually fails in his work. If he accepts a level of work below his capacity, he meets the resistance of his needs to express his creativity and to avoid impotence. He also meets the external resistance of his colleagues, his superiors, and his subordinates (if any) in whom feelings of disequilibrium are stimulated when there is disequilibrium in organization and in payment structure caused by someone occupying a position at a level below the capacity he can exercise. In short, each one is subject to a strong internal and external field of force tending to keep him in a position at a level of work consistent with his capacity. It is our reality sense responding to this field of force which produces our unconscious awareness of the level of work we can successfully carry.

Intuitive or experiential knowledge about capacity and about level of work interact. The psychic yardstick is the person himself.

We sense that this job is too easy, that too difficult, and this one just right. We sense whether we are working at full tilt and right up to scratch, or whether we possess unused capacity for whatever reason – whether for reasons of disinterest, or of pre-occupation with inner psychic conflict, or interference by disturbed home conditions or other worries. This experience through time provides us with the information which allows us to build up our picture of our rate of progress in capacity and in achievement.

Having related ourselves to our work, we are in a position to compare our own job with other jobs, not as we may think by means of job comparisons, but by means of comparisons of our own capacity with that of our friends and associates. I find myself forced to the conclusion that there is great precision in our ability to compare levels of capacity in one another. I think it is done by myriad clues of the way in which the other person talks and thinks, in particular the way in which he organizes his perceptions. In talk and argument and discussions, we learn to sense to what extent the frame of thought within which we operate is broader or narrower, more or less comprehensive, than that of others. It is the sense of talking or arguing on a par with another, or of enfolding the other's capacity or being enfolded by it.

Using ourselves as the yardstick, we are each able to compare our own rate of pay with that of others. My data lead to the conclusion that this judgement is two-dimensional. First, it is a judgement whether a person is earning the same as others of lesser or greater capacity. Second, it is a judgement whether his earnings give the same relative degree of abundance as the earnings of others.

These judgements of current equitable earning levels in relation to work and capacity are, I believe, built up in the first instance from contacts with immediate friends and associates. These contacts very quickly build up into an industry-wide experience of earnings. Friends work within a widely-flung network of jobs. They work in other offices, or shops, or factories, in other occupations, and in other industries. They move. New friends move in from other communities. There is consequently a flow of information about other types of work. The same process holds for work associates. They discuss their work. They change. New associates join the firm from other places. Other associates leave, and maintain contact after having gained employment elsewhere. Or they may apply for advertised jobs, and give information about the jobs after interview. Or a person himself may apply for other jobs, or change jobs, or move to another community.

Over the years, by virtue of this flow of information induced by the steady stream of labour turnover, a great deal of knowledge is gleaned about various jobs and the payment associated with them – jobs in different conditions, different industries, and different communities. The level of work in these jobs is judged by the assessment of the level of capacity of the friend or colleague who does the job. A coherent intuitive awareness is gradually accumulated of the extent to which other individuals and ourselves are in receipt of abundant pay, or under- or over-abundant pay. Norms of the degree of deviation from abundance that is equitable are thus gradually constructed.

The norms of abundance can be looked for in the experience of the individual himself. Given an under-abundant income, we experience unused capacity for discriminating expenditure. Given an over-abundant income, difficulties, uncertainties and the disorganized sense of promiscuity in spending are experienced. For most people, however, experience is limited to under-abundance, and phantasies about how much one might spend if one had the money remain unmodified and untempered by the test of reality. Nonetheless, the sense of equity which I have observed in individuals leads me to conclude that, even under conditions of chronic under-abundance, there exists in the reality-tested areas of the mind a pretty precise standard of just how much higher a standard of living would be required for the demands of personal satisfaction to be met.

CHAPTER 12

Dynamic progression and incentive

I

OUR assumptions lead to a systematic formulation of the nature of incentives in work. It is this. We each do our best at our work when we are doing work which interests us, under conditions of dynamic equilibrium between our level of work, our capacity, and our payment; that is to say, dynamic $\boxed{\text{C-W}}$-P conditions. An optimum 'incentive system' is therefore one in which there are mechanisms for facilitating the movement and progress of individuals in line with their interests and level of capacity, for paying in accord with equity, and for ensuring the continuous availability and allocation of the quantity of work that it is expected should be done. I shall consider separately each of the two main components of this formulation: first, the concept of working at our best; and second, the concept of dynamic equilibrium between work, payment and capacity.

II

What do we mean by incentive? The use of the term in the phrase 'incentive systems' has debased its value by attaching to it the meaning of encouragement to work at some abnormally fast pace. Even though this crude conception of employees working physiologically faster and faster may not be universally held, it is, nevertheless, a sufficiently widespread caricature of the truth to be worth getting out of the way.

In order to get at the question of rate of work, we must first distinguish sharply between a person's rate of work referring to his physiological pace, and his rate of work referring to the amount of work he turns out. In order to avoid any possibility of confusion, I shall use the terms 'physiological pace' and 'quantity of output', and shall not use the phrase 'rate of work' at all. Second, it is essential that we distinguish clearly and unequivocally between *physiological pace, intensity of physical and mental concentration*, and *level of capacity*. Physiological pace refers to

254

the actual rate of movement in work; for example, the difference between walking slowly, walking quickly, and running. Intensity of physical and mental concentration refers to the degree of application to the job. It includes the continuity of thinking about it, and the continuity of physical application, with minimum interruption for thoughts about other things or through minor unnecessary absences from the job during the working day. Level of capacity refers to the capacity – the physiological and mental skill – to carry higher or lower levels of work.

All these three factors – pace, application and capacity – combine to determine the quantity and quality of a person's work. The important thing to note, however, is that none of the factors can be as readily influenced by outside conditions as may often be thought to be the case. In particular, we each have a normal pace of work which we cannot easily depart from – either by slowing down or by speeding up – for any length of time. The level of capacity we exercise remains relatively fixed unless affected by emotional disturbance – it being impossible to exercise more than the capacity we possess, and difficult purposely to exercise continuously less.

Intensity of mental and physical application is probably rather more influenced by external circumstances than is either of the other two factors. But again it is important to note that we each have a normal level of intensity of application. The effect of outside conditions is to interfere with our normal concentration, to disturb or inhibit it, rather than to spur us on to maintain an intensity of application at a level above our norm. The same inhibitory effect is true also for physiological pace.

In short, we each have our normal level of output in work, determined by our normal pace, concentration and capacity. External conditions may pull us down from our normal output, mainly by disturbing our inner state of mind and interfering with our physiological pace, and our intensity of physical and mental concentration on the job. The importance of external conditions – so-called incentives – is to facilitate the expression of normal pace, concentration, and capacity in work, and to prevent interference with their expression.

Over and above the continuous expression of normal pace,

concentration and capacity, it is possible for individuals to achieve above normal rates of output in work, but for very short periods of time only. Everyone will have experienced such spurts, or bursts of special effort. But they cannot be maintained for more than a few days at a time – perhaps longer in exceptional circumstances – without fatigue and slowing-up. But the notion that incentive systems can encourage individuals to maintain such spurts continuously in the normal course of their work is a fallacy.

This line of argument may seem to be contradicted by the fact that two different individuals doing the same kind of work (let us assume that analysis and measurement have shown the jobs to be identical) may differ considerably in the amount of work of given quality that they continue to turn out. Such differences, which are easily enough demonstrated, cannot, however, simply be interpreted as showing that one must necessarily be working harder than the other, in the sense of putting more effort into it or working at a faster physiological pace. If the difference persists – if it is not just a passing phase – then the main factor causing it is likely to be a difference in their levels of capacity. For given a level of work consistent with capacity, and equivalence of interest and experience, I would assume that any two persons of the same capacity will continue to turn out the same amount of work of given quality. Conversely, if one of them has a higher capacity than the other he will, under the same conditions, turn out a greater amount of work. In my experience, this factor of differences in level of capacity of two such individuals must be taken into account as the main factor determining differences in output, before any conclusions can be drawn as to possible differences in physiological pace or intensity of concentration.

This assumption – that the higher the level of a person's capacity the greater the amount of work he will do under otherwise similar conditions – serves to explain the common observation that, of two individuals doing the same work, the one who continuously turns out the greater amount of work of given quality, or the same amount of work of better quality, often appears to be exerting less effort, is less rushed, and may not be working at a greater physiological pace than the other. He is working in a more organized fashion, goes more directly to what has to be done, spends less time in trial and error, arrives at decisions more quickly and confidently, and generally gets on with greater ease and certitude. These characteristics are all the expression of higher capacity.

Returning to our formulation of the nature of incentives in work, we may define 'doing our best at our work' as applying our normal physiological pace, our normal intensity of physical and mental concentration, and our capacity, with special effort or spurts as might be required from time to time in order to cope with emergencies which might arise. Our level of output cannot be stimulated to remain consistently higher than its normal level.

III

Let me now briefly consider the action of a dynamic equilibrium between level of work, capacity and payment. By a dynamic equilibrium I mean a movement in level of work and in the equitable payment that goes with it, at a rate commensurate with the rate of movement of a person's performance in his work. That is to say, as a person's capacity in his job increases and his performance improves, his level of work is correspondingly increased, and so, too, is the level of his payment.

This equilibrium is not difficult to maintain as a person moves up through the bracket of his existing job, so long as his payment is progressed with his performance (the procedures for this purpose are described in the next chapter). The problem is somewhat more difficult, however, when he reaches the upper bracket of his job. At that stage, promotion to another job is called for and clearly cannot always be arranged just at the appropriate moment. Nevertheless, so long as there is a felt initiative in the firm to tackle these progression problems with serious intent, the main conditions for a dynamic C-W-P equilibrium can be met.

The effect of securing a dynamic C-W-P equilibrium is that we are in a literal sense pulled along in our jobs. Not only is our work at the right level for our capacity, but it stays there as we advance or recede in capacity. And we are equitably paid, our payment being adjusted in accord with adjustments in our work.

In connexion with payment, one other feature must be mentioned. I have linked level of payment with level of work. What then of the reward for the time-to-time spurts which a manager may ask of his subordinates? These spurts are special occasions, and as such call for special payments – that is to say, for *ex gratia* payments to be made at the time of the spurt as a special bonus for a special intensity of concentration and pace. I shall discuss this question of *ex gratia* payments in more detail in the next chapter, simply emphasizing for the moment the importance of not mixing the process of assigning normal wage and salary payment for the normal course of work with that of making special payments for special occasions.

The condition, then, which provides the main element of incentive is the arrangement of opportunity and encouragement for each person to use his full capacity in his work with equitable payment for that work, and to be presented with the opportunity and the challenge to increase his responsibilities as fast as his capacities will allow. In extreme form, it is the condition which obtains in societies in times of crisis – such as war – when manpower is short and each person is called upon to exercise his talents to the full. Under more ordinary circumstances we refer, in common parlance, to the opportunity and encouragement to 'get ahead', a conception which is relevant to everyone, not only to young men just beginning their careers, so long as we free it from the connotation of the fulfilment of glittering adolescent dreams.

If this point of view is correct, then we should expect that most incentive schemes, if not all of them, are not really what they appear to be. I refer to all types of incentive scheme – piecework, group bonus, commission payment, etc. They are more likely to turn out to be schemes whose real action is to reduce the inhibition and bottling up of application and resourcefulness, rather than schemes which somehow get more than normal work out of employees. For example, two of the common factors in piecework schemes which contribute to this effect are, first, that they lead to the setting of quantitative targets, and, second, they stimulate operators to demand that their managers maintain an efficient flow of work. To the extent to which they are successful – and as I shall endeavour to show, they have their negative effects as well – these schemes would show evidence that they diminish lethargy and carelessness, and bring about mental and physical concentration and application of capacity somewhat nearer that which a person might normally be expected to manifest if he felt interested in his work, and was not put off by feelings of inequitable treatment and of lack of opportunity for recognition and progress.

In line with these expectations, I would assume that incentive schemes would be based upon any or all of three main elements. First, where a rate bracket in a role is an under-equity bracket, these schemes may allow individuals to obtain equity levels in payment by spurts and special effort – the cause of equity in fact being defeated because of the special effort required. Second, they may, without appearing to do so, allow individuals to progress at their own rate in level of work and to receive increasing payment as they do. Third, they provide the opportunity for time-to-time increases in earnings by spurts. These three elements can be demonstrated to hold true of the common incentive payment schemes, as I shall try to illustrate in the following analysis of piecework bonus incentives. This analysis may serve to illustrate that the conditions which I have described as essential for sound incentive in work are general in that they apply equally to manual, clerical, managerial, technological, and specialist types of work at all levels from top management to shop floor.

IV

Let me consider some of these matters in more detail by reference to piecework systems.

The commonly expressed stereotype of the effect of piecework bonus systems is that they encourage greater effort in the sense of maintaining a faster pace of work. Pieceworkers are assumed to work harder and faster than timeworkers. I have met few pieceworkers or production engineers, however, who do not really consider such a view to be over-simplified. Whatever the manner in which they may publicly discuss piecework and argue about it, they hold to a rather more complex view of the matter, in which four main factors are involved in increasing piecework earnings – pace of work, continuity of application, methods improvement, and an even and regular flow of work. Of these four factors, the first three correspond to the three factors of pace, intensity of concentration, and level of capacity, which we have already considered. The last is concerned with the stimulus to managers from their operators, to ensure a steady flow of work to the operators.

Piecework earnings can definitely be increased by speeding up the actual pace of movement, but such increases can be carried out only for short periods of time. They are spurts. These spurts may be put on towards the week's end if earnings have been low, or before holidays or other periods when extra money is needed for special purposes. They cannot, however, be maintained. Good continuity in application can, however, be kept up, earnings being slightly increased by avoiding time wastage, for instance between jobs, or when getting out drawings, or going to the washroom. Such increases are limited in amount, however, by the control exerted through the use of standard time allowances which characterizes piecework systems.

The two factors of overriding importance in increasing earnings are ensuring that managers keep the work flowing, and methods improvement. Pieceworkers do not stand idly by if their next job is not ready as soon as they have finished the one they are working on. They tend to keep managers and supervisors on their toes. They look for continuity in their work. A piecework system, therefore, seems a simple way of overcoming slackness in management. It is not my purpose here to dwell on problems of management organization. But I must at least comment that my experience leaves me in no doubt whatever that the use of piecework systems to stimulate managers and supervisors weakens leadership in the long run, and disrupts effective manager-worker relationships*.

Of these two factors, therefore, methods improvement must attract our attention. It has to do with the pieceworker finding

*This issue is discussed in 'The social and psychological impact of a change in method of wage payment' (Jaques et al.), 1951. This reports a two-year follow-up study of a change from piecework to timework in an engineering shop. See also Wilfred Brown: *Piecework Abandoned*, 1962.

ways and means of organizing and doing work which are an improvement upon the standards of method and of performance established by the planning and time-study engineers. Methods improvement is associated with growth in capacity, and comprises any or all of such factors as: organizing the layout of tools and work in such a manner as to minimize the amount of physical movement required; achievement of greater facility in the use of tools, in particular of ordinary tools like hammers, wrenches, spanners, files, so that work can be mounted, set, assembled, handled, with greater ease and dispatch. As the capacity of the pieceworker grows, so too does his ability to get on with his work more effectively.

V

If the main factor under an operator's own control for increasing his piecework earnings is the amount of methods improvement he succeeds in accomplishing, then his earnings are dependent not upon his pushing himself to work faster, but upon the level of capacity he brings to his work. The greater his capacity, the better will he organize his work; without any increase in physiological effort, he will get through his work more rapidly and efficiently; and the greater will his earnings be.

According to this view, as an operator's capacity grows, and as he becomes more proficient in his work, his average earnings should show a gradual increase. Although I must emphasize that my sample is too small to allow of any very positive conclusions, this type of increase is precisely what I have found. Over the months and years, with upward and downward deviations during periods when the times on jobs have become loose or have tightened, or periods when a spate of easy or difficult jobs come along, I have found a trend in the actual weekly earnings of piecework operators. These trends in earnings tend to conform to the capacity growth curves, as shown in figure 19. In this figure is shown the progression of the quarterly average of standard weekly earnings for a piecework operator for whom I had been able to establish a reasonably accurate potential progress assessment. His actual earnings, and his assessment of what he would be earning in five years' time, were consistent with the

P.P.A. This finding is typical of the small samples of analyses of earnings of pieceworkers I have done, in which I was able to establish a P.P.A.

The hypothesis that the trend of increase in the earnings of piecework operators is mainly due to growth in capacity, is consistent with the common finding that piecework operators have weekly earning targets to which they adhere. They may put on

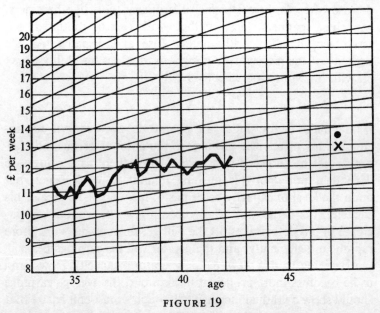

FIGURE 19

spurts if towards the end of the week their earnings threaten to be below this target. If their earnings are above the target, they may slacken off towards the end of the week or try to avoid booking in some of their already completed work until the beginning of the following week. Analysis of the course of these target figures shows that they increase with time, and if corrected for movements in the wages index they fit in with the capacity growth curves. Young pieceworkers (say, under 32 years of age) pitch the rate of increase in their target figures higher than do older workers. The greater the capacity level, the greater the rate of increase planned for. The older workers (say, over 50 years of age) tend to want to come off piecework. They are quite aware

262

intuitively of falling capacity, and anticipate the unsettling effect of earning capacity which may fall at a rate which will not reflect fair recognition of years of service. The older timeworker is in a better position in this respect, for he can count upon receiving national awards which will at least keep his real earnings differentially steady.

This relationship between individual capacity and quantity of work has an important negative effect in piecework types of incentive system which it is worth noting. The way for a person to make such systems yield the highest pay is to get into a job – and hang on to it – which is below his level of capacity. That is to say, a person might be capable of carrying a job with a work bracket, say, of two weeks to one month – implying, of course, that he would be able to turn out a standard amount of work at that level. If such a person can keep himself in a piecework job of, say, one week to two weeks time-span and with a low machine-paced factor – and especially if he is the only worker in that section with a higher capacity than the level of work – then he can beat the system. For his capacity can enable him to turn out a quantity of work well above the standard. The time study cannot be altered, however, for the times would then be far too tight for the average operator working with average effort used as a rate-fixing standard. Under such conditions, an operator can achieve over-equity payment, although it is at the expense of the exercise of the full scope of his capacity.

VI

With regard to equity in payment, I have data which suggest that the reactions of pieceworkers to deviations between the actual wage bracket and the equitable bracket for the work they do, can be analysed in precisely the same way as for timework. This concept of a wage bracket for a piecework job may require a word of explanation.

All piecework rates have a concealed but definite wage bracket. There is a basic rate for the job (or often a basic bracket) – let us say, for example, 2s. 6d. per hour plus 2s. 6d. national bonus. But there is also a negotiated minimum earning level below which the pieceworker's earnings are not allowed to drop, it being assumed that special difficulties or bad time study caused this result. If, for example, this minimum bonus level is 40 per cent, the minimum rate for the job is 2s. 6d. per hour, plus 40 per cent bonus, plus 2s. 6d. national bonus, or 6s. per hour.

At the other end of the scale there is a maximum rate imposed by the standards of any particular management or manager for what constitutes a maximum likely bonus earning, without the times as set having been loose or having become loose. These maximum figures have varied in my experience from 70 per cent to 200 per cent bonus, but commonly range between 60 per cent and 100 per cent bonus. A kind of artificially constructed ceiling comes into being. If this ceiling is, for example, at 100 per cent bonus, then the maximum practicable continuous rate for the job we have adopted for illustrative purposes is 2s. 6d. plus 100 per cent bonus plus 2s. 6d. national bonus, or a total wage of 7s. 6d. per hour.

Thus the actual wage bracket for the job discussed is 6s. to 7s. 6d. per hour. These figures represent a 42-hour weekly wage bracket of £12 12s. to £15 15s. They constitute just as real a wage bracket as the more explicit wage or salary brackets that attach to timework and staff positions. This actual wage bracket may then be compared with the range of weekly piecework earnings which pieceworkers consider would be fair for the job they are doing.

I have carried out analyses of this type, analyses which included time-span assessment of the range of level of work in the piecework jobs concerned. The results are entirely consistent with those I have described for timework jobs. Pieceworkers state equitable wage brackets for the range of level of work in their jobs, which conform to the equitable work-payment scale, despite the fact that their earnings are made by means of a piecework system of payment. Indeed, there is good evidence to suggest that piecework methods of payment are frequently resorted to under conditions where time-honoured and hidebound traditions and practice dictate that one type of work – say, job category A – must be paid more than another – say, job category B – although intuitively it is known that changes in methods of production have led to the level of work in job category B outgrowing the level of work in job category A. By means of piecework, prices can be set which make it possible for a pieceworker in job category B to take home a greater weekly income than a timeworker on job category A, while yet giving the appearance of the stereotype being adhered to and tradition upheld, because job category A is paid at a higher rate than the basic rate for B. Comparisons between the actual earnings in the two categories is held to be out of court, because, as is commonly argued, if the pieceworkers take home more pay, it is because they have worked abnormally hard for it. By such fictions, face is saved all round.

VII

With respect to payment, therefore, we may note that timework and piecework are comparable in many important respects; they both have identifiable payment brackets; similar norms of equity apply; the level-of-work bracket can be measured in time-span; and, negatively, there is no greater guarantee of equitable payment brackets attaching to the one or the other. But there are three great and important differences: (1) a timeworker or salaried staff worker can increase his standard weekly wage or salary only by being given merit increases by his employer; a pieceworker is in a position to progress himself through a wage bracket at his own pace, and at a rate consistent with his rate of growth in capacity, although he must depend upon his employer for any promotion into a higher wage bracket; (2) a timeworker must rely on his manager to grant him *ex gratia* bonus payments in recognition of periods of special intensity of application; the pieceworker can put on spurts when he chooses, and get an immediate reward in his pay packet; (3) as against these two advantages in piecework, the timeworker does not lose out in payment if the flow of work to him slows down, or if there is a flow of troublesome work, or machine breakdowns.

I thus find myself led to the conclusion that, to the extent that piecework systems have an incentive effect, that effect lies in the financial encouragement it gives to applying normal capacity with continuous application of normal physical and mental concentration. It is not an incentive towards working harder in the sense of straining physical effort or pushing the pace of physical movement beyond that pace which is normal for the individual – other than for occasional spurts. It is an incentive to creativeness and to the mobilizing and use of increases in capacity as the individual himself grows and develops. As such, it gives a certain satisfaction, even where conditions of equity in payment are not completely fulfilled. If, however, the flow and character of work is unsteady or the times badly set, piecework systems begin to break down, because the operator loses the partial control he had over his pattern of earnings.

These considerations lead us back to the view of incentives which I put forward at the beginning of this chapter. Zest, enthusiasm, interest in work, manifest themselves in continuous application to the job, and in the full-out use of imagination and initiative. They may result in a higher level of output because they produce better and more efficient work, but not because the individual works physiologically faster. Indeed, as common sense would have it, and as many pieceworkers and piecework managers would aver, if a person puts on pressure to increase the physiological pace of his work, he is more than likely in the long run to diminish his efficiency and rate of output, to do work of poorer quality, and to be subject to fatigue.

We may suspect that piecework is not a very efficient means of facilitating the exercise of normal concentration and ability. It makes the pieceworkers a group apart. It encourages friction between managers and operators over the issue of tight and loose times. It assumes incorrectly that time studies can be objectively conducted, and leads as a result to endless argument. It encourages workers to hold on to jobs just below their actual level of capacity. And it weakens the fabric of sound management and leadership. If the damage caused by this last factor to efficiency and to sound industrial relations could be calculated, it would, I think, be seen to be extremely serious.

VIII

If, however, the above formulation of incentive is correct, it points to a simpler and more direct way than piecework and allied incentive systems, for encouraging good work at a reasonable rate of output – a way that is common to manual and non-manual work, to shop floor and high executive level, and to operational and specialist work. It depends upon the provision of a foundation of equitable payment for work, and a superstructure of opportunity to obtain progress in work and in financial reward in relation to one's progress in capacity.

This method – which implies a dynamic $\boxed{\text{W-C}}$-P pattern of payment and progress for each individual – I shall consider in part six, under the heading of the standard payment and progression method. It envisages a common motivation for everyone, since for anyone to achieve an equitable and abundant income, everyone has to do so. The topmost salaries are linked to the bottom by the equitable work-payment scale. The possibility is removed of any group enjoying equity or over-equity payment and abundance or over-abundance, at the expense of other groups who are not. Each individual would be equally exposed to the economic state of his society, since his own well-being would be linked to it in a manifestly observable way.

In short, each one would share in the group morale, participating in his society in the sense economically of being geared into it. This type of group morale is very different from that connected with group payment schemes and group bonus incentives. In such schemes each individual's situation is mechanically tied to the group, in the sense that each one's progress is the same. The non-requisite character of group bonus schemes is exposed by the fact that the contract to work cannot requisitely be a contract in a group. It is between each individual and his employer. Work is not done in genuine groups. It is done by individuals, or by collectives of individuals, the work of each one being identifiably his own. The instances where a task is done by more than one individual under conditions where the contribution of each is not identifiable are extremely rare. And, in my experience at least, the circumstance simply does not exist where a group of individuals works full-time as a group without possibility of separately identifying the work of each one.

It is of the very essence of executive work that a manager must assess the work of each of his subordinates individually. It is his responsibility to bind their work together by common policies and work-planning. Group bonuses are a concealed technique for foisting these managerial coordinative responsibilities on to the subordinate command, just as piecework foists managerial initiative on to the operators. I would distinguish genuine group morale, therefore, from these artificial and non-requisite procedures.

The group morale I am referring to is one which is built upon a procedure which recognizes individual differences and allows for different rates of individual progress, while yet linking individuals into a coherent social network. In such circumstances I believe a sophisticated sense of individual and group incentive may grow. It will be free from the individually frustrating 'groupishness' which sometimes masquerades under the heading of group psychology; and from the florid individualism and anti-social splitting off of the individual from his society which is brought about by individual bonus and commission schemes.

PART SIX

Problems of implementation

CHAPTER 13

The standard payment and progression method
I – Organization

I

In this concluding part of the book I have two aims. The first is to pull together the various threads of the theory I have presented, by considering the problem of its practical application within industry. The second is to consider some general social implications of the theory.

The practical implementation of the theory centres on what I shall term the *standard payment and progression method*. This method uses the time-span method of measuring level of work, the equitable work-payment scale for assigning payment levels, and the capacity growth curves as the basic datum line for administering individual progress. It is aimed towards achieving dynamic C-W-P equilibrium. It assumes that C-W-P equilibrium gives the optimum foundation for economic efficiency and for individual satisfaction.

I shall first outline the method. Then I shall consider in some detail the implications for executive organization in industry. For implementation of the standard payment and progression method throws into sharp relief some of the shortcomings of the methods of control of organization and manning currently practised in industry, especially the limitations in personnel methods and the policies governing personnel management. A considerable reorientation in personnel work is called for, and will be described. Following this description, I shall mention briefly the problem of modifying the equitable work-payment scale as necessary in the light of economic conditions and changes. In the succeeding chapter I shall refer to a number of questions of policy which arise in connexion with the details of the procedure (see also appendix 2).

In my concluding chapter I shall turn to the more general theme of the social implications which might follow from the theory of differentials in work and in payment, and of economic equity viewed in the light of the theory. In doing so I shall also touch upon the problem of the unconscious resistances which are likely to be encountered against progress towards explicit modes of achieving equity in economic relationships.

II

The standard payment and progression method is this:

1. Determine the level-of-work bracket for each role, and assign to it the equitable wage or salary bracket corresponding to the level of work.

2. Plot on an Earning Progression Data Sheet the achieved earning progression of each individual, along with the level-of-work bracket of the role he occupies.

3. Let the manager-once-removed (or higher) determine a potential progress assessment (P.P.A.) for each person on the basis of performance or work history, and express this as a capacity growth curve on the Earning Progression Data Sheet.

4. Adjust payment as necessary in accord with movements in the wages index.

5. Independently of these wages index adjustments, let the immediate manager assess the individual's performance in his work during the period under review:

   (a) if he judges his performance to have shown that he has worked at full capacity and at full stretch, then let his wage or salary be maintained at or brought to that level called for by the P.P.A.;

   (b) if his actual performance is judged to have fallen short of his potential, then let his wage or salary be placed at a level correspondingly lower than the level called for by his P.P.A.

6. If the continued performance of the individual gives evidence that his P.P.A. has been pitched too high or too low, then let the manager-once-removed alter the assessment in accord with the more comprehensive information and experience available.

7. If at any time, in response to a call for a spurt or special effort, an individual works beyond his normal pace and appli-

cation, then let him be paid an *ex gratia* payment over and above his wage or salary, at the time the spurt is made.

8. If the level of work in the role is undergoing permanent authorized change, then let the manager-once-removed sanction this change, record it, and alter the payment bracket accordingly.

9. If the level of capacity of an individual is too high or too low for the level of work in his role, consider whether to pay above or below the bracket or whether it is possible to adjust the work in the role to match the individual – while still conforming to the demands of the work situation – before deciding to remove the individual from the role or to indicate to him that further progress would require a change of role.

10. In the case either of a change in P.P.A. of the individual, or a change in the level of work of his role, the alteration and its implications for his progress and career future should be considered, and discussed with him.

III

There are certain minimum organizational requirements for the standard payment and progression method to be used. In order to describe these requirements, I must first state my view of the requisite structure of the executive organization concerning payment and progress.

The manager in charge of a role allocates work into it. The manager-once-removed authorizes the allocation. A similar and dependent principle can be seen to be at work in the case of the assessment and progress of subordinates. The manager assigns work to his subordinate, relies upon him to do work, and reviews the quality of his work. He is in a position to assess his performance and actual achievement, and his potential capacity for doing the work which he assigns to him. The manager is not in a satisfactory position, however, to assess his subordinate's potential for progress to higher levels of work. The next higher level of work is the manager's own level, and it would be unrealistic in general to rely upon a manager to be able to assess the potential capacity of subordinates to do work at his level – although there are undoubtedly some managers who are capable of doing so.

If we now move upwards to the level of the manager-once-removed a different type of responsibility emerges in connexion with the potential progress of subordinates. He is directly responsible – as are his own managerial subordinates – for assessing the accomplishment of his own immediate subordinate. But in the case of his subordinates at one remove, he is more concerned with potential. He sets policy or limits within which subordinates-once-removed are appointed and progressed – to avoid nepotism, to ensure that minimum personnel standards are maintained, to provide for future manpower requirements within his own immediate command, and (within policies set in turn by his own manager) to contribute to the manpower needs of other areas of the company*.

Against this background, responsibilities for rewarding current accomplishment and for assessing potential assume the pattern described. The manager-once-removed is responsible for deciding the potential progress assessment (P.P.A.) of individual members. This potential progress assessment having been made, it becomes the basic datum line against which the immediate manager constructs his assessment of his subordinate's actual performance, and in terms of which he rewards him. These organization notions are embedded in the standard payment and progression method which I have outlined.

The significance of this way of looking at the progression and payment policy can be illustrated in the diagram in figure 20. This diagram shows two subordinates, M and N, working in roles with the same level-of-work bracket of six months to one year. This level-of-work bracket has been authorized by the manager-once-removed who authorized the work content of the roles, and the form in which the work is allocated. He has thereby also allocated the salary bracket, which follows from the equitable rates current at any given time.

Both M and N are currently judged as performing at about the same level in the bracket. They are about one-fifth of the way up.

---

* An elaborated account of the structure and operation of this particular conception of the selection and manning responsibilities of the immediate manager and the manager-once-removed will be found in Wilfred Brown: *Exploration in Management*.

The manager-once-removed (assisted by his Personnel specialist, if he has one) must decide in the light of this current performance, past performance, his judgement about M's and N's future performance, and any other information he may have, whether to fix M's P.P.A. at 1.6 and N's at 1.0, as is implied by the current performance. If he does so (or if he confirms a previously decided P.P.A.), then the combined use of level-of-work brackets, the P.P.A. and the Earning Progression Data Sheet, allows the progression policy for M and N to be stated in explicit terms.

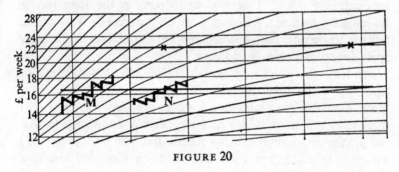

FIGURE 20

If M's performance is judged satisfactory, he may expect to progress at a rate that will take him to the top of his role in about five years' time, at 38 years of age; after that time, he will have to seek promotion, unless the level of work in his role has increased. Subordinate N, on the other hand, may expect slower progress towards the top of the bracket, settling out at that level when he is about 55 years of age. These prognostications can be discussed with M and N. They can form a framework for the manager's salary review of M and N. And they can be altered if either M's or N's performance in work should indicate that the existing P.P.A. is inaccurate. The P.P.A. is not a fixed and unchangeable assessment. It is a *pro tem.* assessment – the best that can be made at any given time in the light of the performance and work history of an individual.

IV

The application of these conceptions requires more, however, than simply a change in outlook towards certain aspects of

275

executive responsibility. It requires technical work of a highly specialized kind: to carry out level-of-work analyses, and job specifications, based on the time-span concept; to maintain earning progression data, and to analyse and interpret these data; and to assist in the appraisal of individuals for purposes of establishing their potential progress assessment. This technical work might ordinarily be considered to fall within the scope of personnel management. For it to do so will call for a pretty radical reorientation of personnel work. The achievement of this reorientation would, I believe, contribute in the long run to building the technical foundation which is necessary if personnel work is to become fully professionalized at the level of the other specialist technologies in industry.

For reasons which I shall explain, I shall refer to this specialist function as the organization and manning type of personnel work. I use this phrase because it states precisely the content of the function I have in mind. It is, perhaps, unfortunate that the phrase is so similar in sound to the title of the already well-established organization and methods function, and that the letters O and M apply to both. However, confusion need not arise if we avoid abbreviations and stick to the phrase itself.

The phrase organization and manning type of personnel work says what it means; it need come as no surprise, for example, that use of the standard payment and progression method requires the closest coordination within one executive function of specialist responsibility for executive organization and for manning. It might be said, however, that personnel work as presently established does include just such a range of responsibility. If it does, it does so in my experience in only the most limited and superficial way. Personnel work in most firms has tended to remain confined to three areas; first, labour relations; second, recruitment, selection and training; and third, welfare. It tends to be oriented exclusively towards people and away from the work of the enterprise, as many critics have pointed out. A revolution in its outlook would be implied in its shifting its orientation squarely on to people in relation to work and its organization; that is to say, on to the person-work relationship.

Personnel work is an incomplete function. It lacks its primary substance – the blood that genuine responsibility for work and efficiency would give it. This divorce from the day-to-day working life of the enterprise is reflected in the divorce between personnel work and organization. In firms which have established specialized responsibilities concerned with organization – with the structure and pattern of work roles, and their relation one to another – these responsibilities are very rarely indeed allocated into the personnel function. The general pattern is the setting up of an organization and methods department, or a work study department, or a straight organization department – none of which has very much to do with deciding on the work content of roles, or on role structure. The personnel function is not ordinarily considered suitable to carry such responsibilities. In most cases this judgement is not unfair. Personnel management itself often tends to reject – or at least tacitly to avoid – any responsibility for the organization of work systems, and remains withdrawn into its manning work. Even where this withdrawal is not sought, there are very few firms, if any, which have set up personnel departments with the establishment necessary to carry a full-scale organization and manning responsibility.

The effects of the splitting of specialist responsibility for personnel work from specialist responsibility for executive organization work are manifold. They can be readily seen if we examine for a moment the common procedure for filling a vacancy. The manager responsible for the vacant role requisitions for a new person to fill it. He sends the requisition form to the personnel department. If it is a role that has been well established and has an existing job description and payment bracket, then the personnel department may proceed forthwith to recruit possible candidates. If there is no established job description, the personnel department may have to help the manager to make one out, by helping him formulate the work he wants to get done and the kind of person he wants to do it.

But what then if selection is bad? Who is to be held responsible if an applicant recommended by the personnel department is accepted and then fails? And then another applicant. And then another. Is it the selection that is at fault? Or is the role not what it appears to be on paper? Or, if the role has been accurately described, is it one of those roles (not in the least uncommon) with conflicting responsibilities, which no normal person could easily cope with? It may be a combination of any or all of these factors and others besides. But it is difficult to tell so long as personnel work is split away from organization.

Under these conditions, it is not at all surprising that roles are so often described in terms of the person required to do the work, rather than in terms of the details of the discretionary responsibilities which must be discharged in connexion with the actual work task. Non-work-oriented personnel staff will usually specify jobs in that way. They have little choice, since their own responsibilities do not ordinarily bring them into contact with the details of the work system which they are helping to man.

This separation of manning from organization precludes the growth of a systematic basis for payment and progression. Those who are responsible for the organization and assessment of roles are not responsible for the payment and progression system. Conversely, the personnel function with specialist responsibility for the payment and progression system, is walled off from effective contact with the assessment and organization of the work content of roles which sets the level-of-work bracket, which in turn sets the limits of equitable payment and of individual progress in the role. The fixing of payment and of progression limits therefore comes to be based upon an intuitive judgement about the type of person who is sought to fill the role.

V

The organization and manning type of personnel work necessary for the application of the standard payment and progression method brings together into one specialist function the divided responsibilities which I have described. Under this conception the personnel specialist is accountable for assisting his operational manager to maintain an efficiently deployed executive organization and to keep it effectively manned. Before elaborating further this organization and manning function, I must mention briefly the conception of specialist responsibility which I am using. It is one worked out in social-analytic work with the Glacier Metal Company*.

I regard work as having three main dimensions: a person in a role, employing a technology, in accord with a programme, the whole occurring through time. The manager in charge of the work must himself set the objective of work and the targets for his subordinates, including time targets. He can use specialists to assist him with the control and coordination of the work of his subordinates along the dimensions of technology, programming, and organization and manning.

The three specialist functions are best considered as lateral extensions of the managerial role, concerned with advising the manager, and exercising staff authority to coordinate the work of the manager's operational subordinates within policies established by the manager himself. Within this framework, the personnel specialist, responsible for the organization and manning dimension, is involved in the same way as his colleagues in other specialist fields in assisting their manager to keep the work in his command flowing smoothly and efficiently.

Organizationally the structure of the situation is as illustrated in figure 21. The personnel specialist, AS, assists his manager,

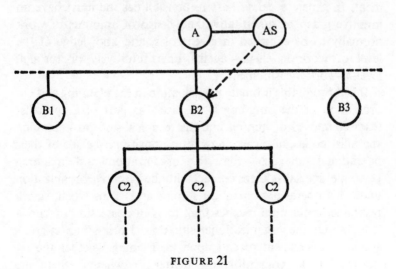

FIGURE 21

*See Wilfred Brown: *Exploration in Management*.

279

A, by coordinating the work of A's operational subordinates B^1, B^2, B^3, etc., with regard to the executive organizations they control, i.e., executive layers C and below, and the manning of those roles.

To begin with, therefore, AS must have a sophisticated knowledge of the work objectives which A has been set. He must help A in his planning to reach those objectives. He must have that intimate grasp of the content of the work, of the techniques which are to be used, and of the kind of work-mix and programming of work-flow which will enable him to coordinate his own work with his specialist colleagues and to influence methods design and programming.

He must know of the work which A has allocated to B, and the establishment which A has authorized B to employ in getting his work done. He must be able to assess the adequacy of this establishment in relation to the work task, taking into account the technology and the programme of work-flow and work-mix. More, he must keep himself apprised of any changes or impending changes in work-input, programming, technology, or supply of personnel, which are likely to be of such size or quality as to require modification in organization or establishment. In order to carry these responsibilities, he must have an intuitive grasp or quantitative knowledge of amounts of work normally to be expected in given roles, and knowledge of the level of work in them – again either intuitively or through level-of-work measurement.

It is through this intimate participation in the planning and co-ordination of the on-going work task – as part of a specialist team composed of himself and his technical and programming specialist colleagues, carrying staff authority on behalf of their operational manager – that the organization and manning personnel specialist keeps contact with the executive organization under his operational manager's command. Thus when, say, a personnel requisition reaches him, he is in possession of knowledge about the organizational situation. He has his on-going specialist assessment to call upon in deciding whether the requisition is a straightforward matter or whether there are accumulating changes in the situation – or forthcoming changes in connexion with their manager's forward plans – which call for him to get in touch with the requisitioning manager, and to review the whole matter with him with a view to agreeing any necessary modifications in organization.

He is in a position to keep abreast of the structure of payment throughout his manager's command because of his knowledge of the current work content of roles in that command. He knows of required changes in payment because of his direct involvement in work planning and his resulting knowledge of change in the work content of roles. Payment brackets for jobs can thus be modified on managerial initiative as and when permanent changes in work have occurred of sufficient size to be reflected in a change in the bracket. The personnel specialist thereby assists his manager to assume genuine managerial leadership in connexion with payment structure, rather than waiting for initiative to come from below in the form of piled-up grievances and complaints.

The manning of roles follows from the deep involvement with his manager's work task, and the organization of the work system to carry out that task. In the first place jobs are specified in terms of the targets or objectives of the work, and the discretionary and prescribed responsibilities to be carried in reaching those objectives. Such a specification points up both the formal knowledge required for the work (expressed in the prescribed content) and the kind of experience and interest needed (in order to exercise the discretion called for). Application of the standard progression method then puts the personnel specialist in possession of systematic information about the progress of individuals in their roles and the potential rate of change of personnel, and lays a basis for the development of systematic manpower plans.

In short, the operational manager, A, determines the work his subordinates B^1, B^2, etc. are to do. He authorizes an establishment of subordinates, C^1, C^2, etc., as necessary for them to get their work done, and lays down policies within which those subordinates are to be selected, paid and progressed. The organization and manning personnel specialist, AS, advises A on the establishment he needs to allocate to B for B to be able to get his work done; he advises on the optimum organizational structure;

ensures that B stays within A's policies on selection, payment and progression; keeps an up-to-date assessment of the potential capacity of C^1, C^2, etc.; and watches the progress of the whole of the C layer of personnel in order to discover those who are likely to outgrow their present roles and become available for promotion, or who may leave, and to formulate future manpower needs.

The other activities of a personnel specialist grow requisitely out of these central responsibilities for organization and manning. Training is that activity carried out to instruct members in the prescribed content of their roles and to familiarize them with the discretionary content including the communication of information on newly-introduced techniques and policies, or to prepare members for advancement and promotion by introducing them to the responsibilities they will have to carry. Counselling and welfare activities relate to helping individuals to formulate their future career plans and to overcome personal problems. Labour relations have to do with negotiating and legislating the policies on individual entitlements which set an important aspect of the prescribed framework for the organization and manning dimension of the work of the enterprise.

This formulation of personnel work may at first sight appear less humane and welfare-oriented, to have less human relations in it, than ordinary personnel work and its rather removed position from the work of the enterprise as an economic entity which must operate efficiently. The opposite, I would strongly hold, is in fact the case. Genuinely good human relations and individual welfare in work organizations arise from recognizing the reality of the work contract; that is to say, the reality of the fact that each individual's relation to the enterprise is founded on his contracting to do work in exchange for payment. If the enterprise organizes requisitely, fills its jobs soundly, pays equitably and progresses its individual members on a systematic basis and in accord with performance, then the basis is laid for serving the needs of both the enterprise and the individual. If this basis is soundly constructed, good personal and working relations are encouraged, and individual satisfaction may be heightened. The responsibility in the organization and manning type of personnel work is to give specialist assistance in keeping such a state of affairs in being.

VI

What steps then might have to be taken in order to establish the norms of equitable payment? Is legislation required? I am not at all convinced that it is. Governmental recognition of the existence of the norms of equity would be required, but legislation is not the only means for doing this. At least two other methods present themselves: assessment and publication of the norms by an appropriate ministry; and fixing the payment pattern for the civil service and nationalized industries in conformity with these norms.

Publication of the norms of equitable payment by an appropriate ministry would require a feed-in of information about reactions to payment, especially in the light of shifts in the wages index which might from time to time occur, and changes in the degree of abundance of the economy. How much the norms of differentials would be likely to change as a population became used to them is a matter which must remain open to conjecture, although the analysis which I have presented suggests that they would not change very much except with large changes in the abundance of the economy. In particular, if the norms of equitable payment were being used I would expect inflationary shifts in payment gradually to cease.

Implementation of the equitable work-payment scale in the civil service, nationalized industry, or other industrial or commercial enterprises could in no way be a matter of simply laying it on, even where there was a strong managerial desire to implement and an employee consensus in favour of doing so. Systematic experience with time-span measurement, and the assessment of a sufficient number of roles, are required. There is much experience to suggest that slow and technically sound growth in the early stages makes for rapid growth and implementation in due course if the conceptions prove reliable and valid, and become more widely understood.

In the presence of nationally recognized and published norms of equitable payment for the level of work in any given role, it would fall to individual enterprises to carry out the actual job of implementation. These norms are not like nationally negotiated minimum or standard wages or salaries. They cannot be foisted en masse on an entire industry by applying them to all jobs which have the appropriate title and an apparently similar work content. They must be applied in terms simply of the level of work in each role, regardless of its title or its apparent similarity to other roles. The aim is equal payment for equal levels of work, and not equal payment for the same title or for any other appearances which may cloak the true level of work or changes in level of work in a role. In practice it does not appear to be necessary to get out a full-scale time-span analysis of every single role. Measurement of a well distributed sample of key roles provides a basis for keeping all roles in line by reference to the known datum points.

CHAPTER 14

The standard payment and progression method
II – Policies and procedures

I

THE standard payment and progression method changes the frame of reference of wage and salary review from the question, 'By how much – if anything – should I increase A's salary as compared with B's?', into the question, 'Has A's performance shown a reasonable achievement during the period under review?'

By a reasonable achievement is meant an achievement that is reasonable for the subordinate in question in the judgement of the reviewing manager. It is the kind of performance which would be expected from that particular subordinate if he were working at his full capacity. A manager, to be worthy of his position, must be able to pass judgement on this question of achievement in performance, and it is my experience that competent managers can do so. The judgement demanded requires simply that a manager should know his subordinates and should know how they are doing their work, matters which ought to fall well within the scope of normal and straightforward managerial responsibility.

This reliance upon managerial judgement in assessing a subordinate's level of performance may seem to destroy any objectivity there might be in the procedure. It would appear to do so only if one believes in the first place that complete objectivity in judgement of behaviour is possible. I do not believe it is possible, even theoretically. Only partial objectivity is achievable. Some factors must be left to human judgement. The factors which can be objectively determined are the level of work and the equitable work-payment scale. The capacity growth curves are a construction which may be brought increasingly into approximation with the objective reality of the pattern of growth of human capacity. But performance is not, and cannot be, objectively measurable. Even if there existed an objective measure of capacity, this measure could not indicate whether or not a given individual had exercised his full capacity without inhibition during the period under review. Performance has to be judged by the manager*.

It might be argued that this procedure is surely stretching managerial judgement too far. But what other choice is there? In fact, an organization is no better than the capacity of its managers to judge the work of their subordinates. There is nothing automatic about these matters. The standards of efficiency of the organization are involved. If managers' judgements are too severe or too lax – if they demand too much or too little – efficiency will suffer either through disaffection or lassitude. Managers must, requisitely, judge their subordinates. The standard payment and progression method not only takes this fact into account; it prevents its being lost sight of.

In making these judgements it is important that managers confine their attention to performance and achievement, and disregard intentions. Good or bad intentions neither make nor mar a business if they do not show in performance. Thus to separate intentions from achievement is not to say that intentions are unimportant. The personal merit, character, or integrity of a subordinate are of great importance in terms of the wisdom and desirability of retaining his services. A person of lesser capacity may well be worth keeping in preference to a person of greater capacity and performance but lesser personal merit and integrity. But the reward for personal merit of this kind ought requisitely to be reflected in security of employment and not in payment level.

II

If managers are capable of doing their job of assessing the performance of their subordinates, the standard payment and pro-

---

* There are many in industry who still cling to the false hope that the performance of an individual may be assessed by some financial or other index or indices. These quantitative data may give a measure of output or the result of work. They do not, and cannot, give an assessment of how well the subordinate has performed in overcoming the multitude of unpredictable difficulties in achieving that result. They can help a manager in making his judgement of performance. They cannot themselves make that judgement.

gression method ensures the rewarding of these subordinates within a common frame of reference, which is at the same time a differentiated one. For example, due weight can be given to differences in age: if an older man and a younger man have demonstrated equal cooperativeness and willingness, a common tendency is to give the same size of increase to each, and to overlook the fact that the younger man is usually increasing more rapidly in capacity and requires a correspondingly more rapid rate of progress. Equivalent treatment of their subordinates by managers in different parts of the firm can be ensured, because the potential progress assessments of individuals are controlled at a higher level.

The sensitivity of the capacity growth curves to age can be seen by reference to the difference in progression curves of individuals at, say, 28 and 32 years of age at the one-year time-span level. It is essential that managers have a differentiated picture of the age and normal expected rate of advance of all their immediate subordinates. I have found that plotting the current salary levels (corrected to June 1955) of all a manager's immediate subordinates on the same Earning Progression Data Sheet, has a salutary effect in helping him to achieve just such a differentiated perception.

As a result of a systematic policy, methods of control which make use of artificial and stereotyped criteria may be avoided. Among these artificial criteria is the use of automatic annual increments which progress all individuals through a given bracket at the same predetermined rate, regardless of the age at which each particular person entered the job and his rate of potential progress at the time of entry. I would include also those intuitive references to 'market values' by which increases are so often justified: the argument being to bring the wage or salary paid into line with changes in outside market conditions.

Avoided also is the common procedure whereby a person is progressed until he reaches his so-called level and then flattened off. This practice often applies in a particularly deleterious way to higher-level personnel. Thus a man reaches, say, a general manager position at £5,500 per annum at the age of 48. If the employing firm regards this as his true level, he is then continued at that salary, with occasional adjustments for cost of living*. The findings I have described lead to the opposite conclusion; namely, that such a person normally continues to grow in capacity and performance, and that this growth should be recognized in salary progressions. Indeed, given normal development, such a person as I have indicated is likely to progress to one further rank in capacity and to seek promotion.

III

There is a special problem worth noting in connexion with the potential progress assessment of younger men of high potential – under the age of 32/35. The earnings of many of these individuals – from hourly-rated to senior managerial positions – appear, both to the individuals concerned and to their managers, to be fitting so far as concerns the money they might earn elsewhere, but incorrect so far as concerns the potential progress assessment they seem to imply. That is to say, while the earnings seem to be fitting for the present, if they are extrapolated into the future along an earning progression curve, they point to a level which is far beyond what seems to be the potential capacity of the individual.

There is a point in connexion with such curves that needs watching. At the present time, there is a pretty intense scramble in industry to find young men of high potential. As I indicated in chapter 10, the general tendency in large organizations is for groups of younger men of possibly high potential capacity to be specially selected and to be progressed along a fairly rapid *trial progression* in the early stages of their careers (often on a salary-for-age scale). By the end of this period of trial progression, those who are deemed to have the potential to maintain this rate of progress in their work and earnings are picked out. Those who are considered not to have the potential they were at first assumed to have, may then find themselves being progressed more slowly until they find a rate of progression consistent with their real potential capacity.

This trial progression of selected groups of younger men of high potential in large organizations has its repercussions

* This practice may be noted in the progressions shown in figure 27.

288

everywhere in setting an automatically high earning potential for all such men until they prove themselves and settle into their normal progression. Because of the incorrect picture of potential progress which may get built up in the minds of both managers and subordinates, it is unwise to consider fixing other than a trial potential progress assessment for them. The higher the level of work involved, the later the age to which the trial P.P.A. should extend: up to 30 years of age for men whose eventual progress may be to a two-year time-span level of work, increasing to up to the age of 35 for men who appear to be moving eventually beyond a ten-year time-span level of work.

It may also be noted that in the case of younger men (say, under 35) being rapidly promoted into high-level positions (say, rank 3 or 4*), these appointments are sometimes made at a point before they are quite ready for the job. Their rapidly developing capacity, however, and their potentially high conceptual ability may enable them to carry the role for an initial period on a quasi-training basis. In considering whether to assess such individuals as being at, or above, or below, the bottom bracket for the job, the possible existence of a training and induction element should be kept in mind.

On the other side of the coin, as I have described in chapter 10†, is the fact that managers are sometimes influenced not to progress young men of high potential at a rate consistent with their growth in capacity, because they somehow feel them to be either too young to be given certain levels of responsibility, or, if they are given them, too young to be paid the salaries that might ordinarily go with them.

IV

The procedures I am outlining have a not inconsiderable effect upon the relations between various levels of managers, and between a subordinate and his manager. Thus, the manager-once-removed can keep a check upon the capacity of his subordinate managers to assess and review their subordinates.

* The concept of ranks is described in my paper 'A preliminary sketch of a General Structure of Executive Ranks' in *Glacier Project Papers*.
† See description of case of Mr. B, p. 222.

Given potential progress assessments set by the manager-once-removed, his subordinate manager must either grant increases which keep his own subordinates' payment in line with those assessments, or else state the reason why he has not. Nor can the subordinate manager avoid this scrutiny of his assessment work merely by automatically progressing his subordinates at the rate called for by the potential progress assessment. For if he does so, he is saying that his subordinates have been working right up to scratch, and so the results achieved by his command ought to reflect this happy situation. Moreover, those of his subordinates who are moving up through their payment bracket will eventually reach the top, in which case, if their performance does not justify promotion, the inadequacy of the judgement underlying the regular payment progression will come to light.

I have frequently encountered the following situation. A manager avoids the responsibility of assessing his subordinates by giving them all a common moderate increase, the implication being that he is satisfied with their work. The effect of such a policy is to under-progress the young subordinates and to over-progress the older ones. If any of his younger subordinates feel entitled to a larger increase, he gets out of doing anything about it by referring to the increase already granted. The manager will of course get no complaints from the older over-progressed members.

The standard payment and progression method may serve to obviate such difficulties. The subordinate who is being reviewed is provided with a means of evaluating his manager's true opinion of him. If his manager does not grant him increases which keep him on a line of progress corresponding to his potential progress assessment, he may expect to know the reason why.

Contrariwise, if a manager commends his subordinate and tells him what good work he has done during the period under review, then the subordinate may expect financial progress at a rate which corresponds to his potential progress assessment. Should he not get it, he has available an objective basis on which to raise the matter with his manager.

In short, objective procedures for paying and progressing in-dividuals support sound managerial work, and expose managerial evasiveness or *laisser-faire*. They require a manager to commit himself to make judgements, to support them, to be open about them, and to modify them if he is wrong. Equally, they require that subordinates face up to the fact that judgements of their performance, and their career prospects, are requisitely the judgements of their manager and of managers higher up. These are very human matters with no absolute standards to call upon to resolve disagreements between a subordinate and his manager on the subject of the subordinate's performance. The basic safeguard of the subordinate's rights lies in mechanisms which require that the manager's judgements be openly made both to the subordinate and to the higher managers.

V

Let me now consider the methods of rewarding performance below assessed potential, and performance at potential but with special effort producing a greater quantity of work than normal.

A person's work can be inhibited for many reasons – among them physical illness, emotional disturbance, preoccupation with personal problems outside work, lack of interest in work, ageing or premature deterioration. Under such conditions, his performance may continue below his potential for long periods of time, or, indeed, indefinitely. We usually describe such a person as not matching up to his potential, as not realizing his full potential, as not achieving what he showed promise of being capable of achieving. It seems to me to be realistic to express this circumstance by maintaining his potential progress assessment unchanged, and reflecting his actual performance in earnings correspondingly below his potential. I am, of course, distinguishing this situation from that in which the potential progress assessment itself clearly proves to have been inaccurate and calls for a downward modification.

It does not seem to me to be realistic, however, to reflect special effort in a wage or salary above the potential progress assessment. Individuals can work up to their potential capacity, and not above it. They can, as I have discussed, produce greater than normal output by intensive concentration and acceleration.

They can do this not indefinitely, but intermittently for short periods of time. When such special effort has been executively called for, reward in the form of a special bonus or *ex gratia* payment is a sound means of recognizing a good response, without introducing the complications of establishing a person's wage or salary at a level above that which his continued performance will be likely to warrant. The proper time to make *ex gratia* payments is at the time the special effort is made. It shows immediate appreciation. It avoids the danger of forgetting. It prevents confusion with normal progress review.

If the person shows evidence of being able to maintain the higher rate of output without special effort, then the most reasonable assumption is that his potential progress has been assessed too low. It ought to be correspondingly increased, and his actual earning progression raised also.

There is much evidence – for example in wartime – that some individuals are capable of rising to unexpected heights of capability. There are at least two possible reasons for this: one, that under conditions of high national morale, inhibitions against the expression of normal pace, concentration and ability are removed, and normally vigorous attention is directed towards the task; second, that individuals with unrecognized potential get and take opportunities for higher responsibilities because of high personal morale and weakening of social and personal restrictions and barriers which might previously have stood in the way of progress. Probably both these factors are at work together, the implication being that under ordinary conditions there is a significant amount of human talent which lies wasting in the community, a loss to the country and a source of festering disaffection.

VI

Realistic and practical career assessment and planning for the individual, and manpower planning for the enterprise, become possible when progression is systematically considered. I use the adjectives realistic and practical to indicate that I am not here speaking of vocational guidance provided by a firm on a welfare basis, the expected return being the goodwill of the employee.

Career assessment is as much a practical necessity for the employing organization as it is for the individual. It is the necessary foundation for manpower planning.

Once potential progress assessments and level-of-work analyses exist for any section of a firm – whether a department, or an immediate command, or a particular occupational group spread throughout the firm – an estimate can be made of the rate at which particular areas are likely to be affected by individuals rising to the top of their current roles and outgrowing them*. Such an estimate will be of the nature of a first approximation (and may take into account executive plans for expansion or contraction of activities in departments or in spheres of work). This first approximation can then be pursued in more detail, however, by discussion of their future with individuals, particularly in areas which appear to be likely to be subject to high labour turnover.

Moreover, plans for organization and manning and for individual careers can be considered in a dynamic frame of reference; that is to say, under conditions where the level-of-work bracket in a role may be undergoing movement upwards or downwards as a result of changes in the work content of the role.

If the level of work in a role goes up as a result of a permanently established change in its work content, the wage or salary bracket would have to be appropriately increased. It must not be assumed, however, that the increase in payment bracket for

* It is outside the scope of this book to go into detailed elaboration of these techniques for manpower assessment and planning. For those who are particularly interested, however, may I mention two examples. (1) Plot as points on one Earning Progression Data Sheet the current earning level of all the members of one department, or all engineers, or all accountants, etc. You will get a comprehensive picture of future growth which, while perhaps not exact in each individual case, will nevertheless be significant for the total population. (2) Set out on one single sheet (single-cycle or two-cycle semi-logarithm paper is ideal) the names of all, say, your immediate subordinates and subordinates-once-removed, ordered in accord with their P.P.A. index. It will give you a systematic comparison of your judgement, as reflected in payment, of their relative capacities with the age factor removed. See Elliott Jaques: *Progression Handbook*, for a detailed description of these methods.

the role must necessarily imply an immediate increase in payment for the person occupying the role. Quite the contrary. If he is already being paid at a level consistent with his performance, within an equitable payment bracket for the role as it was, then there would be no call for an increase in his pay. I can illustrate this point in the accompanying diagrams in figure 22.

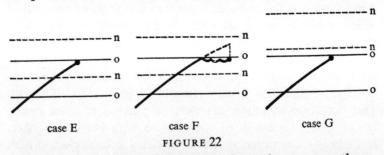

case E   case F   case G

FIGURE 22

If o-o represents the old bracket and n-n the new one, then a person progressing as shown in E would warrant no immediate increase. He has gained the opportunity for further advance in his current role. A person who, as in case F, had already hit the ceiling of his role, would warrant an immediate increase should his performance merit it. In the situation represented by case G, however, the role can be seen to have outgrown its occupant, and reorganization and shifting of personnel will be required if the work is to get done and the individuals concerned are to avoid being subjected to the breakdown pressures of a $\boxed{\begin{smallmatrix} W \\ I \\ C \end{smallmatrix}}$ -P pattern of employment.

But what happens if the level of work in the role goes down, also as a result of a permanently established change in its work content? Would the policy be for a person's wage or salary to be reduced? This question is one which has aroused a considerable amount of anxiety, for it would appear that my conclusions lead automatically to a policy of reducing payment if the level of work in a role drops. In order to answer this question, it must first be recognized that it is really two questions: one, would the payment bracket for the role be decreased? And, two, would the individual in the role have his wage or salary reduced? The answer to the first question is yes. The second is simply not answerable as formulated – there is more to it than the question of payment brackets alone. I can elaborate this point, by reference to the three diagrams in figure 23.

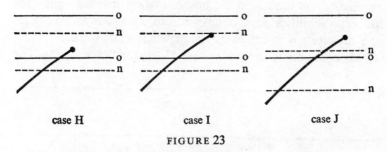

case H   case I   case J

FIGURE 23

In the situation represented by case H, the occupant of the role would not lose out in either money or position, but his opportunity for progress without changing roles would have been diminished. This restriction is more marked in the type of circumstance represented in case I. Here the occupant – who, before the change, had scope for further advancement – has been brought hard against the ceiling of his role as a result of the decrease in its level of work. It is only the third case – J – that presents the immediate problem for the individual, as in G above, for the occupant finds himself in a role that has grown too small for him; i.e., he is in a $\boxed{\genfrac{}{}{0pt}{}{C}{W}}$-P situation, and thus threatened by payment beneath his capacity. Whether or not such a reduction occurs depends mainly on whether alternative work is available at his current level of capacity. In order to go into this question more thoroughly it will be useful to consider it together with case G above.

VII

It is the two cases G and J that have the potential hardship in them. But, within the framework of the present theory, it will be manifest that the basic problem in both cases is one of getting adequate employment for the individual, and not one of payment. Both cases are familiar; they occur often enough in real life. Being outgrown by one's job may come about, for example, through growth of business or technical changes. What is frequently experienced as a painful change, and one not very often openly acknowledged, is that an older man, in an expanding and technically advancing organization manned by young colleagues, may eventually find himself in the position where his colleagues and his responsibilities have outgrown him, and he must give place to a substitute who can carry the higher level of work.

This situation is shown in case K (figures 24 and 25). The

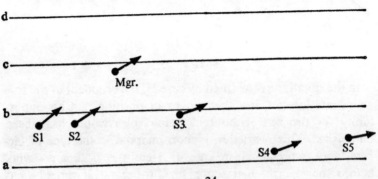

FIGURE 24

manager is about to progress into the next higher rank c–d. His three subordinates S_1, S_2, and S_3, are also about to progress into a higher rank, b–c – the rank just being left behind by the manager. Subordinates S_4 and S_5, however, while still progressing in capacity, are nevertheless not likely to advance beyond their present rank. Thus, when the inevitable organizational shift illustrated in figure 25 occurs, S_4 and S_5 must, requisitely, be left behind. The usual procedure, however, is to maintain the team,

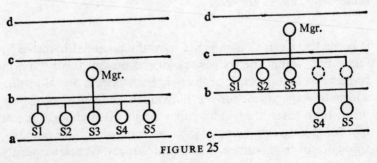

FIGURE 25

and to let S_4 and S_5 break down at the higher level demanded of them, and then to remove them from their roles*.

These circumstances are ordinarily not talked about or faced up to. The fact that some members of a group of colleagues may outgrow the others is a taboo subject. Contrariwise, however, decrease in the level of work in a role is more frequently talked about. It may come about through change or contraction in business, or through reorganization of responsibilities, or through change in method such as increased mechanization or automation.

Before considering redeployment of individuals, however, there is one possibility which must first be explored – that of a partial restructuring of the role so that there is once again a sufficient match between the occupant and the role. In stating this possibility I am not suggesting the proposition that executive organization should be designed around the individuals employed in the organization. Executive organization is fundamentally a function of the work that is to be done†. But work is dynamic, and its dynamics must be reflected in organizational flexibility and change. There is always some opportunity, therefore, for modification of the work content of individual roles. Sometimes the opportunity is great. Sometimes it is very small. But the degree of opportunity is always worth investigating if the employing organization is to avoid being guilty of merely pushing

*There is an implied assumption here that the growth of a firm is a function of the time-span capacity of its top management group. That assumption is intended. I believe that this factor is the prime factor in the growth or contraction of firms. My experience leads me to believe, moreover, that the rate of growth or contraction of the individual firm can be predicted by taking into account the time-span capacity and age of its top management. To do so requires that this group, including the Managing Director, be plotted on an Earning Progression Data Sheet, and the individual progressions extrapolated, say, two to five years ahead. Look especially for movements of individuals across the 1-year, 2-year, and 5-year time-span boundaries, as these broadly delimit managerial ranks (see *Measurement of Responsibility*). Predictions about what is likely to happen may then be derived by scrutiny of the internal consistencies or contradictions which the constructed future picture throws up. This exercise may prove a useful one for managing directors.

†This point was set out in *The Changing Culture of a Factory*, and is pursued in depth by Wilfred Brown in *Exploration in Management*.

people around. Where a reorganization of the work is possible, it may be accomplished by the manager freeing himself for other duties by allocating some of his own responsibilities into the role. Or, conversely, he may take back certain responsibilities and increase his own duties. Or he may redistribute some of the responsibilities to other subordinate roles, or allocate additional responsibilities from other roles.

Under such conditions, the subordinate may be left in his role. The level of work is held intact, or nearly so, and so, therefore, is the payment bracket. If, however, an adequate degree of restructuring is not possible because of the dynamics of the work situation, redeployment becomes necessary. Given that a sufficient endeavour to restructure the role has been made, redeployment cannot reasonably be regarded either as irresponsible or as counter to individual rights.

VIII

When restructuring of a subordinate's role to make it fit him is not possible, the requisite solution is to be able to transfer the occupant of the role to another role – at a higher or lower level than the new level of the one he is in, as the case may be – so that he is working once again in a role consistent with his capacity. Given such a solution, the problem of what happens to a man's payment simply does not arise. He continues to receive the same payment, since he is receiving equitable payment for the level of work he is carrying.

This solution to the problem throws the emphasis where it ought really to be. If a man's job outgrows him, or drops beneath him, the problem is to provide a suitable job. This simple fact is unlikely to be very widely accepted at first. Too many emotional obstacles are in the way. In the first place, it is argued, no-one readily accepts a lower position if his job outgrows him. This argument is a powerful and common one, although, of course, its formulation is a distortion of the facts. If a person's job outgrows him and he moves into another role at his own level, he is not dropping in actuality; but he may feel himself to be dropping relatively to others who may be advancing more rapidly than he is. It is this appearance of falling behind that produces a sense of loss of face or of self-esteem.

My experience, although limited, bolsters the theoretical conclusion that this emotionally distorted reaction is less likely to occur under conditions where there is an active policy of placing people in roles whose level of work matches their capacity. Loss of face takes a back seat to reality, when the reality is one in which the manifest value – both to the individual and to the enterprise – of each person working under $\boxed{\text{C-W}}$-P conditions is not only recognized but is the object of known and agreed practices and procedures.

In like vein, the most intense problems can and do arise when level of work drops. The most familiar type of disturbance is that associated with the drop in level of work when work is mechanized or standardized as a result of technical advances or of work study. The introduction of such changes and innovations is frequently resisted, even when the number of roles will remain unchanged, on the grounds that the individuals are likely to suffer a loss of earnings. Often compromise solutions are arrived at, with an agreement to keep the earnings at a level artificially high for the new reduced levels of work. But trouble still continues because the character of the work is no longer up to the calibre of the employees. A $\boxed{\begin{smallmatrix} C \\ i \\ W \end{smallmatrix}}$-P situation is created. Discontent with the new processes is stirred, which becomes particularly strong if there is no opportunity for a drift to occur to other employment.

If faced squarely, technical progress of the kind outlined requires to be accompanied by a planned redeployment of those members who will be precipitated into a $\boxed{\begin{smallmatrix} C \\ i \\ W \end{smallmatrix}}$-P situation as a result of the change. Redeployment of this kind is requisitely an integral part of the development programme itself. Attending to the payment side may alleviate temporary distress, and where special financial arrangements are made as a temporary tiding-over measure, then they are all to the good. But they cannot in the long run make up for the basic requirement of an agreed policy of planned redeployment.

Failure to tackle the redeployment issue on an explicit and worked-out basis leads to the notoriously strangling resistances to change which characterize many sections of industry. These resistances occur just as much in the form of unconscious sabotaging of development plans by high-level personnel who have intuitively sensed that they are among those likely to be left behind by the developments, as in the more open form of resistance expressed by manual or office workers. A society must accompany its technological inventiveness by an equally realistic and concrete policy of enabling satisfactory redeployment shifts to occur. In the absence of such a policy, and without the capacity of individual enterprises to plan and work out in detail the necessary redeployment shifts and transfers, the deeper unconscious as well as conscious anxieties are stimulated and aroused. Technological progress is obstructed, and hatred and suspicion are built up against the very processes which could in the end lead to an increase in economic abundance.

IX

In thus outlining the standard payment and progression method, I am not intending to speak of perfection in arrangements. But some of the common gross and unnecessary difficulties ought readily to be avoidable. It is not necessary, for example, for a firm to remain unaware of the fact that one or more of its members has reached the ceiling in his job (whether an explicit or implicit ceiling) and is bouncing against that ceiling with opportunity for further progress inhibited because of his desire to remain with the firm. It is true that mere explicit recognition of the situation does not automatically remove the problem. But it could prevent what so commonly occurs – the resentment and disaffection which are stirred in an individual on those occasions when the employing organization blindly and incorrectly maintains that it is providing a reasonable rate of advance for him and cannot understand what it calls his unreasonable or even neurotic dissatisfaction. It is disturbing enough in itself for an individual to find that there is no opportunity for advance when he is ready for it. It is like rubbing salt into wounds, however, when the employer at the same time remains blind to the capacity of his subordinate and, by not openly recognizing and admitting that he is for the time being under-employed, makes what is tantamount to the explicit judgement that that individual's capacity is no higher than his current status or level of work.

There are few circumstances more galling to a person than this combination of under-employment of his capacity and the failure of his employer to recognize it. Yet many managers would nevertheless maintain that it is better to deny that a subordinate is capable of a higher level of work or deserving of higher reward or status for his current work, than to admit this fact if there is no possibility of advancing him. They would argue that to let the subordinate know that he is capable of carrying greater responsibility than he has would be to upset him unnecessarily. There is much familiar experience which shows this desire to let sleeping dogs lie to be unrealistic and escapist. The real disaffection which results causes disturbance and inefficiency which outweigh the temporary peace of mind which the manager believes he may gain from keeping quiet.

A typical example of the disaffection described is that of the employee who had come to be regarded as a chronic malcontent and a ringleader of malcontents. He was experienced as a constant thorn in the side of management. For his own part, he held that he was trying to establish not only that he was being unjustly treated, but that the management tended pretty consistently to be tardy in giving due recognition and reward to its employees. Analysis of his job and of his potential progress showed him to be both under-employed and under-rewarded. He was capable of a higher level of work; and his current level of work warranted his having a higher salary and a higher status than he had. Eventual promotion to a job consistent with his capacity, together with recognition in salary and status, changed his relationship with the firm. He settled down and got on with his job.

In citing the foregoing example, I am not trying to say that militancy in individuals arises only from the shortcomings of managers; nor that the person concerned underwent a personality change; nor yet that managers should recognize the worth of their subordinates just in order to avoid militant retribution from them if they do not give this recognition. I wish simply to make the point that this single instance is a quite typical illustration of the tensions which are set going when the capacities of individuals are bottled up. If this circumstance occurs on any scale within a department or a factory, then it is pretty certain that low morale will result, which may express itself in mass disaffection.

Herein lies the great hidden disease in unemployment. Some economists speak of the need for something like a three per cent level of unemployment in order to avoid inflation in a capitalist economy. The human wastage in such a figure is in itself appalling. But at that level of unemployment, another equally devastating effect occurs. The freedom for each one to seek and find his own level in work and in reward is greatly diminished. Indeed, it is precisely this diminution in freedom which is held to be essential to reduce the pressure towards wages inflation, and hence towards a general inflationary trend in the economy. What gets overlooked is the under-utilization and under-recognition of the employed sector of the population which comes into force just as soon as the doors to alternative employment begin to shut. Those who do have jobs do not complain out loud about their work and progress when work is scarce. They burn inside with resentment against a society which can under-value the worth of human beings. Spontaneous recessions create difficulties enough for both employers and employees. Planned under-employment, apart from its inhumanity, is planned social disincentive and inefficiency*.

X

If payment is to be held to equitable levels throughout industry, it may be asked how then is satisfactory mobility of labour to be achieved: for example, into those industries which might be especially important for the total economy of a nation or its security? First, by the provision of good working conditions and special attention to sound progressing of individuals. These conditions – especially that of sound progression – are possible

*The connexion may be noted with the chronic under-employment of native populations in colonial countries, which has such crippling effects when these nations achieve independence.

in prosperous expanding industries with their great attracting power, given a fixed equitable payment system, because of their great opportunities for individual progress. Second (as was mentioned in chapter 1), by payment, where called for, of special bonuses, but without tampering with the wage and salary structure. These actions may be supported by appeal to that loyalty and integrity of citizens which can be called upon when work and an equitable income are in any case available to all. Reduce anxiety, and individuals simply do become more realistic and socially cooperative in behaviour.

It will be noted that this policy precludes over-equity payment as a means of attracting labour. I realize that with full or abundant employment, collusive over-payment might be stimulated. The situation would not be quite the same however, as at present. When over-payment occurs now, there are no objective standards which permit that fact to be explicitly recognized by all concerned. Self-justified denial is easy. Under the policy I am describing, a firm could offer over-payment, and employees accept it, only as a conscious and wilful anti-social act.

But what about the enterprise that cannot afford to pay in accord with the equitable differential pattern? How is it to attract the necessary labour? There is no easy answer. It must pay in accord with equity, like every other enterprise, or take its chances on failing. So long as an enterprise is conducted within the private sector of industry rather than the governmental or nationalized sector, then it must be capable of standing up to the normal forces of competition. True, inability to pay equitably would show up immediately, rather than remaining obscured for long periods of time in the absence of a known equitable differential payment structure. Inefficiency would be exposed more quickly, and whatever else the effects, the inadvertent taking of money from employees to subsidize the work of an enterprise would be eliminated. If the employees wished to contribute part of their incomes by accepting less than equitable rates, that would be their prerogative, but at least they would know what they were doing.

In the case of non-profitable enterprises considered by the government to be necessary to the national economy or to national security, the government ought itself to subsidize equitable payment. If the doing of certain work is in the interest of the nation, then the nation as a whole must support it.

CHAPTER 15

Requisite law and the equitable society

I

IT is my hope that the findings I have presented, and the theory built up from these findings, may contribute to a more orderly and objective way of dealing with the disordered state of industrial relations, differential payment, and the employment of individual talent. In order for them to do so, certain fundamental responsibilities will have to be recognized as belonging respectively to the State, the enterprise, and the individual.

To the government of the nation falls the responsibility for seeking to achieve and maintain abundance of employment, and to manage the economy so as to move towards economic abundance. In connexion with payment, the government would keep the current equitable work-payment scale under scrutiny and announce any change in it. It would have to govern the relation between personal taxation and payment levels to keep a proper balance between public and private spending.

To the employing enterprise goes the responsibility for pursuing its economic aims with realism and creative initiative. It must be requisitely organized and manned, in the way that effective organization and manning type of personnel work may help to achieve. It must know its work sufficiently well to keep an explicit appreciation of the level-of-work brackets for its various roles by reference to level-of-work measurement datum points. It must administer equitable payment brackets for the level-of-work brackets in those roles. To the employing organization falls also the responsibility for taking initiative in progressing its members at a rate consistent with their performance, within the limits of the work which it has available – recognizing that no employing organization can hope to guarantee to have just the right role at just the right time to suit the growing capacity and interests of every one of its employees. It would be charged with helping people for whom it could not provide adequate opportunity for progress, to leave and to find appropriate jobs in other firms.

It is this responsibility for payment and progress which resolves the problem of managerial leadership which I touched upon in the first chapter. It is the manager's responsibility to know his subordinates and the work allocated to them. The equitable work-payment scale then gives him the datum line needed for making fair payment. Initiative and responsibility for ensuring fair payment and appropriate progress thus become an integral part of the leadership situation in managing subordinates. They are an essential part of the process of getting an efficient organization.

To the individual falls the responsibility for deciding on his career and training. He must choose which work he wants to do, and seek out the training relevant to that work. He must seek appropriate opportunities at change points in his career. When, for example, he reaches the limit of potential for progress in his current role, he must decide which new line to try to follow, as in the case of the manual worker who reaches the point where he must make a switch to some kind of technical, supervising, or office work, if he is to make further headway in his career. And he must discharge his responsibilities in his job.

In short, the nation and the enterprise may be responsible for maintaining the external conditions necessary for effective work and progress. The individual must direct his own use of these conditions in following the career he chooses, and deploy his capacity in fulfilling his work obligations. If, under these conditions, he finds he has doubts and anxieties, then he carries the further and important responsibility of not foisting these personal problems on to his work relationships. He must take them to where he can get professional assistance if he wants help with them.

II

Two sets of conditions are of paramount importance for achieving the acceptance of these responsibilities by the state, the enterprise and the individual. First is the explicit and conscious social recognition of the human aspiration towards differential equity and of the existence of norms of equity. This condition I have discussed at length. Second is the establishment of optimum socio-economic conditions – or at least an observable movement towards such conditions – comprising abundant employment, an equitable differential distribution of earnings, and opportunity for individuals to advance in work at a rate consistent with their capacity.

The provision of optimum socio-economic conditions includes two factors which are well beyond the scope of the present study, although their effects have been taken into account in my analysis. These are the achievement of abundant employment, and some hope of movement towards an abundant economy. These conditions, or at least an explicit governmental policy and programme designed to achieve them, are fundamental to my considerations.

Although my work and my analysis are within a more limited frame than would allow for consideration of how abundant employment is to be achieved, one comment may be made. It has become a widespread and deeply ingrained belief that we work most efficiently when we are driven by economic fear. This type of argument is at the core of the reasoning behind the destructive assumption that unless there is a certain amount of unemployment – say, two to three per cent – there will be three serious consequences: first, wages inflation due to the increased bargaining power of labour; second, a let-down in the incentive to do a fair day's work; and third, difficulty in attracting and retaining an optimum labour force.

The present analysis leads to precisely opposite conclusions. It underlines the critical importance of equitable payment differentials, abundantly available work, and abundant opportunity for progress, as conditions which arouse the objective and realistic sense of equilibrium in us. When this sense is tapped by external conditions we work at our freest and best, and our hate, greed and envy are least aroused. Under these conditions, the scrambling for differential improvement of one's position at the expense of others is reduced. And even though a nation's economy may be under-abundant for the time being, constructive social endeavour to improve the position can be maintained because economic privation is equitably shared.

I emphasize these points because I wish to turn to consider

some of the psychological difficulties in the way of achieving equity. These difficulties are strong enough in themselves without the situation being further confused by what I believe to be inaccurate assumptions about what human behaviour is likely to be if equity and abundant employment are achieved. Thus, nothing I may say about the importance of psychological factors in any way gainsays the importance of the objective reality of abundant employment, economic equity, and the opportunity to take part in creating economic abundance and to share in it. To bring the reality of internal psychological factors into the picture is in no way to push to one side the social and material reality of the external world. It is the interaction between our inner lives as individuals and the outside surround of human beings and the physical world which is crucial to any analysis of obstacles in the way of social change.

III

The general problem which we are treating – that of differentials – touches upon the deepest layers of anxiety and concern in the individual. A moment's thought reveals why this should be so. In the issue of differentials lies the vexed question of comparative position and economic and social status – of security, prestige, esteem and recognition. The most powerful rivalries are stirred. It is a situation which gives opportunity for social creativeness or for mass hostility and social disruption: social creativeness if the problem is tackled and regulated in such a way that equity and justice are seen to be served; social disruption if power-bargaining is the mode of regulation, and if there are real grounds for suspecting inequity.

To the extent, then, that pockets of under- and over-equity payment exist in society, suspicious hostility, individual and group rivalry, and lack of regard for the interests of others, are to be expected. The prospects of achieving a swing towards regulated equitable differentials under such conditions are considerably reduced. A long history of favoured and unfavoured groups leaves a deep social impression that is difficult to eradicate from the mental outlook of both those who have enjoyed the advantageous position and those who have suffered the disadvantageous one. Various political platforms are presented to overcome these problems. Political difficulties apart, however, there are other large obstacles in the way which are less readily observable, and which will have to be taken into account if progress towards social sanity is to be facilitated.

I have indicated in earlier chapters* that human beings are torn by conflicting constructive and destructive impulses. Love, generosity, fairness, gratitude, trust and a sense of the common good, are in constant conflict with hate, greed, envy, jealousy, destructive rivalry, suspicion, and omnipotent grandiosity. I have mentioned how this conflict shows in the conflicting realistic and phantasy-dominated views we each have about our capacity and our economic needs, and in the determination of actual payment levels. It shows equally in a vacillating and ambivalent attitude towards the lawful regulation of differentials.

To the extent to which constructive impulses dominate in the members of a society, the problem of differential status and reward becomes one of arranging for fairness all round – equity for everyone. Constructive social impulses reinforce the will to find means to ensure that everyone gets the same relative treatment as everyone else – and to do so in such a manner that everyone can rest assured that this is happening.

To the extent that destructive impulses enter, the problem of differential status and reward takes on quite a different hue – that of the destructive impulses themselves. Differentials become matters of personal prestige, vanity and conceit, omnipotent selfishness, feelings of persecution by the greedy or the envious, desires for special treatment or advantage over others, suspicion of the motives of others, malicious rivalry, grudges and spiteful revenge. The will to get an equitable regulation of differentials is dissipated by the suspicion and inter-group hostility which is generated. Bargaining is the mode of choice, for bargaining gives freer rein to the expression of destructive feelings, and scope for wresting a favoured position if the necessary power can be mustered.

I have frequently seen this conflict between the sense of equity and the inclination towards power-bargaining in sharp relief in

* And see Jaques: 'Psycho-analysis and the current economic crisis', 1958.

discussions about the possible application of time-span measurement and the equitable work-payment scale*. Lack of agreement on the grounds that these instruments are new and relatively untested would be readily understandable. But the strongest criticism that is usually expressed by managers and elected representatives alike is that the instruments might work. For if these instruments were to prove practicable, runs the argument, payment would be systematically fixed within an equitable framework. Equity or not, each person would thus lose the opportunity to bargain for what he thought he might give or get for his work or for a particular category of work. Underlying this paradoxical criticism is an unconscious persecuted feeling of loss of personal freedom – the loss of the freedom to look after one's own interests in a situation where one is suspicious of the other's envy, avarice, and desire for selfish exploitation.

Individually, of course, no-one (or at least, very few) will admit that he is personally motivated by conflicting impulses. We are readily aware of much of the positive or constructive side – and of our phantasies about our good points – but the negative or destructive side tends to remain unrecognized or denied. It is always the other person or group whose motives are suspect. In reality there is always some evidence of the destructive side of that other person or group, and of the constructive side of ourselves or our own group. It is not difficult, therefore, for our unconscious constructive and destructive impulses to fix upon these split-off aspects of reality, and to cause us to see these aspects as though they were the whole story – the other side becoming totally black and our own side white. This familiar process of blackening and idealization leads to the extremes of emotion in group processes which add irrational and therefore pernicious burdensome obstacles to the resolution of social problems – the reality problems themselves being difficult enough to solve.

This projection of our own unconscious feelings of idealization and of persecution into the group situation, so that personal

---

* I am here referring to reactions in organizations other than the Glacier Metal Company. The reactions inside that firm have been described in chapter 7.

310

feelings get merged by absorption into group consensus and ideologies, is a common feature of all group behaviour*. There occurs an unconscious collusion between individuals to live out in their group behaviour the conscious and unconscious motives which might otherwise arouse feelings of guilt and loss of self-esteem if experienced personally. The group processes thereby become the carriers of irrational unconscious impulses, and are distorted and disturbed by them. For example, in their attempts to avoid and to deny their personal desires to give and to get preferential treatment, it is not uncommon for groups of employers and of employees respectively, to maintain that they want to abolish differentials altogether – an attitude which is in fact implemented in industries where workers in given categories all receive the same pay regardless of the fact that the category – say, all fitters, or carpenters, or moulders – will contain a variety of roles with different levels of work requiring individuals of different skill levels.

Another illustration of the resulting inconsistencies between the private and public feelings of individuals is the difficult position in which they place employers' and workers' representatives during negotiations. In the negotiation situation neither of the negotiating representatives behaves as an individual. Each expresses a complex of attitudes and feelings: some of these have to do with the negotiations; but many of them are the expression not only of explicit political views, but also of the unconscious idealizing and destructiveness of the members of the groups represented. The bargaining situation provides a socially accepted outlet for these impulses in the groups represented by the negotiators; hatred, suspicion, mistrust, concern for one's own interests, are all taken for granted, 'the other side' being a fair target for such feelings. Individuals whose personal relations may normally be friendly, may become exasperated or vindictive opponents for the duration of the negotiations. Where the negotiators on either or both sides want to behave reasonably, and strive to do so, they are defeated by the lack of any rational framework within which to couch their arguments, and by the fact that they are caught up in a complex group process in which concise argument to the

*See Jaques (1953), Bion (1956) and Menzies (1960).

point is not the only aim*. Eventually, when, in spite of the negative forces, a solution is arrived at, the fact that systematic principles have most probably not been considered is commonly lost sight of in the heat and haze of the debate. The large-scale evasion of the basic problem of the differential pattern of payment remains relatively intact.

The foisting of negative and destructive unconscious impulses on to the social situation is stimulated and increased in intensity by any existing inequity in differentials. Inequity in payment differentials thus acts as a strong force to defeat socially cohesive impulses to establish equity. It gives grounds for suspicion and mistrust in reality. It thereby hinders and undermines constructive negotiations, stimulating greater use of them for the projection of the unconscious greed, envy, hate and destructiveness which have been strengthened by the inequity. It encourages the retreat into crude bargaining.

These questions of differential entitlement, then, make contact with the most profound and disturbing rivalries and anxieties within us all. If the regulating conditions are such that these rivalries and anxieties are stirred, then problems of social reality interact with unconscious psychological processes to create a vicious circle. Inequity provokes an objective sense of guilt and injustice. Anxieties – both conscious and unconscious – are intensified. These anxieties are played out into the disruption of mass social relationships by the destructive rivalry and hostility. The objective difficulties in resolving the problems are markedly

* If the negotiations are taking place within one firm, instead of two sets of negotiators acting in a representative capacity there is a set of representatives negotiating with an employer acting in his normal executive capacity. An unbalanced situation arises. The elected representatives are forced by their position to carry out the group processes I have described. How deeply the employer may be involved in such processes will depend more upon his personal outlook and make-up. I think this fact explains the particular type of argument which tends to ensue in which representatives are faced with the task of expressing a complex and sometimes inconsistent set of views, while the manager is faced with the executive task of getting a solution which will somehow reconcile the need to keep costs down with the need to maintain an adequate and effective labour force. The meeting place for these diverging approaches needs the greatest goodwill on both sides if it is to be found without formal dispute.

increased by the ensuing confusion and suspicion, and the fogging of reason and constructive endeavour. Inadequate social mechanisms become fixed and resistant to modification. Group solidarity forms within sections of society around hatred of other sections. Unless the whole process is at least temporarily reversed from time to time, national duty and responsibility are pushed to one side, and national morale and unity are undermined and weakened.

Under such conditions it becomes difficult for the constructive desires of individuals for differential equity to be expressed in group behaviour and other social institutions and procedures. These desires are kept inside the individual, the group being retained more as an outlet for fight and for argument. Fighting negotiation based on power thus has functions beyond the resolution of payment differentials. The possible loss of the current negotiation methods is thus likely in and of itself to arouse considerable anxiety. Time-span and the equitable work-payment scale aside, therefore, any mode of socially acceptable regulation of payment differentials is likely to meet heavy resistance.

My point in raising these psychological issues is that they are the ones which are ordinarily overlooked. It is unrealistic to operate on the assumption that conscious goodwill is sufficient to bring about equity: power bargaining has its strong attractions. It is equally unrealistic to assume that inequity is the product merely of conscious ill-will and exploitation. The unconscious destructive forces in individuals have a powerful effect on social processes, and the expression of these unconscious forces is general in all groups. It is not peculiar to any particular group. Recognition and understanding of these forces may facilitate social progress by helping to release the equally powerful unconscious constructive forces of which human beings are capable.

IV

Even if these resistances can be overcome, there still remains the question of how general is the analysis. It is my view that it applies quite generally in the sense of being independent of politico-economic system. It can be applied to any type of economy in which employment contracts are used. In particular, it is applicable equally to capitalist economies, socialist economies, or intermediate forms of welfare economy.

The fundamental difference between capitalist and socialist economic organization has to do with the character of investment and directorial work, but not of employment work. Capitalist economy is built upon private entrepreneurial work and share-holding. A fully socialist economy excludes these types of work, substituting for them investment carried out by the elected members of the state, and direction carried out either by them or by their appointees.

These differences in ownership and control do not extend, however, to employment work. Capitalist and socialist enterprises alike depend upon organizations of employees under contract to carry out the work necessary to achieve the objects of the enterprise. The two types of economic organization have in common the use of identical executive hierarchies, employing smaller or larger numbers of people within manager-subordinate relationships. What is perceived as a fair pattern of payment differentials for the hierarchy of employment work from chief executive to shop or office floor is connected with fundamental human characteristics concerned with the capacity to work, the capacity for discriminating expenditure and satisfaction level of consumption. Given such a connexion, the problems of arranging a fair differential payment structure and fair individual progress for those engaged in employment work will be the same in both types of economy. Politico-economic systems do not in and of themselves provide a rationale for any particular differential wage and salary structure for employment work. There is evidence, for example, that the pattern of distribution of wage and salary differentials in the U.S.S.R. is very similar to that of the United States*.

I may return now to one of the main points I raised in the first chapter – that of the relationship between payment levels and the

---

* David Granick: *Management of the Industrial Firm in the U.S.S.R. (A Study in Soviet Economic Planning)*. I would suggest that it is also because of these basic human characteristics that the Pareto coefficients in different economies over long periods of time show such a very considerable consistency. See Colin Clark: *The Condition of Economic Progress*, 1951.

profitability of an enterprise. Whatever the type of economy, the two issues must be treated quite separately. By so doing, the relative payment levels can be treated in terms of the equitable work-payment scale, the size of the equitable payments being the product of the aggregate amount of money being distributed in the form of wages and salaries.

In a completely socialist economy, where nearly all personal income is income from employment, the problem is one of what portion of the total national income is retained by the State for further investment and development, and what portion is distributed in wages and salaries. It is a matter controlled by national policy. The fixing of the differential pattern of distributed income still remains a problem. My findings suggest that equity is better served by payment related to level of work, than by payment linked to productivity of enterprise, as practised in some socialist countries. By keeping payment related to level of work, the problems of relative advantages gained through capital investment favouring some enterprises or industries do not arise.

In a capitalist economy, or a mixed economy such as in Great Britain with its nationalized and private sectors, there is the same need to keep the question of profitability separated from that of equitable payment distribution. The equitable work-payment scale would be established in common for the Civil Service, nationalized industry, and large corporations having the character of public utilities, in conjunction with the large representative industrial and commercial organizations, especially the trades unions. This scale would apply to all employment work, and would thus determine the total amount of the national income to be distributed in wages and salaries. Changes in income connected with increase or decrease in national prosperity would be arranged for all, not by separate negotiation in different industries, but by national negotiation or legislation of changes in the equitable work-payment scale. These changes would at the same time regulate the relationship between dividend and income distribution.

Under such an arrangement, individual enterprises would continue to be more or less profitable. But there would be a considerable difference, through taking the question of wages and salaries right away from the market mechanism – by ceasing to treat labour as a commodity with a variable price to be bargained over. Profitability could not then be increased by driving hard bargains with labour, nor by keeping individual wages and salaries within enterprises at under-equity levels; nor could it be threatened by labour achieving favoured over-equity payment. The capacity to make a profit would arise only from acuity in the entrepreneurial work itself – that is to say, from sound judgement in what goods and services to provide, and in the efficient running of organizations for the production, development and marketing of those goods and services. The operating profit or loss would be the asset or liability of the controlling interest – whether the nation or private shareholders. If individual employees wished to share in this profit or risk a loss, they could do so by investing in the enterprise (they already do so, along with all other taxpayers, in nationalized industry).

In short, keep the risks of shareholding and investment work separate from the contract of employment, and from the issue of the equitable distribution of wages and salaries. The basis for sound industrial relations would be strengthened by doing so.

More, keep the members of the nation joined together by a common payment structure so that the prosperity of each and every one is tied to the prosperity of all. Give no favoured individuals or groups the opportunity to exploit either tradition or disequilibria in the labour market in order to enjoy or accumulate wealth by means of over-equity payment. The moral fibre of the nation would be toughened.

V

I would like finally to draw together the threads of my presentation, and to state as succinctly as may be two defining characteristics of what I mean by the equitable society. First, it possesses and employs objective means for expressing the rational unconscious norms of fair differential sharing of work and of wealth, and regulates the differential economic entitlements of its members in accord with these norms. Second, it possesses and employs a common and agreed method and policies for progressing its members in work, and therefore in the economic returns for that

316

work, at a rate consistent with progress in their level of performance in work. I am defining not a political aspiration, but a mode of social operation designed to make manifest the natural laws of psycho-economic equilibrium in the individual and the society.

The aspiration towards the discovery of inherent norms of justice in mankind has been a recurring theme in the theories of law propounded by jurists for the past two thousand years – through Aristotle, Cicero, St Augustine, Aquinas, Locke, Hume, and Kant, to the present. It is the theme of natural law. To the extent, however, that the concept of natural law has been founded upon moral, ethical and political imperatives, it is not of use for our present purposes. In its place, I would substitute the concept of requisite law – that is to say, law based upon scientifically discovered and objectively demonstrable generally occurring human norms. It is law which springs from the inherently orderly parts of the mind of man and which, when correctly understood, is as immutable as is his basic psychological make-up.

One of the main tasks of law and of legal procedures and institutions is to establish in a manifest and external form the conditions governing the duties and entitlements of individuals and corporate bodies in relation to each other and to the state, when interests overlap and encroach upon each other. In its fullest sense, requisite law should not only express what we might consciously consider reasonable and just in the sorting out of conflicting needs and requirements, were we not ourselves personally involved in the matter. It ought also to express the deep unconscious sense of order and norms of fairness which we possess. This sense, given unfettered outlets, would suffuse our conscious awareness with the impulse to achieve what is sane and balanced in human relations. It would provide the solid intuitive foundation for that conscious achievement.

In our minds, the sense of law and order coexists with the impulse towards lawlessness and chaos. By verbalizing our inner sense of law and order into statements of requisite law, we are enabled to employ our intellect and exert conscious effort to negate the effects of these unconscious destructive impulses. We

can thus prevent their being poured into our social relationships.

The most useful way of looking at the general question of
implementation of the findings I have presented is within the
framework of requisite law. The equitable work-payment scale
constitutes one such law which may perhaps be of special interest.
It comprises a set of lawful norms of economic differentials which
can be defined in terms of an objectively measurable variable, that
of level of work measured in time-span. In this manner, the
unconscious creative norms of individuals can be transformed
into the verbalized formulations of society.

The equitable society, then, is a lawful society in the deepest
sense of lawful. Its laws bolster the rational constructive strivings
of its members. And they inhibit the dumping into its socio-
economic relationships of the irrational hate, envy, greed and
omnipotence phantasies which undermine those relationships and
the institutions which mediate them.

It is under conditions of economic abundance that the equitable
society comes into its own. Under these conditions there is
opportunity for work and a career for each one of us at a level
consistent with the growth of our capacity, and an abundant
income and rate and intensity of expenditure. The socially and
emotionally disruptive effects both of poverty and of over-
abundance are eliminated. These are the necessary economic
foundations for full-scale social justice and for sanity.

In the abundant equitable society we must each individually
find our own destiny. The opportunity exists for us to do so.
Whether or not we succeed is much more a matter of our own
state of mind than it is when lack of abundance and economic
inequity disturb our adjustment and progress, and conceal the
contribution of our own internal psychic conflicts to the troubles
we encounter. We are gripped more firmly in contact with our
inner selves, in a setting of external economic security. These conditions are among those essential to psychological health and
integration. They support the strengthening of character and the
growth of moral courage. The good society will be less of a
utopian dream when once we learn to understand the reality of
the power of our unconscious destructiveness, and equally learn

to trust the power of our unconscious strivings towards justice and to express those strivings in the form of conscious and explicit norms and requisite social institutions.

Appendices

1

APPENDIX TO CHAPTER 9

Plotting of earning progressions in the United States

I

Concurrently with the completion of writing this book, I received earning progression data from seven companies in the United States*. Preliminary work on these data gives a strong indication that the capacity growth curves empirically arrived at from British data, apply equally in the United States. In this appendix I shall describe how the data from the American firms were analysed and plotted, present the results, and discuss how the curves can be used in the United States. I shall also indicate how the curves may be tried out for use with other currencies.

II

In order that the data obtained from the United States could be plotted for comparison with data obtained in the United Kingdom, two main corrections had to be made†.

(i) *Correction for changes in general levels of wages over the course of time.*

In principle, this problem was dealt with in the same way as in the case of British data. For this, wages were corrected by means of the wages index which measures the average movement from

---

*I am indebted to Mr H. D. Rossman, of the Missile and Space Vehicle Department of the General Electric Company, for arranging the collection of these data. The seven companies who gave their cooperation were: The Atlantic Refining Company; Federal Reserve Bank of Philadelphia; International Resistance Company; The Penn Mutual Life Insurance Company; Philadelphia Transportation Company; Scott Paper Company; Vertol Aircraft Corporation.

†This material, and the correction factors used, were prepared by Mr J. M. M. Hill.

month to month in the level of full-time weekly rates of wages in the principal industries and services in the United Kingdom. Thus, a change in any individual's salary over the course of time may reflect both differential career progression *and* movement arising from general increases. By removing the latter, only those increases due to differential career progression are shown.

The United States, according to my information, has no precisely analogous measure, but the nearest equivalent seemed to be the 'average hourly gross earnings' given in dollars which could be corrected to a base-line at 1947 in the same way as the British index. The index of average hourly gross earnings, however, reflects not only changes in basic hourly and incentive wage rates, but also such things as premium for overtime payment, late shift work, changes in incentive basis, etc. There was a further index which excluded overtime, but this was not available for 1957 onwards. When, however, the two indices were compared so far as movement over time was concerned, only insignificant differences were perceptible in the figures.

As a further check, the American index (corrected to a base-line at 1947) was plotted for comparison with the British wages index, and a broadly similar rate of increase over time was revealed. The movement of these two indices is shown in figure 26.

Accordingly, an index based on the average hourly gross earnings was used to correct the raw salary data to a base-line of June 1955 – the same base-line as had been used for the British data. The yearly figures which were available were treated as applying to June 30th each year, and a December figure obtained by averaging consecutive mid-year points.

CORRECTION FACTORS – U.S.A.

1947–1959, *taking June* 1955 *as* 1.00

June 1947 1.52	Dec. 1950 1.23	June 1954 1.04	Dec. 1957 0.90
Dec. 1947 1.45	June 1951 1.18	Dec. 1954 1.02	June 1958 0.88
June 1948 1.39	Dec. 1951 1.15	June 1955 1.00	Dec. 1958 0.86
Dec. 1948 1.37	June 1952 1.13	Dec. 1955 0.97	June 1959 0.85
June 1949 1.34	Dec. 1952 1.09	June 1956 0.95	
Dec. 1949 1.31	June 1953 1.06	Dec. 1956 0.93	
June 1950 1.28	Dec. 1953 1.05	June 1957 0.91	

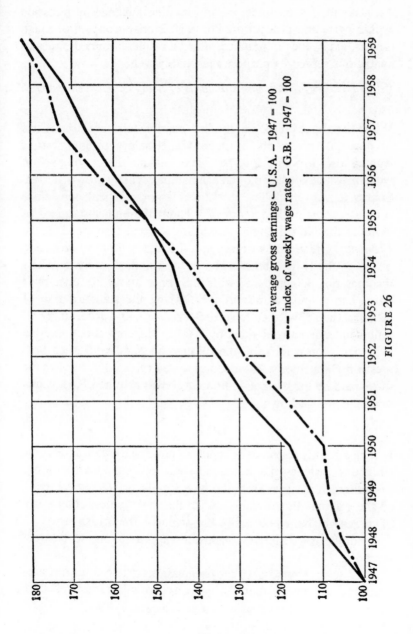

FIGURE 26

average gross earnings – U.S.A. – 1947 = 100
index of weekly wage rates – G.B. – 1947 = 100

I recognize that this method is fairly rough and ready. It takes no account, for example, of any relative advance or recession within particular occupational or professional groups. But rough as it is, experience in practice with the results obtained indicates that it has served its purpose reasonably well.

(ii) *Correction for differing standards of living as between the U.S. and the U.K.*

While the above correction made it possible to remove the effects of national increments from individual salary progressions, I wanted also, if possible, to be able to make a direct comparison with British data when plotted against the capacity growth curves. Simply to convert dollars to pounds is not sufficient here, since such a conversion leaves out of account the higher standard of living in the United States. According to results obtained by the *Economist* which táke into account differences in the purchasing power of the two currencies and in the standard of living, U.K. incomes can be compared with U.S. ones about $2\frac{1}{2}$ times their size when expressed in sterling*. Taking the standard rate of $2.80 to the £1, we then have $2.80 \times 2.5 = 7$, and accordingly all dollar incomes were divided by 7 (after the corrections to June 1955 had been made) and then plotted on standard Earned Progression Data Sheets. All incomes were expressed per week; for those paid by the hour, a 40-hour week was assumed. The results obtained are as shown.

III

In figure 27 are presented the results of plotting the data as described. The consistency of fit of the individual progressions is striking. The progression curves from the American firms, treated as I treated the original British data, lead to the construction of an array of curves which are practically identical with the British array.

A number of tentative conclusions appear to me to be warranted.

1. The close similarity of the progressions in two countries supports the conclusion that the capacity growth curves reflect a

*These calculations refer to the year 1960.

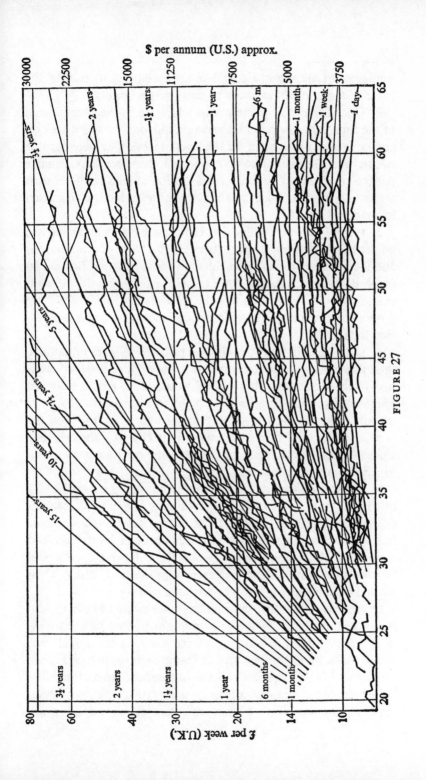

FIGURE 27

fundamental characteristic of human development, that of the pattern of growth of capacity to carry responsibility.

2. One of the basic assumptions which led to the construction of the capacity growth curves was that individuals would seek an equitable level of payment for the level of work they were capable of carrying. The assumption is supported, therefore, that a similar pattern of norms of equitable distribution applies in the United States as applies in Great Britain, but at a higher level, as discussed in chapter 8.

3. It is a likely possibility that the capacity growth curves can be used for other currencies where the patterns of employment and income distribution are similar to those in Great Britain. In other types of economy – for example, where grossly different employment systems obtain – the progression array for that economic system would have to be constructed from raw progression data.

4. If the capacity growth curves apply for a number of nations, then they may be used for comparing the relative levels of earnings in those nations. The method would be to plot a sufficient number of earning progression curves to establish the capacity growth curves for any given nation. The currency value on the vertical scale could then be compared directly with the currency values on the vertical scale of the capacity growth curves established for any other nation.

In this last connexion, it may be noted that the factor of $2\frac{1}{2}$ obtained by the *Economist* for comparing U.S. and U.K. incomes expressed in sterling, appears to be confirmed. For if the factor had been either too high or too low, the array of curves obtained would have shown the same pattern as the U.K. array, but would have been relatively higher or lower than the U.K. array, when plotted on the Earning Progression Data Sheet.

In making these brief observations I am aware of having side-stepped many very large questions; for example, would one necessarily expect that a feudal type of economy, or a colonial one, would throw up the same pattern of progression as in the U.K. or the U.S.A.? Or, are the data so small in number as to hide possible differences in the steepness of the capacity growth curves between the U.K. and the U.S.A.? These and other equally serious questions remain untouched for the moment. I decided, nevertheless, to include the material in this appendix, even if only in tentative form and even if it serves only to raise these and other major questions for scrutiny and further study.

Those who wish to work with American data can use the standard Earning Progression Data Sheets simply by multiplying the vertical scale by 7 to convert it to U.S. dollars.

Some organization and manning procedures at the Glacier Metal Company Limited

These notes outline some of the procedures which are being developed in the Glacier Metal Company, which employ the conceptions set out in this book. They are in the form of draft memoranda setting out the procedure for reviewing organization and manning, and the procedure for reviewing staff progress and salaries. The procedures are being tried out in some parts of the firm.

A short comment on the conception and structure of the organization and manning review may be necessary. This review is an annual meeting between a manager, A, and one of his subordinates, B, to review B's immediate command – from the point of view both of its organization and of the occupants of the roles. Thus, a manager who has several subordinates who in turn are managers, will have to conduct several reviews in the course of the year, one with each subordinate. Each review takes about half a day.

ANNUAL ORGANIZATION AND MANNING REVIEW
Objectives of annual organization and manning review

1. The annual organization and manning review is a formalized and scheduled occasion for a comprehensive review of present organization and manning, and of future requirements and plans.

2. The points to be covered in the review comprise:
(a) confirmation or modification of work policy
(b) review of requisiteness of organization, present and future, in light of the work policy
(c) review of each role, present and future
    (i) work content – prescribed and discretionary
    (ii) subordinate establishment
    (iii) level-of-work bracket
    (iv) salary bracket
(d) review of present occupant

    (i) performance during period under review
    (ii) confirmation or modification of basic assessment
    (iii) consistency of actual earning progression
    (iv) future progress in the role, and potential career development in the Company
  (e) review of future manning of the role, if not by present occupant, and of potential replacements.

On-going organization and manning work

3. The annual organization and manning review is one part of the total procedure by means of which a manager maintains his continual responsibility for the personnel dimension of the work he controls. Other aspects of this responsibility include, for example, problems of filling vacancies or dealing with the organizational reflection of expansion or contraction, the on-going staff work of his personnel specialist, wage and salary reviews, promotions, etc.

4. As a part of their on-going day-to-day responsibility, the Personnel Staff Officers carry out normal visits and inspections to the commands of their managers' subordinates. They ought to settle outstanding problems of organization or of manning via normal staff work procedures.

5. By these means, organization and manning problems are dealt with as they arise, and not accumulated to be dealt with in organization and manning review meetings. The organization and manning review meeting is thus freed for its task of a general review of the year's work and experience, and an appraisal of future trends and requirements.

6. Thus, the preparatory work for an organization and manning review meeting should be directed towards crystallizing out the implications of the year's experience, so as to aid the job of setting a satisfactory direction and objectives to govern the day-to-day personnel work during the ensuing year.

Review meeting

7. An executive meeting, under the control of the reviewing manager, who will make decisions on each of the points listed in para. 2.

8. The subordinate manager (or co-managers) is present as the person with whom the reviewing manager is carrying out the review, and whose own organization and manning work is being assessed.

9. The reviewing manager's personnel specialist is present in his normal staff specialist role *vis-à-vis* the reviewing manager. His own staff work is under review. He ensures that adequate personnel records are kept, and picks up emergent problems for staff work follow-up with the subordinate manager and with his own technical subordinates.

10. The personnel specialist from the level above the reviewing manager shall be present. He is not in charge, but is there for the purpose of:

   (i) reviewing the efficacy of his own screening and manpower planning;

  (ii) reviewing, as co-manager, the work of the reviewing manager's personnel specialist;

 (iii) adding to his specialist knowledge about the reviewing manager's subordinates, in line with his specialist responsibility in connexion with that stratum of members;

 (iv) giving technical support and control;

  (v) ensuring that higher policy is implemented;

 (vi) finding out about any difficulties which might be arising from the implementation of current policies.

11. Other persons may be brought into the meeting on the recommendation of any of the members of the meeting, and the agreement of the reviewing manager.

Documentation

12. Reports on organization, and on manning in general, may be circulated among those concerned.

13. Personal information and reports on individuals are kept by Personnel Division. The reviewing manager and the subordinate manager (or co-manager) may have access to them, but copies are not made and circulated.

14. Those parts of the personal information about individuals which would ordinarily fall under the heading of clinical information, are retained in confidence in Personnel Division, and are

submitted to the managers concerned in a form appropriate for executive usage. Clinical psychological reports by outside consultants are submitted to Personnel Division, and held thus in confidence.

STAFF PROGRESS AND SALARY REVIEW

Definitions

1. *Performance*: level of a member's actual achievement in the job; rated on an eight-point scale: -2, -1, 0, 1, 2, 3, 4, 5 (see guidance note on page 342).

1.1 *Normal performance and progress*: judgement by a manager that a subordinate has worked effectively in the sense of having made full use of his capacity on the job.

1.2 *Sub-normal performance and progress*: judgement by a manager that a subordinate has failed to make effective use of the capacity he possesses; not 'working up to scratch'.

1.3 *Special effort*: judgement by a manager that a subordinate, in response to the manager's special request, has put in concentrated effort and application of a kind that can be maintained only for very short periods of time.

2. *Potential progress assessment (P.P.A.)*: assessment (or re-assessment) by an authorized manager of the rate of progress in work which a member is likely to make, and whether he will be capable of moving into a higher job or rank. The P.P.A. is expressed as a capacity growth curve at age 55. It is a *pro tem.* assessment, and may be changed by the appropriate manager.

2.1 *Trial progression*: a temporary P.P.A. assigned to younger members who have not proceeded sufficiently far in their careers for a sound judgement to be made of their potential performance.

3. *Normal % salary increase*: the salary increase a member would receive if he were given an increase in accord with the capacity growth curve which expresses his P.P.A.; always stated in % per annum.

4. *General salary adjustment*: an increase in salary given to all staff members at the time of implementation of a nationally negotiated hourly-rated increase.

POLICY

1. Staff progress and salary reviews shall be carried out in two stages:

(a) in conjunction with his organization reviews, the reviewing manager shall set a tentative increase for each member reviewed; and

(b) at the annual staff salary review, the tentatively set increase will be implemented, unless a member's performance is judged to have changed significantly since his assessment at the organization review.

Conditions for progression and payment

2. The general policy for the progression and payment of members is as follows.

3. Adherence by managers to this policy is a prime condition for encouraging maximum incentive in work.

4. The policy requires a shift in thinking from wage and salary review to review of progress in performance.

5. The main conditions to be fulfilled in progression and payment are:

(a) employment of members in jobs which are consistent with their exercised capacity;

(b) maintaining an explicit appreciation of the level-of-work bracket for each job (whether intuitively, or by reference to work measurement datum lines);

(c) fixing of payment brackets consistent with the level-of-work brackets in jobs;

(d) payment of individuals at a level within the bracket which accords with their manager's assessment of their level of performance in the job;

(e) progression of individuals in work and payment at a rate consistent with their progress in level of performance;

(f) rewarding exceptional performance (i.e., exceptional concentration and application which it would be impossible for anyone to keep up for more than very short periods of time) in response to special demands, by *ex gratia* payments made at the time.

Progression review

6. Wage and salary reviews are requisitely reviews of a member's progress in performance. If progress in performance is settled, the wage or salary review follows automatically.

7. Progression review requires:

(a) a potential progress assessment* fixed by the manager-once-removed (or higher) and stated in terms of a work progression;

(b) judgement by the immediate manager as to whether the member, during the period under review, has been:

  (i) performing up to scratch (i.e., in a manner consistent with his expected performance)

  (ii) performing below what he was judged to have been capable of doing

  (iii) showing evidence of capability above or below the potential progress assessment made by the manager-once-removed.

8. Therefore, if you are the immediate manager and you assess your subordinate's performance to be up to scratch, a wage or salary adjustment consistent with the potential progress assessment should be recommended.

9. If you decide that the potential progress assessment is correct, but that your subordinate's performance has been substandard – that is, below what you expect he ought to be doing – indicate by how much you judge his payment should be allowed to fall below that called for by his potential progress assessment (by recommending no increase, or less than a normal increase, and not by actually decreasing his wage or salary).

10. If you assess your subordinate's performance to be showing evidence of capacity above or below the potential progress assess-

*A progression review may include a full-blown potential progress assessment on each one of a manager's immediate subordinates. It may, at the other extreme, as in the case of a unit manager reviewing some two to three hundred operators, be a review based on the unit manager's detailed knowledge and potential progress assessment of, say, the twenty per cent with the highest potential, the rest having been systematically reviewed but not brought forward by section managers for personal consideration by the unit manager.

ment, make recommendations to the manager-once-removed to revise the assessment.

11. If your subordinate has reached or is approaching the top of the work and payment bracket, then make up your mind whether, in your judgement:

(a) there is an increasing level of work available in the job, which you want to get done, and by that subordinate – in which case recommend a raising of the bracket;

(b) there is no likelihood of the level of work in the job increasing, but you wish to be able to keep the man after his performance would ordinarily warrant progression above the bracket – in which case, recommend that his payment be raised over the bracket;

(c) there is no likelihood of the level of work in the job increasing, and no particular need to break the top of the bracket – in which case point out to your subordinate that he is reaching the top of the bracket in his present job, and report to the manager-once-removed.

12. If you consider that he has shown bursts of exceptional performance (as defined above) on one or more occasions, you ought to have recommended the award to him of *ex gratia* payments at the time, and should exclude these considerations from wage or salary review which should deal exclusively with the level of performance maintained throughout the period under review.

ASSESSMENT OF INDIVIDUALS IN ORGANIZATION REVIEWS

13. Organization reviews shall be conducted by the Managing Director and by all General and Divisional Managers.

14. They shall be held throughout the year, except during the months of June, July and August.

15. Both the persons and the roles shall be considered in the course of organization reviews, but this directive deals only with the assessment of persons.

Preliminary steps

16. Prior to an organization review, the Personnel Manager acting for the reviewing manager shall ensure that:

(a) each member's E.P.C. is brought up to date;

(b) the basic data are entered upon the Personal Assessment Forms (see figure 28);

(c) his Command Folder (containing job descriptions, Role Assessment Forms, Personal Assessment Forms and the E.P.C.s) is circulated to each manager concerned in the Review.

17. The *immediate manager* shall record his assessment of the performance of each of his subordinates during the period under review. He shall confine the assessment to his subordinate's actual achievement on the job. He may separately record his subordinate's good intentions, reliability, soundness of character, etc., under the heading of personal merit.

17.1 If he assesses his subordinate's performance as subnormal, he shall indicate how and when he has taken this up with the subordinate.

17.2 He shall give a rating of his judgement of each subordinate's level of actual performance in the job bracket, in accord with the criteria listed in para. 2, p. 329.

17.3 He shall record if he has granted any *ex gratia* payments during the year, and indicate what they were for.

17.4 He shall recommend what salary increase he would want his subordinate to get, on the basis of that subordinate's performance.

17.5 If he judges that a subordinate's P.P.A. is either too high or too low, he shall state his reasons, and recommend what he judges an appropriate P.P.A. to be.

18. The *specialist co-manager* (if any) shall comment on his subordinate's technical abilities and capacity to handle the job, and his technical performance, and shall make recommendations with regard to salary and P.P.A.

19. The *personnel manager* shall record his appraisal of the member's potential capacity, and comment on the relation between the member's potential capacity and his performance as assessed by his immediate manager (and co-manager).

19.1 He shall fill in the Assessment Cross-Check Data for use at the review.

20. The *reviewing manager* shall consider the views of the

immediate manager (and co-manager) and the personnel manager, and record any comments.

Action at organization review

21. The *reviewing manager* shall conduct the review, and shall decide:
   (a) whether to confirm or change the member's P.P.A.;
   (b) the tentative salary increase for the annual salary review (taking into account whether any interim salary adjustments have been or are to be granted, or whether the individual will have been with the Company for less than one year at the time of the salary review);
   (c) whether or not to grant other salary adjustments, either immediately or in the course of the year.

22. The *personnel manager* shall record the reviewing manager's decisions, as appropriate, on the Personal Assessment Form and on the Personal Progress Record (see figure 29).

23. Where a P.P.A. has been established or changed at an organization review, the reviewing manager shall decide who shall discuss this with the member concerned.

ANNUAL STAFF SALARY REVIEW

24. The procedure by which annual review of salary will be carried out will be as follows:
   24.1 During the month of April, each manager will receive his immediate command folder, and shall complete the Review portion of the Personal Assessment Form for each of his subordinates.
   24.2 In the case of attached specialists, the operational co-manager should complete the form in the first place, and subsequently both co-managers should discuss the matter and jointly complete and sign the Personal Assessment Form.
   24.3 In recommending the amount of increase for any subordinate, managers shall take into account whether that subordinate has received any increases during the year under review, or whether he has been with the Company for less than one year.

NAME...

Age.................................... Salary Bracket of Job:

I. **Immediate Operational Manager's Assessment**

    1. *Performance.*   (a) Comment:

    (b) Rating: −2, −1, 0, 1, 2, 3, 4, 5.

    (c) *Ex gratia* payments during year: No............. Amount £............

    (d) Recommended Tentative Increase: Amount £............ ....%

    2. *P.P.A.* (reasons, if recommendation for change):

                    Signed: Date:

II. **Assessment by Specialist Co-Manager and by Personnel Specialist** (to be signed and dated).

Personal Assessment Form. The Glacier Metal Co. Ltd. GLW 1750

FIGURE 28

IV. Reviewing Manager's Assessment

Signed: Date:

V. Reviewing Manager's Decisions

(a) *Comments and Actions:* (training, career discussion, etc.):

Assessment Cross Check		
Recommended Salary Adjustment	*Amount*	%
Immediate Manager	£ : :	
According to Rating	£ : :	
According to P.P.A.	£ : :	
Tentative Salary Adjustment	£ : :	

(b) Summary: (i) P.P.A. decision ....

                (ii) Immediate Salary Adjustment, if any: £ : :

                (iii) Tentative Salary Adjustment: £ : :

           Signed: Date:

VI. Annual Salary Review Recommendations

Immediate Manager	*Specialist Co-Manager*	*Manager-Once-Removed*

Comments (if any) by Managers concerned, (signed and dated):

NAME: _____   Date of Birth: _____

Potential Progress Assessment		Salary Data							Formal Qualifications:
Date	P.P.A. Index	Date	Age	Increase Granted		Normal % Increase	Actual New Salary	Corrected Salary	Notes and Remarks
				Amount	%				
								▨	

Personal Progress Form.   The Glacier Metal Co. Ltd.   GLW 1749.

24.4 Unless there is some special reason, no member will ordinarily be granted an increase unless his progress warrants an increase of 2% or more.

24.5 Nil returns shall be completed in all cases where no salary increase is proposed.

24.6 Each manager shall then complete the Group Recommendation Form for his immediate command.

24.7 Many lower-level staff, and members who have joined the Company since an organization review at which they would have been considered, will not have either a P.P.A. or a tentative salary review, and may not be in a job with an established bracket. The Personal Assessment Form will be made out with as much data as possible, and the authorizing manager shall proceed as far as he can with the cross-checks ordinarily used at organization reviews.

Collation of Group Recommendation Forms

25. The manager at the bottom of each line of command shall pass his command folder to his own manager.

25.1 Each manager receiving command folders shall discuss individual recommendations with his immediate subordinates, and adjust if necessary.

25.2 He shall, if necessary, adjust his subordinate's Group Recommendation Form, and make a collated Group Recommendation Form covering all his staff subordinates more than once-removed.

25.3 He shall then pass to his own manager:

   (a) all the command folders of his subordinate managers, including their group forms;

   (b) the collated group form for his subordinate managers' commands;

   (c) his own command folder, including the group form for his own subordinates.

Final authorization of increases

26. On receiving recommendations from General and Divisional

341

Managers, the Managing Director will decide upon his policy for the review for each General and Divisional Manager.

27. Once their recommendations have been authorized in the light of the Managing Director's policy, managers shall complete the appropriate Salaries Office forms and forward them to Salaries Office by the notified date.

INTERIM AD HOC INDIVIDUAL REVIEWS

28. At any time during the year, a manager may recommend a basic reassessment of the P.P.A. of a subordinate in his direct line of command, or a salary review for him.

GENERAL STAFF SALARY ADJUSTMENTS

29. When hourly-rated wages are adjusted as a result of a nationally negotiated agreement, staff salaries shall also be adjusted.

30. The Managing Director will state the size of the adjustment to be made.

31. All staff members shall receive the general adjustment, except those whose normal salary progressions are not being maintained.

PERSONAL PERFORMANCE RATING AND
ECONOMIC ACHIEVEMENT – GUIDANCE NOTES

These notes give guidance in the use of the personal performance rating scale on the Personal Assessment Form. They set out the relationship of this performance rating for the individual and his degree of achievement of his programmed work target.

In making the personal performance rating, three variables must be kept separately in mind:

(a) the personal performance rating of the person doing the job: stated in terms of a −2 to +5 scale;

(b) the level-of-work bracket for the job, and its salary bracket as related to level of work: stated in terms of a time-span and/or a salary bracket;

(c) the target achievement rating: stated in terms of achievement at, above, or below, requisite programmed target;

i.e., the programmed target to be achieved with the command operating at full efficiency.

Assuming a well-established and running command, with normal work input and programmed targets, and normal operating conditions, the personal performance ratings are defined as follows:

Ratings +4 *and* +5: can be counted upon to sustain programmed target within budgeted expense, without preoccupation by manager or his specialists, even with operating conditions running at the extremes of normal; simply gets on with the job because of his experience and capacity.

Ratings 0 *and* +1: in order to keep the subordinate's command on target, a considerable amount of managerial and specialist attention is required, otherwise normal variations in operating conditions tend to cause a fall away from programmed target; satisfactory for short periods during the induction of a subordinate into a role.

Ratings +2 *and* +3: able to maintain programmed target with some regular attention from manager and specialists when operating conditions are running at the extremes of normal.

Rating −1: achievement tends to be consistently below programmed target, since for the subordinate to keep to programmed target requires a greater intensity of preoccupation and attention from the manager and his specialists than can be sustained, except very temporarily; the subordinate may be considered worthy of a further trial in the expectation that his performance can be improved with training.

Rating −2: subordinate's achievement consistently below programmed target, and his command is running down; replacement indicated.

These ratings must be adapted to take care of variations in operating conditions. Thus, for example, a subordinate may be given a disorganized and inefficient command to rebuild and bring up to requisite programmed target standard:

Rating +5: would imply that although the achievement was below requisite programmed target, nevertheless it was showing a decidedly satisfactory upward trend, and the subordinate was achieving this rate of improvement largely on his own initiative.

Rating −2: would imply that matters were deteriorating further.

Rating +3: would imply that matters were improving but not as quickly as could be.

Contrariwise a subordinate might have a run of relatively favourable operating conditions, in which case a higher than targeted achievement would be required for the performance ratings as outlined to obtain.

Some implications

When manager C agrees with his subordinate B that B's subordinate A has warranted a high or low personal performance rating, he is not necessarily making any statement about whether or not he is satisfied with the achievement of A. Thus, for example, A's personal performance may be high, but his achievement low, because of inadequate support from B and his specialists; or vice versa.

Manager C requires his subordinate B to fulfil the programmed target, regardless of any shortcomings in performance of his subordinate A. If A has a low performance rating, it means that B and his specialists must involve themselves more deeply in A's work, and keep closer tabs on it.

A member's payment should accord directly with his performance rating; i.e., his salary should be at roughly the same point in the salary bracket as his performance rating in the job bracket. His payment is thus in fact dependent upon (even though not simply correlated with) his achievement, since his personal performance rating depends upon that achievement.

If a subordinate's economic achievement is steadily above programmed target without specially favourable conditions, then he ought to be considered for additional responsibilities or for promotion.

Bibliography

BEAL, EDWIN F.
- (1963) 'In praise of job evaluation'. *California Management Review*, 5: 4, 9–16.

BION, WILFRED
- (1956) 'Group dynamics: a re-view'. In *New Directions in Psycho-Analysis*. Tavistock Publications Ltd, London; Basic Books Inc., New York.
- (1957) 'The differentiation of the psychotic from the non-psychotic part of the personality'. *Int. J. Psycho-Anal.*, vol. 38.

BROWN, WILFRED
- (1946) 'Principles of organization'. Monographs on Higher Management, no. 5. Manchester Municipal College of Technology.
- (1952) 'Some problems of a factory'. Occasional Paper no. 2. Institute of Personnel Management, London.
- (1960a) *Exploration in Management*. Heinemann Educational Books Ltd, London; J. Wiley & Sons Inc., New York.
  In Swedish translation – *Forskning i Företagsledning*, Strömberg, Stockholm.
  In French translation – *Gestion Prospective de l'Entreprise*, Les Editions de la Baconnière, Neuchâtel, Switzerland, 1964.
- (1960b) 'Selection and appraisal of management personnel'. *The Manager*, vol. XXVIII, no. 6.
- (1962) *Piecework Abandoned*. Heinemann Educational Books Ltd, London.
- (1962) 'What is work?' *Harvard Business Review*, September. (Also in *Scientific Business*, August 1963.)
- (1963) 'A critique of some current ideas about organization'. *California Management Review*, Fall (September).

BROWN, WILFRED and JAQUES, ELLIOTT
- (1964) *Product Analysis Pricing*. Heinemann Educational Books Ltd, London.
- (1965) *Glacier Project Papers*. Heinemann Educational Books Ltd, London.

BROWN, WILFRED and RAPHAEL, WINIFRDE
- (1943) *Managers, Men and Morale*. MacDonald & Evans Ltd, London.

CLARK, COLIN
  (1951) *The Conditions of Economic Progress.* Macmillan & Co. Ltd, London.

FREUD, SIGMUND
  (1922) *Group Psychology and the Analysis of the Ego.* The Hogarth Press Ltd, London.
  (1922) *Beyond the Pleasure Principle.* The Hogarth Press Ltd, London.
  (1927) *The Ego and the Id.* The Hogarth Press Ltd, London.

GRANICK, DAVID
  (1954) *Management of the Industrial Firm in the U.S.S.R. (A Study in Soviet Economic Planning).* Columbia University Press, New York.

HILL, J. M. M.
  (1951) 'A consideration of labour turnover as the resultant of a quasi-stationary process'. *Human Relations*, vol. XI, no. 4.
  (1957) 'The time-span of discretion in job analysis'. *Human Relations*, vol. X, no. 4; Tavistock Pamphlets no. 1, Tavistock Publications Ltd, London.
  (1958) 'A note on time-span and economic theory'. *Human Relations*, vol. XI, no. 4.

JAQUES, ELLIOTT, RICE, A. K., and HILL, J. M. M.
  (1951) 'The social and psychological impact of a change in method of wage payment'. *Human Relations*, vol. IV, no. 4.

JAQUES, ELLIOTT
  (1950) 'Studies in the social development of an industrial community'. *Human Relations*, vol. III, no. 3.
  (1951) *The Changing Culture of a Factory.* Tavistock Publications Ltd, London; Dryden Press, New York.
  (1953) 'On the dynamics of social structure'. *Human Relations*, vol. VI, no. 1.
  (1956) *Measurement of Responsibility.* Tavistock Publications Ltd, London; Harvard University Press, Cambridge, Mass. In Italian translation – *La Valutazione delle Responsabilità*, Isper Edizioni, Turin, 1966.
  (1958a) 'Fatigue and lowered morale caused by inadequate executive planning'. *Royal Society of Health Journal*, vol. 78, no. 5.
  (1958b) 'An objective approach to pay differentials'. *New Scientist*, vol. 4, no. 85.
  (1958c) 'Standard earning progression curves: a technique for examining individual progress in work'. *Human Relations*, vol. XI, no. 2.

(1958d) 'Psycho-analysis and the current economic crisis'. In *Psycho-Analysis and Contemporary Thought*. Hogarth Press Ltd, London.

(1960) 'Disturbances in the capacity to work'. *Int. J. Psycho-Anal.*, vol. 41.

(1961) *Equitable Payment*. Heinemann Educational Books Ltd, London; John Wiley & Sons Inc., New York.
In French translation – *Rémunération Objective*, Editions Hommes et Techniques, Neuilly-sur-Seine, 1963.

(1962) 'Objective measures for pay differentials'. *Harvard Business Review*, January–February.

(1963) 'A system for income equity'. *New Society*, 12th December.

(1964a) 'Economic justice – by law?' *Twentieth Century*, Spring.

(1964b) 'National incomes policy: a democratic plan'. Pamphlet published by K.-H. Services Ltd.

(1964c) *Time-Span Handbook*. Heinemann Educational Books Ltd, London.

(1964d) 'Level-of-work measurement and fair payment: a reply to Professor Beal's comparison of time-span and discretion and job evaluation'. *California Management Review*, Summer.

(1965a) 'Speculations concerning level of capacity'. In *Glacier Project Papers*. Heinemann Educational Books Ltd, London.

(1965b) 'Preliminary sketch of a general structure of executive ranks'. In *Glacier Project Papers*. Heinemann Education Books Ltd, London.

(1967) *Progression Handbook*. Heinemann Educational Books Ltd, London.

JAQUES, ELLIOTT, RICE, A. K. and HILL, J. M. M.
(1951) 'The social and psychological impact of a change in method of wage payment'. *Human Relations*, vol. IV, no. 4.

KEYNES, J. M.
(1936) *The General Theory of Employment, Interest and Money*. Macmillan & Co. Ltd, London.

KLEIN, MELANIE
(1948) *Contributions to Psycho-Analysis*. Hogarth Press Ltd, London.

(1956) *New Directions in Psycho-Analysis*. Tavistock Publications Ltd, London; Basic Books Inc., New York.

(1957) *Envy and Gratitude*. Tavistock Publications Ltd, London; Basic Books Inc., New York.

(1959) 'Infant conflict in adult behaviour'. *Human Relations*, vol. XII, no. 4; Tavistock Pamphlets no. 2, Tavistock Publications Ltd, London.

MENZIES, ISABEL
(1960) 'A case study in the functioning of social systems as a defence against anxiety'. *Human Relations*, vol. XIII, no. 2.

MISRA, R. and BANERJEE, R.
(1962) 'Use of time-span instrument in job analysis and measurement of responsibility'. *Journal of the Institution of Engineers (India)*, vol. XLII, no. 8, part GE2, April.

MONEY-KYRLE, ROGER
(1951) *Psycho-Analysis and Politics*. Gerald Duckworth & Co. Ltd, London.

RICE, A. K.
(1951a) 'The use of unrecognized cultural mechanisms in an expanding machine-shop'. *Human Relations*, vol. III, no. 2.
(1951b) 'An examination of the boundaries of part-institutions'. *Human Relations*, vol. 4, no. 4.
(1952) 'The relative independence of sub-institutions as illustrated by departmental labour turnover'. *Human Relations*, vol. 5, no. 1.

RICE, A. K., HILL, J. M. M. and TRIST, E. L.
(1950) 'The representation of labour turnover as a social process'. *Human Relations*, vol. 3, no. 4.

RICE, A. K. and TRIST, E. L.
(1952) 'Institutional and sub-institutional determinants of change in labour turnover'. *Human Relations*, vol. 5, no. 4.

SEGAL, HANNA
(1957) 'Notes on symbol formation'. *Int. J. Psycho-Anal.*, vol. 38.

Index

and work-payment-capacity nexus, 201, 251
Dishonesty (failure in prescribed content), 84 (see also Negligence)
Disputes, 32, 42
about payment are differentials disputes, 31, 193
productivity argued in, 38
profitability argued in, 38
Dissatisfaction: see Disequilibrium
Distribution
absence of agreed principle of, 31,
of aggregate real wage, 31
egalitarianism, 178–9, 192
of goods and services, 53
of income: see Income
of payment: see Payment
of payment differentials in U.S.A. and U.S.S.R., 314
and production, 53–4
of roles, and equitability of payment, 159–61
of wealth, 30
of work and income, and psycho-economic stability, 23
'Disturbances in the capacity to work', 88n. 243n
Dividends, 32, 33
Draughtsman, 91, 92, 95
Duties, conflicting, 317

Earnings
and capacity, 241, 250
comprise total emoluments, **147**, 203, 209
forecast of own future, 230–31
levels in other nations, 326–7
Earnings progress of individuals, 172, 201–2 (see also Capacity growth curves; Progression; Standard payment and progression method)
achieved earning progression, 209, 221–2, 229, 230, 272
and capacity growth curves, 209, 213, 214
in overcrowded occupations, 230
reconstruction of, 232–6
analysis and plotting of, 202–9
curve representing equilibrium

situation, 202, 208
distinct from average earnings of groups, 203n
review of consistency of, at Glacier Metal Company, 330
in U.S.A., 321–7
Earning progression data, maintenance and intepretation of, 276
Earning Progression Data Sheets, 208n
for U.S.A., 272, 327
Economic circumstances and destructive impulses, 30
Economic conditions providing equilibrium, 14
Economic depression and unrewarding work conditions, 250
Economic distress and fair shares, 177–8, 179
Economic equity, importance of, 307–8
Economic environment affecting behaviour, 243
Economic fairness and differential payment, 165–6
Economic inequity, 177–8, 318
Economic insecurity, 47
Economic needs, conflicting impulses about, 309
stated in terms of capacity, 187
Economic unrest, 38
Economic work, 50–60
entrepreneurial (q.v.) and employment (q.v.), 54–5
and quality standards, 85
three main types, 21
Economy
abundant economy, 246, 305, 308, 318
defined, 181
differential reward under, 177
equitable distribution of income in, 189
and equitable society, 318
responsibility of government, 305, 307
and work-payment-capacity reactions, 246
British, distribution of income in, 189–90
capitalist, 314–16
socialist, 314–16

content of work, 77, 86

responsibility and authority of, 17

and review of discretion: see Review

and review of work: see Work

selection and manning responsibilities of, 274n

setting up new role, 107

sharpening perception of task, 127

and staff progress and salary review at Glacier Metal Company, 332–44

standards, changing, 140

standards of discretion expected by, 126

and standards of quality, 103, 104, 105

  unfamiliarity with, 102

and subordinate

  capacity too close, 109

  disagreement about activities, 101

  intuitive understanding between, 102, 108

  must decide what he holds subordinate accountable for, 106

  open-ended instructions to, 109–10

  review of subordinate's performance, 102

  setting unrealistic tasks for, 105

  with experienced subordinate, 102

  with inexperienced subordinate, 102

and sub-standard discretion (work)

  accountable for discovering, 101

  anger at implication of, 136

and successive approximation, 104, 105, 109, 126

and (target) completion times, 103, 104, 105, 108, 109, 110, 119–20

  unfamiliarity with, 102, 108

unfamiliar with tasks allocated, 102, 108

and time-span measurement

effect on, 105

helped by, 102, 103, 105, 115

of new role, 106

of occupied roles, 106–7

steps for, 100, 101, 119

of unoccupied roles, 107

work sanctioned and allocated by, 69, 71–2, 77

Manager's decision

an objective fact, 103–4

and subjective judgement, 140–41

Managerial contraction, 44n, 71–2, 77

Managerial decisions

basis of time-span measurement, 103

effects on subordinate behaviour, 103

time-span measurement without access to, 104

Managerial instruction

essence of genuinely prescribed, 85

prescribed and discretionary elements of, 79

re work, 78–9, 83

Managerial leadership

and piecework systems, 260, 266

in wage bargaining, 43–6

and work, payment and progress of subordinates, 306

Managerial personnel, salary levels of, 32

Managerial review, 90–98 (and see Discretion; Review)

of subordinate's work, 91

and sub-standard discretion, 90–98

Manager-once-removed

authorizing manager's work allocation and methods of review, 102

authorizing payment level, 101, 134

authorizing time-span measurement, 101, 102, 134

and change in level of work in a role, 273

and open-ended instructions, 110

responsibility for potential progress of subordinates, 272, 273–4, 289, 334, 334

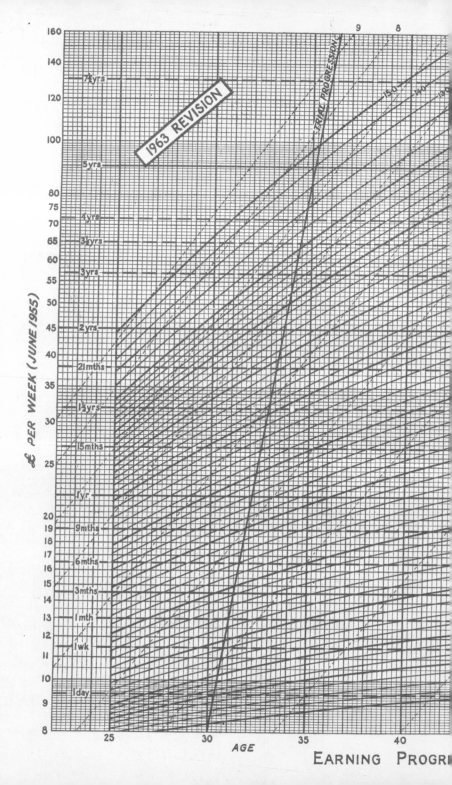

1963 REVISION

EARNING PROGR[ES]